How to Build a Life
in the Humanities

HOW TO BUILD A LIFE IN THE HUMANITIES
MEDITATIONS ON THE ACADEMIC WORK–LIFE BALANCE

Edited by

Greg Colón Semenza
and
Garrett A. Sullivan, Jr.

First published in 2015 by
PALGRAVE MACMILLAN®
in the United States—a division of St. Martin's Press LLC,
175 Fifth Avenue, New York, NY 10010.

Where this book is distributed in the UK, Europe and the rest of the world,
this is by Palgrave Macmillan, a division of Macmillan Publishers Limited,
registered in England, company number 785998, of Houndmills,
Basingstoke, Hampshire RG21 6XS.

Palgrave Macmillan is the global academic imprint of the above companies
and has companies and representatives throughout the world.

Palgrave® and Macmillan® are registered trademarks in the United States,
the United Kingdom, Europe and other countries.

ISBN: 978–1–137–51152–2 (hc)
ISBN: 978–1–137–42888–2 (pbk)

Library of Congress Cataloging-in-Publication Data is available from the
Library of Congress.

A catalogue record of the book is available from the British Library.

Design by Newgen Knowledge Works (P) Ltd., Chennai, India.

First edition: April 2015

10 9 8 7 6 5 4 3 2 1

This book is dedicated to Marti Semenza and Garry and Lorry Sullivan

CONTENTS

Part III   Diverse Lives

Part IV   Life Off the Tenure Track

FOREWORD: LIVING THE HUMANITIES IN THE TWENTY-FIRST CENTURY

Tony Grafton

We have heard the news, and it isn't good. Politicians and pundits, creative destroyers and creative writers all seem to agree: the humanities are on the chopping block, and it's a good thing. Since the 1960s, they point out, humanities enrollments have crashed, and about time. We humanists deserved to lose our students. Our subjects just aren't practical. Pundits agree that college should prepare students for the world of work—while the humanities prepare them for something more, like irresponsible, and impractical, intellectual play. Even our professorial president, Barack Obama, cited a humanistic discipline— art history—when he needed an example of the kind of study that doesn't lead to a job. But our subjects aren't idealistic either. For, in the 1980s and 1990s, we gave up on teaching great texts and urging students to debate about great ideas. Instead of feeding the young bread, the best that has been thought and said, we handed them something worse than a stone: a sausage machine, named Theory, that transformed everything we put into it, from Homer to Walcott and Sappho to Woolf, into a single, uniform, and displeasing product.

No wonder, then, that we're on the way out. We should expect no sympathy, and we get very little. As an editorialist in the *Harvard Crimson* put it when a report about the decline in humanities majors appeared, "Let them eat code." In too many states, attitudes like this flow not only upward from the college paper but also downward from the governor's mansion. Many university administrators make clear, by actions if not by words, that we don't bring in outside money and, therefore, can hardly expect to receive much internal support. A fair number of them make common cause with the prophets of the massive open online course, who offer to replace the Sage on the Stage with the Vox in the Box, and urge us to replace our own courses with MOOCs, for which we would serve not as expensive professors—why pay ordinary humanists salaries when you can stream the stars?—but as modestly compensated coaches.

It's not just bean counters and MOOC makers who spout this invective. Novelists—many of whom double as creative writing professors—identify us, most of the time, as privileged heterosexual white males (Philip Roth, always original, at least made his professor an African-American male who was passing as white). Whether they depict us as sterile pedants obsessed with research or charismatic lecturers obsessed with teaching, they agree on the nature of our central occupation: persuading students to sleep with us. Michael Chabon's *Wonder Boys* and Richard Russo's *Straight Man* delight us for many reasons—and not least because their male protagonists somehow manage not to sleep with their beautiful, seductive female students.

All the invective adds up to something truly terrible: a vast and monstrous set of accusations that seems impossible to escape. Many of the assertions that compose it are false. A number of humanists—from the senior literary scholar Michael Bérubé, who has an essay in this volume, to the junior historian Ben Schmidt—have done fine work, correcting the mistakes. They have shown that humanities enrollments shot up in the 1960s, when large numbers of women, who traditionally studied the humanities, entered previously male colleges and universities—and fell off again almost at once, as women found their way to the full range of academic disciplines. They have pointed out that, since the fall, enrollments have recovered, and held steady until the recent crash, which does seem to have frightened students and their families in large numbers into looking for more practical majors. They have noted that enrollments rose, not fell, in the age of theory, and that the normal humanist nowadays is female, not male, and often neither white nor heterosexual. Moreover, they have made clear, again and again, that while humanists don't bring in a lot of grant money, we do a lot of teaching and don't cost very much. In fact, in many colleges and universities, we're cross-subsidizing the natural scientists, whose work costs more than their grants pay and who do less teaching than we do.

But these systematic answers, although necessary, are not sufficient. They don't, and can't, offer the details that bring a world into focus for those living outside of it. Even those who read some of these arguments with understanding still find themselves baffled when they try to imagine what professors actually do all day, all weekend, and all summer. And there's a good reason for this. We humanists have argued at length, in recent years, with real and imaginary critics. But, we have told far too few stories in the course of these debates: stories about what we actually do all day, about how we work with administrators, colleagues, and teachers. The few exceptions to this rule—such as Bérubé's *What's Liberal about the Liberal Arts?* (2006)—are invaluable. But they also necessarily focus on the disciplines their authors know and the situations they have experienced.

One of the many good qualities of the essays in this book is that, collectively, they offer a panorama of humanists' lives. In them, every major step in the humanist's career, from graduate school to retirement, comes in for imaginative, sympathetic, and precise description. Even if you are not a humanist—especially if you are not a humanist—let me urge you to read this book from end to end. Do it, and you will learn a great deal—much of it the sort of thing that no polemic could teach you. You will see that many humanists in many disciplines write sharp, vivid, and accessible prose, totally devoid of the jargon and containing none of the obfuscation that critics of the academy describe as universal. You will learn that humanists come in many forms—female as well as male, gay as well as straight, with fears, with depression, with disability—and with confidence, with joy, and with health.

Soon, you will see that humanists are not the scarecrow figures of academic fiction or the scary ones of political polemic. They can be fearful—fearful, in many cases, that they do not deserve the jobs they hold, the rewards and privileges of which they deeply appreciate. They can be depressed—depressed, in many cases, because of the peculiar series of stages into which humanists' careers fall, which impose stress and isolation on many. They can be nervous—nervous, in many cases, because they know they can't do everything and they very much want to choose the activities that will be most valuable to their colleagues and their departments. Humanists, in other words, are often their own sharpest critics, and when they discuss the need for downtime and leisure activities, they often do so because they almost burned themselves out before realizing that work cannot and should not cannibalize life.

Above all, however, you will realize that humanists—whatever discipline they practice and whatever sort of institution they teach at—have core values in common. If they do research—and many do—it's because they are deeply committed to their subjects and believe that pursuing them energetically and intelligently is an activity of high intellectual worth. Further, when they teach—and they almost all do that—they feel loyalty and affection for their students, and a strong desire to help them by giving them the fullest set of skills they know how to provide. The humanists represented in this volume take pride in their practices as lecturers, seminar leaders, and readers of work. The grades and comments they dish out are designed not to discourage their students but to inspire them—and provoke them—into doing better.

But replying to the outside world—although vital—is not enough. We have other constituencies as well—from the alumni and parents who want to believe that they have not put their children into the hands of crazed pedants and vile lechers to the students for whom we are responsible. And their questions—although by no means all of them are hostile—are harder to answer than the criticisms of those who have written us off. Consider, for example, a graduate student in a humanities field who wants to know what it's like to have a baby while still working on her dissertation—and has only male advisers to consult. Or a more advanced graduate student, who has passed general exams and written all or most of a dissertation, and has been offered a position at a community college—although he himself has never studied or taught except at private, selective institutions. Or an undergraduate, who has done superb work in courses, written a dazzling capstone paper, and wants to know if he or she might possibly be able to make a career in the humanities—and what that might be like, especially for someone who has a diagnosed partial disability.

Humanists—real humanists, not the scarecrows imagined by the polemicists—want to be helpful to their advisees. Late in the afternoon, when a student comes into the office, his or her face eloquently expressing a need to lay out a problem or a possibility for a reliable adult, we rapidly change our plans, sit back down in our cut-rate office chairs, listen, and offer the most sensible and accurate advice we can. But our ability to carry out that vital task is limited, in every case. Those of us who have studied and taught only in private research universities—my own case—can't give very realistic advice on what it would be like to work at a community college or a small liberal arts college (students of mine do both). Those of us who have never served as chairs can't give realistic counsel about what doing that entails—or about what possibilities it offers. Moreover, those of us who were young in a different world can't give realistic advice about what it's like to make a career and a life now—to say nothing of the next decade or two.

No single person or book can carry out all of these tasks. But this book can and will do an enormous amount of good. Its articles have the feel and the texture of lived experience accurately conveyed.

In some cases, they will confirm justified fears. In others, however, they will bring reassurance. They show that colleagues—and administrators—are often understanding, generous, and can be supportive. They show that what can be ordeals, like being considered for tenure, can turn into comprehensible, even constructive, tests of ability and accomplishment. Full-time, tenure-track positions at research universities have become so rare that students treat the prospect of getting them as a bitter joke. From these essays, they will take away one final lesson: that jobs of many kinds and at many levels can prove immensely rewarding—so much so that those who hold them can't imagine giving them up to move. It turns out that even what looks like an abyss looming at the end of the academic road—retirement—can actually offer new possibilities for learning and teaching.

Few informed humanists are broadly optimistic about the state of their disciplines or that of the university. The rise of corporate management strategies—strategies that seem to come from corporations of a very old vintage, rather than from Google or a contemporary advertising agency—threatens freedom of speech. So, more surprisingly, can an articulate and fierce public, easily offended by what seems to a professor common sense or straightforward history. Some members of the ordinary public greet our efforts to craft exhibitions and other forms of accessible programming with warm enthusiasm. Others wage concerted campaigns against individual professors whom they have identified as enemies, pursuing their targets with all the energy and ferocity, worthy of a better cause, that writing at a distance seems to inspire. Meanwhile, the replacement of tenure-track jobs with contingent positions moves on apace, and with it the erosion of traditional campus cultures and relationships.

The authors of these essays are far too canny, and have seen far too much, to give way to optimism. What they display instead might be called an earned confidence: confidence that most humanists, whatever the difficulties they face, can leap the hurdles, negotiate the hard passages, and gain the perspective and experience to be good teachers and colleagues. Confidence also that many humanists find, and more will find, the elusive balance between care of their selves and their children and care of their students, colleagues, and books: they can, in short, live a version of the lives that most people want. This is a book I wish I could have read when I was much younger. Because nothing like it existed then—and nothing like it exists now—I'll be very happy to recommend it to my students and colleagues, as well as to administrators, trustees, and general readers.

Acknowledgments

We first met when one of us was a graduate student and the other a newly minted assistant professor. By the time we both had tenure-line appointments, we'd already enjoyed multiple conversations about the vagaries and complexities of academic life. One key question that continuously emerged, whether directly or indirectly, had to do with how on earth today's academics—from graduate students to adjuncts to professors of all ranks—are supposed to build a good life *and* a good career. Is it even possible to balance the demands of a serious academic position and a life fully lived? In the years that followed, we continued to discuss these and other issues, sometimes with several of the contributors to this volume. *How to Build a Life in the Humanities* is a product of this dialogue as well as its extension into print. Our hope is that it will engender new conversations and contribute to already existing ones among its readers—and, just maybe, help some of those readers to answer that question for themselves.

We are grateful, first of all, to our contributors for the fine work they have done. Each of them has taught us a great deal about our peculiar profession, and has responded with intelligence, good humor, and grace to every editorial request. We feel lucky to have had the chance to work with them on this volume. Tony Grafton has not only been kind enough to write us a foreword but also to do it in record time; his generosity and professionalism are truly exemplary. Brigitte Shull is an ideal editor, one to return to again and again. It's a privilege to work with her and others at Palgrave Macmillan, including Ryan Jenkins. The press's readers have also offered useful advice that's made this a better volume. Bob Hasenfratz and Mark Morrisson, our department heads, have been most supportive.

We would additionally like to thank our students. Because this book focuses on the complexities and challenges of academic life, it doesn't have much to say about its pleasures. Indeed, to stress those pleasures might seem ethically questionable—might we help lure unsuspecting undergraduates into the academy at a time of diminished opportunity and resource scarcity? Yet, if we don't acknowledge our students, we slight the positive contributions they make to our lives every day. They justify our faith in the value and power of a humanities education, and we feel lucky and privileged to work with them.

Additionally, Garrett would like to thank his mother Cathy and his sisters Tracy, Amy, and Sheila for their unwavering support. Non-academics all, they have always encouraged him in, and occasionally mocked him for, his bizarre choice of career. His partner, Marie, *does* know the madness of which he speaks; he is forever grateful to her for building her academic life in conjunction with his. He happily dedicates this volume to Garry and Lorry, his father and stepmother, for their exuberant enthusiasm for projects such as this one.

Greg is especially grateful to Simon and Brendan for their willingness to confirm—through a restorative year of lively conversation—the need for this book; here's to Mt. Washington, guys. His sons, Benjamin and Alexander, have taught him more about life than he'd managed to learn in his previous 30+ years on this Earth, and Cristina—poor thing—who's lived with him through so many of those years, is his witness. He's thankful for all the support they provide. Additional thanks to his father, Greg, to Geri Semenza, and to his brother, Matt. In dedicating a volume with the word "life" in its title to his mother, Marti, he's had to suppress every cheesy, punning instinct in his body. Hopefully, "thanks" will do the trick.

Introduction

Greg Colón Semenza and
Garrett A. Sullivan, Jr.

This volume is the by-product of an ongoing conversation between its editors. It attempts to answer a question that preoccupies us both: How do you build a life in the humanities? The book is both a companion to and the logical outgrowth of Greg's earlier work, *Graduate Study for the 21st Century: How to Build an Academic Career in the Humanities*. And yet, the questions of constructing a *career* and a *life* are distinct, if inevitably interwoven. It's one thing to say that scholars should work many hours each week, for example, but how are they to do so while trying to raise children, maintain a home, deal with personal crises, or manage the daily stresses of the office? Just as the practical advice in *Graduate Study* is grounded in the conviction that there's nothing commonsensical about the professional activities of a humanities scholar, this volume approaches the difficulties of managing life as an academic as peculiar and in need of serious discussion. Moreover, while various forms of professional advice are readily available and widely disseminated, the issue of building an academic life remains comparatively underexplored. Graduate students and new junior faculty are amply oriented to their institutions, but not to the possible lives they might construct for themselves within the academy. This book is designed to provide such an orientation. As life-building is less an event than an ongoing process, the volume has much to offer present and future academics of all ranks and positions.

This book, then, performs a detailed and wide-ranging examination of how academics negotiate their humanity in an increasingly bureaucratic academy and manage the personal challenges of working in an extraordinarily complex and competitive profession. The impact on our daily lives of twenty-first-century academic realities—increasing corporatization and administrative oversight, dwindling state support, decreasing employment opportunities for PhDs, and so forth—is too infrequently discussed in professional forums and publications, and almost never in spaces dedicated exclusively to the topic. Graduate students and younger faculty members especially, but also experienced academics navigating the murky waters of the mid-career phase, are often forced to deal with their personal ordeals alone, although such ordeals tend to be quite common. One of this book's foundational premises, therefore, is that collective meditation on the personal side of academic life is both an ethical and practical obligation of those humanists who are in a position to share their experiences with others.

Of course, no two academic lives are the same. For that reason, we have assembled contributors from a range of different institutions (community colleges, liberal arts colleges, and research universities) as well as institutional positions (graduate students, adjunct professors, and tenure-line faculty of all ranks) and asked them to write first-person essays in full confidence that their own experiences and reflections will resonate with a broad academic audience. (They certainly have with us; we've learned a lot.) Consequently, these essays don't tell you how it's done as much as they provide raw materials for your own DIY life-building project.

Such projects aren't undertaken in a vacuum, and one challenge we all face is negotiating the relationship between our lives in the humanities and in the outside world. Most of us have had awkward conversations at family reunions or holiday parties about our jobs. Some of us have been foolhardy enough to try to explain "what we are working on"; others have fallen back on partial and misleading truths. In both cases, we've often been greeted with blank stares or longing glances at the liquor cabinet. If building an academic life is a challenge for us, its workings are, to many of our interlocutors, a mystery they don't care to solve.

Moreover, what we do tends to be undervalued as well as imperfectly understood. In January 2013, *Forbes Magazine* published an article by Susan Adams identifying that year's "Least Stressful Jobs." Alone at the top of the list stands the university professor. As Adams puts it,

> University professors have a lot less stress than most of us. Unless they teach summer school, they are off between May and September and they enjoy long breaks during the school year, including a month over Christmas and New Year's and another chunk of time in the spring. Even when school is in session they don't spend too many hours in the

classroom. For tenure-track professors, there is some pressure to publish books and articles, but deadlines are few.[1]

Adams's laughable caricature of professorial life provoked enough of a *ouch* response to inspire her (to her credit) to add an addendum:

> Since writing the above piece I have received more than 150 comments, many of them outraged, from professors who say their jobs are terribly stressful. While I characterize their lives as full of unrestricted time, few deadlines and frequent, extended breaks, the commenters insist that most professors work upwards of 60 hours a week preparing lectures, correcting papers and doing research for required publications in journals and books. Most everyone says they never take the summer off, barely get a single day's break for Christmas or New Year's and work almost every night into the wee hours.

The comments to Adams's essay nicely articulate some of the stresses attendant upon academic life. For instance, "Anthroprof" notes both that professors are only on nine-month contracts—one reason for their relatively low salaries—and that "summers actually present a break from committee work and classroom time to engage in other responsibilities necessary for me to KEEP MY JOB." As Mary Leech points out, "We may spend few hours in the classroom, but for every hour in the classroom, at least two to four hours are spent in preparation. Tests, papers, labs, and homework are all graded outside of the classroom, and add many hours of work." Ian Durham asserts that "a very small sub-sample of university professors have cushy jobs. The rest of us are overworked and often underpaid." And David Perry (in a comment highlighted in Adams's addendum) observes, "I love my job. It's definitely deeply rewarding. But the stresses are intense and the workload never ending."

If the *Forbes* article misrepresents the lot of the professor, it does so at a moment when the "University Professor" resembles an endangered species. Indeed, those of us with tenure-track jobs are aware that most graduate students, postdocs, visiting assistant professors, or adjunct faculty members would eagerly embrace our stresses. Our cultural moment is marked by a relatively long time to degree for humanities PhD students; a dearth of tenure-track and full-time professorial jobs; relatively low salaries for those lucky enough to hold permanent positions and an absence of salaried jobs for everyone else; and, increasingly, a lack of public and institutional support for what we do, not to mention the types of skills we teach. This is a tough time to be building a life in the humanities. Moreover, even those of us fortunate enough to secure permanent employment are shadowed by the sense that we are not only overtaxed but also culturally marginalized. In proclaiming our stresses, we are also seeking legitimation. At the same time, we think that David Perry got it right: we love our jobs, and we feel profoundly lucky to have them, but they are stressful as all get out. We build our lives around them, but they make it hard to live.

Only over the past 25 years or so has the academic work–life balance become a topic academics are willing to discuss openly. For instance, several book-length studies have addressed the challenges of academe for highly specific populations—a strategy our book also employs in the section on *Diverse Lives.* Examples include *Working-Class Women in the Academy: Laborers in the Knowledge Factory* by Michelle M. Tokarczyk and Elizabeth A. Fay (1993); *Lesbians in Academia: Degrees of Freedom* by Beth Mintz and Esther D. Rothblum (1997); *Ms. Mentor's Impeccable Advice for Women in Academia* by Emily Toth (1997); and *Professor Mommy: Finding Work-Family Balance in Academia* by Rachel Connelly and Kristen Ghodsee (2011). By far, the most impressive forum for the discussion of specific issues related to academic life, however, is the blogosphere. A number of online journals, including *Vitae, Inside Higher Ed,* and *Grad Hacker,* as well as several well-known periodicals such as *The Chronicle of Higher Education* and *Slate,* now regularly publish columns by a growing group of dedicated bloggers and columnists—many of whom have contributed to this volume—who focus specifically on academic work–life issues. This expanding body of literature has gone a long way toward providing the sort of forum for academics that we feel is badly needed. If there's any problem with the blogs and articles, it's simply that there are so many of them, authored by so many excellent people, and appearing in so many different venues. One of our main goals for this collection, therefore, has been to provide in a single, compact volume a range of views on a variety of the most important academic work-life topics.

We have organized this book's chapters into four sections: *Professional Life, Personal Life, Diverse Lives,* and *Life Off the Tenure Track.* The first section focuses on different kinds of postsecondary institutions and the most important professional activities that faculty perform within them. Section two concerns key issues for, and challenges to, maintaining a healthy work–life balance, while the third section centers upon the experiences of academics who don't conform to the stereotype of the tweedy, white, heterosexual male academic from a privileged background. Most of the contributors to these first three sections hold tenure-line appointments. Section four, however, centers upon those (sometimes former) humanities scholars who have built their lives off of the tenure track.

Of course, the boundaries between our section topics are porous, and that is appropriate for a profession in which it can be difficult to separate work from the rest of one's life. This porousness means that individual essays often speak to and resonate with one another in what we hope are illuminating ways. All of the essays in the volume are grounded in authorial experience. They offer not an encyclopedic overview of a given topic, but a single writer's close engagement with a subject of significance to her or him. Most of the essays have a practical dimension: they provide glimpses of the inner workings of different types of institutions; advice for managing specific problems; or fresh perspectives on practices we all engage in every day. Taken together, the essays offer a full picture of academic life—treated here as singular rather than plural only for rhetorical convenience—in all its personal and institutional complexity. At the same time, that picture is far from comprehensive; a single book could not possibly account for the full range of experiences and viewpoints of those in the academy today. For example, the chapter on "Disability" is co-written by two deaf scholars; they share their experiences of what it is like to work in the academy with a disability, but in no way do they claim to represent the experiences of all disabled persons. Moreover, in putting this volume together, we were keenly aware that, in a single volume, there were topics or issues worthy of examination that we were not going to be able to cover. The editors hope our readers will understand this volume to be inaugurating or extending conversations about academic life in the humanities rather than offering the final word.

As mentioned earlier, we believe that our book will be of keen interest to individual professors, graduate students, and undergraduates contemplating a life in the academy. We also designed it with introductory graduate research methods and/or professional development seminars in mind. An awful burden is placed on instructors for such courses to pretend they can somehow cover all aspects of the academic life—an impossible task. *How to Build an Academic Life* is intended to help by marshalling the aid of some two dozen teachers who bring their unique perspectives on a wide range of issues related to working and living as academics. Whether you're lucky enough to be enrolled in such a seminar or you're taking up this book on your own, you'll surely be tempted to skip directly to those chapters you assume will be most relevant. This is fine, of course, although we think you'll benefit from reading the essays in the order in which they're presented and especially from delving into those essays that might seem least relevant to your own interests. Knowing something about the lives and experiences of our fellow workers can help us to understand better the multifaceted professional world we're all a part of, making us more informed, more involved, and, hopefully, more empathetic colleagues. In other words, it can make the humanities a little bit more humane.

NOTE

1. Adams, S. "The Least Stressful Jobs of 2013," *Forbes Magazine*, January 3, 2013, accessed August 1, 2014, http://www.forbes.com/sites/susanadams/2013/01/03/the-least-stressful-jobs-of-2013/.

PART I

PROFESSIONAL LIFE

CHAPTER 1

LIFE IN A LIBERAL ARTS COLLEGE

William Pannapacker

I have been a humanities faculty member at Hope College, a liberal arts institution in Holland, Michigan, for more than 14 years; I also attended Saint Joseph's University in Philadelphia as an undergraduate. (For graduate school, I attended two private research universities—the University of Miami and Harvard—and I taught briefly at a community college: Miami-Dade.) I have been a "Careers" columnist at *The Chronicle of Higher Education* for more than 16 years; more recently, I have been serving as the founding director of an undergraduate program in the "Digital Liberal Arts" and an initiative that seeks to foster collaboration among the 13 liberal arts colleges of the Great Lakes Colleges Association; both are funded generously by the Andrew W. Mellon Foundation.

While I feel at home in the culture of liberal arts colleges, I don't presume that my experiences are representative except in the broadest sense. But, I hope that my thoughts about those kinds of institutions will be useful for readers who are considering employment at one, or who are interested in the experiences of others who have worked in similar institutional contexts. I have found that there is a distinct culture of liberal arts education in the United States that permits a kind of immediate mutual recognition—an unspoken set of shared assumptions and attitudes—among those who have been associated with them for significant periods of time. In many respects, in the last few decades, a life at a liberal arts colleges is one that is caught between hopeful idealism and deepening anxiety.

Today, there are approximately 125 to 250 private liberal arts colleges, depending on the method one counts by, enrolling between 100,000 and 350,000 students, constituting almost two percent of the students in accredited postsecondary institutions.[1] Liberal arts colleges are, arguably, the most diverse of the institutional types: public and private, single-sex and co-ed, secular and religious; they each have their own unique missions, histories, traditions, and curricula. They typically are four-year institutions that focus on undergraduate education, usually in a residential setting, although there are many exceptions. For example, Saint Joseph's University, my alma mater, has numerous master's programs in professional fields, and a large number of commuting students, of which I was one. However, Hope College, where I now teach, is overwhelmingly residential, and it has no graduate programs.

In general, liberal arts colleges are small enough to foster a sense of familiarity and community, although there is disagreement about the scale at which that is possible. St. Joseph's and Hope are large schools by liberal arts standards, with approximately 8,000 and 3,000 students, respectively; colleges such as Earlham and Albion are more typical with approximately 1,200 and 1,350 students, respectively. Many liberal arts colleges, like Oberlin and DePauw, have roots in religious denominations and movements; most, although not all, of those colleges have become secular: Hope, for example, has become an ecumenical Christian college, but it remains affiliated with the Reformed Church in America. Liberal arts colleges often regard themselves as preparing students for leadership, not by focusing on technical or vocational learning, but by exposing students to a wide range of transformative experiences that are both curricular and co-curricular. They typically offer a general education program that includes literature, languages, history, life science, mathematics, physical sciences, psychology, social sciences, the visual and performing arts, philosophy, religion, and various interdisciplinary and area studies. While holding on to that ideal, most liberal arts colleges now provide pre-professional training, too, especially in business, education, engineering, computer science, and the health-related fields.

Even with significant adaptations, and a service ethic among their faculty, many liberal arts institutions are coping with severe pressures that threaten their continuing existence. In the 1950s, approximately 40 percent of US institutions of higher learning were liberal arts colleges, and they enrolled approximately 25 percent of all undergraduates. They have been losing ground ever since, and many of the survivors have seen their missions erode to the point wherein their status as liberal arts institutions is debatable.[2] Many liberal arts colleges are facing significant financial risk, especially the ones with small endowments that are primarily tuition-driven, and that have taken on substantial debt to maintain their competitive position, often through extensive building campaigns. Although endowments have been improving in recent years, many colleges still are recovering from the recession with accumulated deferred maintenance, larger classes, and fewer faculty members—all of which undermines one of the major reasons to attend a liberal arts college rather than, say, a less expensive state university with larger, more impersonal classes.

Increasingly, students and their families are concerned about the relevance of liberal arts degrees in a highly competitive, seemingly winner-take-all labor market. The demographic outlook for the United States suggests that the number of students available to attend college will be shrinking and that the search for talent and tuition revenue will become more challenging than before. One admissions officer described to me the future as one of "fracking for students." Meanwhile, public institutions are attracting a larger percentage of their target students—often by creating honors colleges that seem to replicate the liberal arts experience—and wealthy private institutions are driving many colleges toward unsustainable discounting and an amenities "arms-race" of expensive building campaigns, as students come to expect high-quality residences and athletics facilities. Many liberal arts colleges will no longer exist in the next couple of decades, at least not without some changes in the "value proposition" that they offer their students in terms of cost, the quality of the experience, educational outcomes, and access to various career ladders and alumni networks.

Often, from the perspective of larger educational institutions—especially the major research universities, community colleges, and the for-profit sector—liberal arts colleges are seen as idyllic and laid-back, evoking the imagery—but not the educational struggles—of *Dead Poets Society*. However, like every corner of higher education, liberal arts colleges are struggling to negotiate the contending pressures that I have just described: to remain small or to grow large; to preserve a founding mission or to adopt a more encompassing vision; to expose students to a wide range of intellectual experiences or to embrace preparation for employment. None of those is an either/ or decision, of course, and for that reason, to work in a liberal arts college is to grapple with these issues, among others, on a regular basis. Inevitably, one will find oneself engaged in conversations among the institutional stakeholders—the students, the faculty, the administrators, employers and the larger community—to which we are all accountable. When I was first hired by Hope College, a senior faculty member advised me, memorably, that the nearly 150-year-old institution is like a sailboat—it tacks one way and then the other, adjusting its sails to the changing winds, but still moving forward. Liberal arts colleges have a great advantage in their ability to adapt relatively rapidly, and experimentally, in comparison to large universities that, arguably, move more like oil tankers.

Another crucial feature of liberal arts colleges is that, in general, they are small enough for individual faculty members to have a voice and, eventually, a major role in institutional governance. For most new faculty, that is a significant change. At Harvard, for example, the role of graduate students in setting the course of the institution was vanishingly small; an individual could easily get lost in the immensity of the institution and the momentum of established practices that are the outcomes of battles and compromises that most of those employed today don't remember. It is worth recognizing that, as a candidate for a position at a liberal arts college, it's quite likely that you are being evaluated for your views on the mission, and the controversies about institutional identity, especially as they are reflected in the curriculum and the courses that you might choose to teach. What institutional committees and boards might benefit from your expertise, and what—in the fullness of time—are you likely to become: a program director, a chair, a dean, a useful gadfly? Liberal arts colleges are not just looking for scholars—although that is important—they are looking for a whole person, and search committees are, inevitably, trying to assess what any given candidate might contribute over the course of a career.

Institutional culture, faculty governance, and leadership are not matters that I thought carefully about when I was on the academic job market 15 years ago; like most PhD graduates, I applied for every position for which I could possibly be considered. But I am sure it helped me that I had been a student at a liberal arts college: I understood reflexively the culture of such institutions and believed in them enough to seem like a potential long-term fit. That is not to say that one must have a liberal arts degree to teach at such an institution. However, if you are a graduate student or a recent PhD looking for a position at a liberal arts college, you should have a good idea, first, of why you want to work at that kind of institution, and, second, how you might fit into its specific mission. I have been on at least a dozen hiring committees in English—one of the most desperately competitive fields—and it still surprises me how many job letters are not written for liberal arts positions, in general, and for our institutional context, in particular. Scholarly research is important, of course, and hiring committees want to know that you are likely to have an active, productive career that will complement the needs of the college's curriculum. However, it is essential for candidates to demonstrate that they are committed to teaching and service as well as to scholarship.

The ideal graduate school experience will have lots of time for seminars, research, conferences, and publications. Teaching often gets less emphasis, although that is changing as programs adapt to access employment opportunities for their graduates that demand teaching experience and skills at least as much as an active research program. As a graduate student, I partially qualified myself for a liberal arts position because I had a considerable number of teaching experiences in multiple disciplines in different institutional settings. I wasn't strategic about it; I simply sought teaching opportunities to sustain myself financially in expensive cities. But, the fact that I had taught so much was enough to complicate the suspicion that I was really looking for a research university position, since that's what most PhDs are encouraged to prefer because it can be hard to maintain an active scholarly career in a liberal arts setting. Teaching loads are variable but significantly higher than those at most research universities: Three is the norm (three courses in the fall and three in the spring), but four and even five are not uncommon. I have taught 12 credits per semester (three of the four-credit courses), fall and spring (usually with preparations for at least two courses each semester), and three one-month courses in the summer for most of my career, although I have benefitted from sabbaticals and other releases that have enabled me to remain productive by the standards of our institution.

While new hires often gain traction in their scholarship by teaching aspects of their dissertations, there is seldom much room in the curriculum for highly specialized courses. For that reason, liberal arts faculty typically teach a large number of so-called introductory service courses in their disciplines and general education courses, sometimes outside of their areas of expertise, narrowly defined. One needs to find ways to adapt and stretch scholarly interests to a wide range of contexts, and it often will be necessary to revisit subjects that one last studied as an undergraduate, if at all. For example, the course that I have taught the most—generally five times per year—is a survey of global civilization from the 1500s to the present in three disciplines: English, philosophy, and history (and, to some extent, art, music, economics, and the sciences). It has taken me away from my original scholarly field, but it also has stretched me in many ways, and broadened my ability to be conversant with colleagues across a wide range of disciplines. Although it can be demanding, especially at first, that kind of broad teaching experience requires faculty members to role-model the ideals of liberal arts education in their professional lives.

In addition to the challenges of becoming more of a generalist (or a "super-generalist"), new liberal arts faculty members will, quite likely, encounter students who are different in many ways from the ones they knew in graduate school. You have to adjust your expectations and strategies; for that, your colleagues will be helpful, but the students will teach you even more effectively. In a small liberal arts college, new faculty members quickly establish a reputation among the students, and an empty classroom, even more than mixed student evaluations, is a strong indicator that a faculty member has failed to adapt to the needs of his or her students. Liberal arts faculty are expected to provide a lot of personalized support, too; it's one of the major reasons that families choose such institutions: because they perceive that their children are more likely to be successful in a nurturing environment. That is not to say that liberal arts faculty should not be demanding and rigorous, but that high expectations need to be matched by a high level of personal commitment. Students will recognize that, and, in general, respond positively to it.

In most cases, a poor teacher—with empty classrooms, and no students who can testify to having been positively impacted as individuals—will not get tenure at a liberal arts college unless his or her other contributions are truly extraordinary. There is a wide range of expectations about scholarly productivity, and—with the rise of digital, collaborative, project-based forms of scholarship—there is increasing openness to the various forms that scholarship can take. For the most part, elite liberal arts colleges continue to have the most demanding, traditional expectations: at least one scholarly monograph plus some notable scholarly articles are the norm for tenure; with a second book—and an established reputation in one's field—for promotion to full professor. Beyond those elite institutions, however, there is a great deal of freedom to define what constitutes scholarly productivity, what "counts." One can write for a more popular audience, serve the community as a local expert, or create projects in collaboration with students and colleagues at other institutions. Faculty members are expected to have ongoing research interests, and to publish, but that is not the *sine qua non* of their institutional standing. Liberal arts colleges, with some variation, espouse the same values for their faculty members as they do for their students: everyone should have

time to think and explore questions of ultimate meaning for them- *freedom*
selves and society. To a great extent, that freedom is a source of their
creative energy as distinctive institutions, and I think it is one of the
major benefits of being a liberal arts faculty member.

One of the greatest risks liberal arts colleges face, in the context
of rising costs and a more challenging job market, is the concern that *non-tech*
a non-technical degree—one without an obvious career track—is a *degree*
path to debt and unemployment. But, as I have tried to explain to
many students and parents: you need a liberal arts education because
the job you will want may not exist yet. Liberal arts colleges prepare students to become thinkers, artists, leaders, and entrepreneurs,
among other things, for a future that we can't fully anticipate. That,
of course, does not mean embracing purist notions of the "life of
the mind." For Hope College, like many other liberal colleges, it has
meant constantly exploring intersections between traditional fields of
study and the changing opportunities that exist outside of academe.
For example, I founded and currently direct a three-year "Mellon
Scholars" program for our students in the arts and humanities that
offers a combination of faculty–student collaborative research, experiential education in internships related to that research, and ongoing
engagement with new technology for making their work accessible
and interactive (the "Digital Liberal Arts"). All along, the program
has sought to reconcile employers' appreciation of what liberal-arts
graduates traditionally have to offer—well-roundedness, creativity,
critical thinking, writing, and speaking abilities—with their expectation that new graduates also possess specific experiences, accomplishments, and skills that can enable them to become functioning
professionals without long periods of entry-level training. It's not primarily about embracing "vocationalism," although employability is
important; it is about using high-impact learning practices to enhance
the transformative power of the liberal arts experience. We cannot
remain aloof from the career prospects of our students, but we must
not abandon the values that define what it means to be a liberal arts
college.

Other substantial changes are on the horizon. As Victor E. Ferrall,
Jr. argues in *Liberal Arts at the Brink*, liberal arts institutions are
going to need to work together, more than they currently do, rather
than engage in an ongoing and escalating cycle of unsustainable competition for the same students. Of course, that will be challenging,
given the variability of institutional missions and identities, but we
will need to continue to explore means of sharing resources, including faculty and staff, when possible, and differentiating ourselves

when necessary to preserve the distinctive qualities that attract students to specific colleges. The residential character of most liberal arts colleges—and their emphasis on interaction with faculty—militates against the threat of massive open online courses (MOOCs), but they are moving toward hybrid courses, developed cross-institutionally, especially in lesser-taught languages. Regional consortia are going to be able to do without many kinds of faculty positions that were once considered essential for each institution. Most liberal arts colleges will remain tuition-driven, but they can't keep raising their advertised tuition rates, discounting even more deeply for some, and increasing class sizes while reducing personnel, except through curricular innovation, the creative use of technology, and cross-institutional collaboration. Much of the work in the coming decade, for new faculty in particular, will be in those areas.

Although many things about liberal arts education will change soon, some should not, including: teaching students how to think, broadening their encounters with other kinds of people, stimulating their curiosity and imagination, and instilling a lifelong respect for learning. The liberal arts can address the need for vocational development, but they also are about the ideals of honesty, love, and justice. We are not in any "business"; we are on a mission to liberate the individual through personal transformation. That mission is under great pressure, and anyone who wants to dedicate a career to the liberal arts needs to be prepared for challenging, turbulent times. It's important work; and, as Andrew Delbanco concludes in his book *College: What It Was, Is, And Should Be,* "Democracy depends on it."[3]

NOTES

1. Ferrall, V. E. Jr. *Liberal Arts at the Brink.* Cambridge, MA: Harvard University Press, 2011, 1.
2. Oakley, F. "The Liberal Arts College: Identity, Variety, Destiny." In *Liberal Arts Colleges in American Higher Education: Challenges and Opportunities,* ACLA Occasional Paper 59, New York: American Council of Learned Societies, 2005. 1–14, 5–6.
3. Delbanco, A. *College: What It Was, Is, and Should Be,* Princeton, NJ: Princeton University Press, 2012, 177.

CHAPTER 2

LIFE IN A COMMUNITY COLLEGE:
A DAY IN THE LIFE OF A
COMMUNITY COLLEGE
ENGLISH PROFESSOR

Rob Jenkins

It's still dark as I steer my aging economy car into the parking lot and choose a spot next to a late-model Mustang. Obviously a student's car. This is the smallest and most suburban of my college's five campuses, with students who are correspondingly more affluent than their counterparts at our urban locations. We also don't have separate parking for faculty.

Which is fine, because I'm here at 6:45 a.m., and the parking lot is almost deserted. In approximately ten minutes it will start to fill, mostly with cars driven by teenagers taking an early-morning dual-enrollment class before heading over to the local high school. That's why I'm here bright and early (well, early, at least) on this frigid February Wednesday morning: I have a 7:00 a.m. section of English Composition that's populated almost entirely by dually-enrolled high school kids. I also have several dual-enrollment students in my 8:30 class, and even a few in my 11:00 one.

And no, I'm not being punished by having to teach these early-morning classes or, for that matter, by having to teach high school kids. I chose this. After 27 years as a full-time faculty member, including 14 years at this institution, I have enough seniority to put together my own schedule, within reason. Classes meet on this campus from 7:00 in the morning until 10:00 at night, and some of my colleagues prefer to teach in the afternoon and evening. But I'm a morning person. I like my early classes and, for some odd reason, everybody else seems content to let me have them.

I enjoy my dual enrollment students, too. On average, they tend to be a little better writers than most community college students. At the same time, I also enjoy my traditional-age students, as well as the non-traditional students—many returning to school after years away—that I see in my later classes. I had a lot more of those non-traditional students when I taught on one of our larger campuses in town, back before I transferred to this suburban outpost because it's closer to home. But despite being located in a relatively affluent area, this is still a two-year school, and we still attract a wide range of students, most of them looking to pick up anywhere from a single class to a couple years' worth of coursework before moving on to one of the surrounding state universities.

I throw my backpack over a shoulder, shove my hands into my pockets, and make my way over to the building—we just have one—pausing to hold the door and exchange pleasantries with a couple of early-arriving students. There's just enough time for me to drop my bag by my office, fish out the sheaf of essays I finished grading yesterday afternoon, and get to my classroom with a few minutes to spare for booting up the computer and the overhead projector. One thing I'll say for this campus, small as it is: when it comes to classroom technology, we're pretty much set. But then, that's fairly typical of community colleges, many of which had SmartBoards and data projectors long before most four-year campuses. I can remember, back in the early 2000s, hosting visitors from some of our state's regional universities who were amazed at how well equipped our classrooms were. Two-year colleges might not receive as much in-state appropriations as their four-year counterparts, but what money we do have, we tend to spend on improving teaching and learning.

On the other hand, the truth is I don't really have an office. I have a cubicle in a cubicle farm in a converted classroom. Although our campus is small, it's growing fast, and space is at a premium. I had a nice office at my previous campus, but I gave that up to shave ten miles (16 km) each way—which, in Atlanta traffic, equates to approximately 40 minutes—off my daily commute. That has made a tremendous difference in my quality of life. Between my early schedule, which allows me to leave campus by 2:00 most days, and my shorter commute, I've been able to carve out more time for exercise and writing. Last year, I was even able to make it to my son's 4:30 junior varsity basketball games. I miss a lot of things about my former campus—not least my nice, large office—but the trade-offs have been more than acceptable.

Since it's Wednesday, I have three classes. On Tuesdays and Thursdays, I have two. A five-course load each semester is pretty standard for community college faculty. I can also teach a couple of courses in the summer for extra pay, which I usually do because I have four kids and can't find an orthodontist who's giving braces away for free.

Actually, I earn a pretty good salary, after 27 years in the profession, and my wife teaches part-time for our local school system; so, together, we make a decent living—enough to afford a modest home in a pleasant suburb with good schools. I also have excellent health insurance and retirement benefits, basically the same package my colleagues at state four-year institutions receive. Still, the ability to earn a little extra income in the summer is a nice perk.

This semester, I'm teaching two sections each of English 1101 and English 1102 (basically, comp 1 and comp 2), along with a section of American Literature. That's three "preps," which isn't too bad. Remember, I chose this schedule, although in all honesty it's not much different from the schedules I was assigned as a junior instructor 25 years ago. I could probably hold out for two sections of lit if I wanted to throw my weight around, but I like teaching writing. Plus, while one lit class makes for a nice break, two would mean I was taking one away from a colleague who probably needs the break more than I do.

Besides, three preps is no big deal. At this point in my career, prep time for my writing classes is fairly minimal, since I've been teaching those same classes for nearly 30 years now. Sure, I change things up on a regular basis, trying new teaching strategies, adding new reading selections or decommissioning old stand-bys. However, most of those changes are made in the three or four weeks between terms, when I'm supposedly on vacation. Most days during the semester, I know exactly what I'm going to be talking about in each class and, at least 80 percent of the time, it's something I've talked about many times before.

Grading, on the other hand—now that's time-consuming. Do the math: four sections of composition, with 24 students per section, writing six essays apiece, equates to nearly 600 essays each semester. As a result, I spend several hours every week reading papers. That's probably my least-favorite part of the job, but I've learned to make it manageable by staggering due dates and spreading out the grading instead of leaving it all for the weekends, as many of my colleagues do. In fact, after 29 years of grading essays (including two as a grad assistant), I've developed a system that generally allows me to get all of my grading done in about an hour a day, five days a week (except maybe at term paper time). I would share my system with you, but if there's one thing I've learned in all those years, it's to be careful about telling people what you do, because word will get around and some administrator will probably tell you that you can't do it.

Maybe you're wondering how, after teaching the same courses and reading all those essays year after year, I've managed to avoid burnout. I don't know if I can answer that, except to say that even the worst parts of my job still seem preferable to anything else I could be doing for a living. I have a good friend who's an accountant, and although he makes a lot more money than I do, I can't imagine looking at ledgers and spreadsheets all day. I'll take reading students' essays over that any time.

Further, although I teach the "same" courses, based on the college's course numbering system, they're not really the same. As I said, I try different things, test out new strategies I've picked up in my reading or at a conference, throw in an essay I just came across. And then there are the students, who, of course, change every semester. Each class, just like each individual, has a unique personality. That's not always a good thing, but usually it is. At the very least, it keeps things interesting.

So no, I'm not burned out. But check back with me in about five years.

Today, I've got the 7:00 class, followed by the 8:30, then a break, then an 11:00. At my college, all of our classes (or the vast majority of them, at least) meet for an hour and 15 minutes twice a week, either Monday–Wednesday (MW) or Tuesday–Thursday (TR). On Fridays, we don't have any classes except for science labs and a few other sections that meet once a week. Up until about six years ago, we did have classes that met Monday–Wednesday–Friday (MWF) for 50 minutes each—a pretty common schedule at many colleges, two-year schools included. I found it very difficult to coordinate my syllabi, when I had one section of a course that met MWF and another that met TR. I like this schedule better: all the classes are the same length and meet for the same number of days. The powers-that-be, as I've learned over the years, rarely hand down policy decisions that make faculty members' lives easier, but I'll give them full credit in this case. Oh, and the students like the balanced schedule too, which is probably the real reason the administration decided to go with it.

Besides my three classes, I've got a couple of office hours scheduled today. Full-time faculty members at my institution are required to keep ten office hours per week, which is pretty standard for a community college. Being available to students outside the classroom is seen as one of our primary responsibilities as faculty members at a teaching-intensive, student-focused institution. So I make it a point to be in my office (or close by) two hours a day on Mondays and Wednesdays and three hours on Tuesdays and Thursdays, my "light" teaching days. On Fridays, I occasionally meet with students by appointment, but mostly I leave that day open for grading and for my own writing. I don't even have to be on campus most Fridays, as long as I've put in my required office hours. That's not necessarily the norm at two-year colleges, many of which require faculty members to be on campus for a particular number of hours five days a week. I've worked at a couple of those schools and, as you can imagine, I like this arrangement much better.

Even so, I end up going in on more Fridays than I would like, in part because that's when so many of our departmental and college-wide committees schedule their meetings—you know, because very few people are teaching on Friday.

Speaking of meetings, I've actually got to cut out a little early today. My office hours are supposed to run until 1:30, but at 2:00 I've got a curriculum committee meeting on our main campus, which is 45 minutes away in the best of traffic—and, as this is Atlanta, I never count on the best of traffic. I need to leave by 1:00 to be sure I make it on time. Although I generally despise committee meetings, this is one I don't want to be late for. The topic today is composition textbooks, and if I'm not there when they vote on the selections, I won't have any say in the matter.

A few years ago, the administration made a push to require us all to use the same textbook—as a service to the students, they said, but I think it was really a service to the bookstore. Fortunately, we were able to reach a compromise: the committee selects three texts, and then individual instructors get to choose. One of the books up for a vote this time is the one I like to use, and I need to make sure it stays on the list. Otherwise, well, I'll keep using it anyway, but that will involve circumventing the usual book-ordering process, which is a pain. Much better to be on time for the meeting.

The good news is that this is the only committee I'm on this year. Back when I was a junior faculty member, I often served on three or four standing committees at the same time, plus maybe a search committee in the spring. But, with a little more seniority, I've managed to off-load most of that. It's not that I don't like getting together with my colleagues from across the college—well, okay, there are some of my colleagues I'd just as soon not get together with. But, mostly, I dislike committees because they often seem like a waste of time. Sure, I know all that grunt work has to be done by somebody, and some of it is even useful. I've just decided, unselfishly, to allow my junior colleagues to fill the committee spots that used to belong to me. They probably need more fodder for the "Service" section of their annual reports, anyway.

Meanwhile, I fulfill my contractual service requirement by doing things on campus that nobody else wants to do but that I don't mind, such as staffing the department booth during the spring Open House. My chair regards this as a "win–win" situation: he doesn't have any problem getting people to sign up for the American Literature curriculum committee, but he does have the devil of a time persuading folks to show up on a Thursday evening to glad-hand parents.

Before I leave campus today, though—speaking of my department chair—I've got to remember to stop by his office and start the paperwork to attend a conference later in the semester. This year, for a change, we actually have a little bit of travel money. For several years following the Great Recession, we had little or no funding to attend conferences, but this year I'm told we have approximately $650.00 per full-time faculty member. I say "approximately" because I can probably get more, maybe even a lot more, since some of my colleagues won't use any of their allotment. And I'm going to need it. This conference, once I figure in airfare, registration, and three nights in a hotel, will probably cost the college upward of $1,200.00.

That shouldn't be a problem, since I'm presenting. Community college department chairs, when they have to make tough calls about travel funds, tend to favor faculty members who are presenting at a conference and not just attending. I suppose that's their way of encouraging faculty to present, which is one of the primary forms of "professional development" at most two-year colleges. That's another area in which we're evaluated, along with teaching and service, and can include anything from attending campus-based seminars and "brown-bags" to traveling to (and maybe even presenting at) professional conferences. Professional development also, by the way, includes research, writing, and publishing, although comparatively few community college faculty members engage in those activities. That's not because they aren't qualified or interested; most of them just don't have time, or at least don't feel like they have time—with five courses each semester and all the preparation and grading that entails, not to mention probably serving on three or four committees.

Plus, most community colleges don't require faculty members to publish in order to earn tenure. A handful do, mostly in the Northeast, but most don't. It's true that not all community colleges actually offer tenure; however, the majority do, and most of those just require three to five years of acceptable performance in teaching, service, and professional development. Generally speaking, if you do a good job in the classroom (which is the most important thing at a community college, anyway), serve on several committees, attend a handful of conferences and seminars, and maybe present a couple of times, you won't have any problem getting tenure.

Wow!

Of course, there are some two-year college faculty members who make time for research and writing, usually because it's something they want to do for their own personal and professional satisfaction. For the most part, they're never really rewarded for it; at most community colleges, publishing an article counts no more toward tenure than presenting at a conference. And whatever faculty members do, research-wise, they have to do on their own time, because their "40-hour work week" is taken up entirely by teaching, grading, course prep, and committee work. Sure, the college will probably give them a nice pat on the back if they manage to get something published, maybe even interview them for the campus newsletter. But, in the end, no one else at the institution really cares if they publish or not.

That's because two-year colleges are teaching institutions—first, last, and in-between. Which is not to say that no research goes on there. It's just not necessarily the kind of research that professors at four-year schools are conducting, the kind that gets published in journals. Rather, it's a more practical kind of hands-on research that involves trying new teaching strategies in the classroom to see what works with students. The graduate schools of education might propose the theories, but community college faculty members are the ones who test them out in the field. That's why it seems like we're always at the forefront of every new movement, whether technological or pedagogical. Teaching is what we do, and so we're constantly looking for ways to improve student learning.

teaching institutions

That philosophy extends beyond the classroom, by the way. Advising students—helping them figure out what to take while they're here and, more importantly, what will transfer to their four-year institution—is also a significant part of my job.

Which reminds me—I hope I can get out of here by 1:00 this afternoon, because I just remembered that I've got a student stopping by at 12:30 to talk about her schedule next semester. She's a non-traditional student who's been taking five or six classes a year for the last three years. If she attends full-time in the fall, she can finish up, graduate with her associate's degree in December, and transfer in January. Then again, she's a single mother with two kids who works about 30 hours a week. So, maybe, she just needs to spread those courses out over two semesters and transfer in the fall. At the same time, she's anxious to move on and finish her bachelor's degree, so she can ditch her dead-end job and make a better life for her family. I'm not sure what to tell her. I guess I'll mostly just listen, try to give her a clear picture of her options, including pros and cons, and let her decide. That's what I usually do with students in her situation—and I see a lot of them.

New students, now—those are a different story. They usually need me to do more than just listen. Whether they recently graduated from high school or they've been out for ten years, they show up in the late summer with no idea what going to college actually entails. No one has ever explained to them how it works; in many cases, they're the first people in their family to attend college—yes, even here in this affluent suburb. Even though they're plenty smart enough to earn a degree, once they figure things out, I can't imagine some of those folks going off to a large university, where they'd each likely be just another number, herded through a "cattle-call" registration process into lecture classes with 500 other people.

No, what they need is what we offer them, here at their local community college: the personalized treatment, the small classes. Just enough "hand-holding" to get them walking on their own. That's why we're here. That's why I'm here. That's why, at the end of the day, after all the classes and all the grading and all the driving, I love my job.

And that's why I wouldn't trade places with any other English professor in the country. Not even at 6:45 a.m. on a frigid Wednesday morning in February.

CHAPTER 3

LIFE IN A RESEARCH UNIVERSITY

Barry V. Qualls

When Greg Semenza and Garrett Sullivan requested an essay from me on "Life in a Research University," I replied that my career had little typicality in terms of today's PhD tracks; and, further, that the issues of teaching and undergraduate education that have dominated my 43 years at Rutgers involved choices that few, if any, beginning assistant professors could now make without committing professional suicide. The changing definition and expectations implied— demanded—by the term "professional" now have little relevance to the world of humanities education I entered in 1971. Here I want to address, in the context of my own experience, issues that involve teaching, research and publication, and building an institution. Rutgers has changed vastly since I arrived: from being a collection of liberal arts colleges, it has become a major public research university. Having been a part of Rutgers through all of these changes—as both a professor of English and an administrator in several roles, including vice president of undergraduate education and dean of humanities for the Faculty of Arts and Sciences—I want to describe here what "Life in a Research University" once was, and has become. The trajectory I trace here indicates in some ways, I think, what the future holds for those who might be fortunate enough to work in a university like Rutgers. Though research universities have undoubtedly changed, they still are characterized by the amazing range of professional options they give their faculty—as researchers, teachers, administrators, and even campus citizens.

My own path was relatively straightforward. I went to Northwestern University in 1967, after graduating from Florida State. I came to Rutgers College in 1971 (I completed the dissertation in summer 1972). In my graduate program, no one suggested that graduate students should give conference talks or send papers out for publication. Some faculty wrote on my essays that "you should think of working on this for publication," but that was it. When I began to look for a position, the MLA job list did not exist (the list first appeared in 1971), so I wrote to schools where I thought I would like to teach—to liberal arts colleges and to universities where Victorianists whom I admired taught. I wanted very much to be at a liberal arts college, but I received few replies and no interview requests from them. I did hear from a few research universities. When the chair of Rutgers College English, Daniel Howard, came to Chicago before MLA, he interviewed and hired me. There were no committees, no job talks; just a decision by one person.

Today, merely to be considered a viable candidate for a research university position, one must build the credentials in graduate school that will convince faculty, department heads, and deans at hiring institutions that one is capable of balancing the demands of research, teaching, and service. Since tenure decisions for faculty at research universities will depend mainly on a candidate's research productivity, it is unlikely that a PhD would be hired without a few strong, peer-reviewed articles and a dissertation topic capable of becoming a book in a few short years. Moreover, because the competition for positions in research universities—which constitute no more than approximately 10% of America's institutions of higher learning—is so great, there is little incentive for a department to hire even the most promising ABD candidate. Indeed, some research universities want to see postdocs as part of the candidate's experience before they consider interviewing them.

Years ago, things were different. I found my years as an assistant professor at Rutgers College productive, apolitical, and almost ideal for beginning a career (or so it seemed, and seems still—although now I realize that the gender politics of the time made my career path easier). The expectation for tenure was then a book from a "strong" press, perhaps some talks, and an article or two. But the CV already packed with publications and professional activity *before* one applied for positions—no one imagined this. The expectations for tenure are higher today, even in outline: the book published or in production, articles, and talks are mandatory; and some universities have begun expecting a plan for a second book, perhaps even the book itself.

Furthermore, navigating a university's often dense bureaucracy and complex political terrain has become increasingly difficult for junior faculty, even as many humanities departments "protect" their untenured colleagues from the worst of this, urging them not to accept committee assignments beyond the department. Some departments even urge new faculty not to teach courses outside the department—for example, honors courses and first-year seminars. *research*

Research might be everything in the eyes of administrators and department chairs, but this fact does not lessen the other pressures with which one must contend, the most obvious of which are teaching and service demands. Here I want to dispel two myths about the work of an assistant professor—and, indeed, of tenure-line faculty at all ranks: the myth that teaching does not matter at research universities; and the myth that no one pays attention to service. In the case of teaching, most assistant professors arrive with some training for the classroom, acquired in both the composition and literature programs at their graduate schools. At Rutgers, graduate students have faculty mentors who observe their classes and work with them on teaching. This attention to teaching carries over into the mentorship of new assistant professors. Our History department has a teaching committee that visits every class of untenured faculty members at least once a term and addresses any issues that arise as well as providing a sounding board for new ideas.

As a new faculty member at Rutgers in 1971, each term I taught two sections of composition and one Victorian literature course. (Three years earlier, faculty taught four courses each term.) I had always wanted to teach, but realized very soon after I began that I was not prepared for the classroom and the issues that daily surprised me about what I did not know. I told my colleague Bridget Lyons, with whom I shared an office, my doubts about knowing how to work effectively in a classroom. Her response: "When you begin to teach, you start your education again." That comment has remained one of the keystones of my career; it made me conscious that my real education—from colleagues and students—was just beginning. The writing courses, in the post-1960s world of no common syllabi and writing from "experience," took place in the often charged atmosphere of the civil rights debates and the antiwar movements. I still remember a fist fight in one of these courses as we were discussing James Baldwin's "Fifth Avenue, Uptown"—a Jewish student insisting that the essay was anti-Semitic, a black student asserting that every word in the essay described "the real world." I stopped the fight; we resumed our discussion; another fist fight commenced—and I suspended class for that day. It is hard now to imagine such political passions among most students.

Today, one feature of life in a research university is that full-time faculty rarely teach composition or other courses considered "basic"; that work is done by teaching assistants and non-tenure-track instructors. Faculties teach more specialized courses in their areas of expertise as well as their department's courses required for the major. Further, most teach two courses per semester. Teaching undergraduates has been my passion throughout these decades, and my many years at Rutgers have allowed me to take on a wonderful range of courses. It is not true that faculty only teach their specialties and nothing else. Choice is abundant at a research university—if you want it; some even move into very different fields from their initial specialization. I never wanted to stray far from "my" Victorians; even as a child, I loved the period's poets and novelists. I have taught many different Victorian courses, even one on the sensation novelists. (It was in a class reading Wilkie Collins that I met Greg Semenza in 1993. He heard me declaring that Collins's introduction of Marian Halcombe in *The Woman in White* is one of the great moments in Victorian fiction.) Other courses have focused on poetry required for the major, some I was asked to teach (Eighteenth-Century Fiction), others I designed: on the Bible and literature and, for fall 2014, a course on storytelling aimed at first- and second-year undergraduates; there were also first-year seminars on "Streetwalking in Queen Victoria's England," as much about Mayhew's London as about prostitution, and on "*Uncle Tom's Cabin*: Protest Novel or Racist Novel?" I have always thought of myself as a "cheerleader for reading"—not a comment on my students, but a statement of my conviction that good close reading and clearly focused writing are my first goals for undergraduates. I have taught generations of students using this conviction because I am certain that a vital humanities education begins in alert nuanced reading. I often joke that, when I retire, I will have sold over 5,000 copies of *Jane Eyre* and *The Mill on the Floss*.

One of the most rewarding privileges that research faculty enjoy is the teaching and mentoring of graduate students. Even with the pleasure I have taken in undergraduate education, teaching graduate students is very different from undergraduate teaching and brings rewards that I cannot imagine finding in other professions. You teach in your field and direct dissertations, working with students eager to explore more, think more, and question more. You also prepare future teachers. I used to tell my students in a graduate course on Nineteenth-Century British Fiction that I wanted them to leave the course with the sense that they were ready to teach undergraduate courses in the Victorian novel when they began their careers, and that they had handouts and other course materials already available. Other forms of mentoring include serving on dissertation committees, visiting classes that the students are teaching, and writing letters of recommendation (I have written many "teaching letters" for students who have served as my teaching assistants in undergraduate courses)—all essential to preparing students for careers and, indeed, sustaining them in the early part of their careers. I believe, strongly, that not to talk with graduate students about teaching—and about teaching at different kinds of colleges and universities—is to fail them in preparation for academic careers. I encourage them to apply for jobs at institutions that are not defined by research. I worry that graduate education is too often blind to the possibilities elsewhere.

The second myth I want to address is that faculty at research universities are not expected to do much service. Although some—perhaps most—departments do in fact protect their junior faculty from onerous service assignments, many do not. Resources are simply too tight and so young faculty often are asked to serve on a number of department committees. In addition, the number of "service" activities surrounding teaching increases with each passing year: more letters of recommendation, more advising of graduate students, and more work with undergraduates who are applying for graduate schools or national fellowships like the Rhodes or Fulbright. Then there are the many institutes and research centers on campus that allow faculty to work in "think tanks" with colleagues and graduate students from other departments and other universities. Although outsiders like to think of research faculty spending all of their time in libraries or archives or at conferences, the fact is that the vast majority of their work happens in the classroom and office.

The move toward tenure in a research university is not simple, and it never has been. In my own case, two books on my dissertation topic, Carlyle's role in Dickens's fiction, appeared within the first year of my teaching. Therefore, I began a project that I had planned to work on if I earned tenure—on the Victorians' use of the Bible and Bunyan. I did not have a book contract by the time I was considered for tenure; the manuscript was at Cambridge, but its acceptance came months after the tenure votes. The book, *The Secular Pilgrims: The Novel as Book of Life*, appeared two years later. I doubt that my tenure would be possible now.

My point here is that institutional expectations and the structures that articulate them have changed signally over these last decades. A rewarding career takes advantage of these changes. The freedom to pursue only what you care about—if you care about career advancement—is restricted; you can never ignore research and publication, teaching, or service. But it is true that, after tenure, you have certain freedoms to focus on your critical passions that colleagues at many four-year and most two-year institutions rarely enjoy. For me, administration wound up being the path that I pursued, almost from the beginning, and continued through December 2012. I served over a decade as associate director of English's graduate program. For eight years, I was chair of English. For nine years, I was dean of humanities in the School of Arts and Sciences. For seven years, I served as vice president of undergraduate education. None of this administrative work had I ever envisioned; and only one of the positions, that of dean of humanities, did I ask for. I still loved teaching—and the smartest decision I made throughout these many years of administrative work was to continue teaching every term. This assured that I was always doing what I found the most satisfying, and that I always knew the issues that confronted students and faculty—up close.

So why take these administrative jobs? Clearly, I am not good at saying no. Some colleagues urged me to be "careful about being sucked into administration" at the expense of more lasting scholarly work. I knew then, and now, that the rewards of administrative work—unless you are dedicated to that professional track—are rarely "professional" in terms of making an impact on your field. I know too that, in a research university and after tenure, service is whatever a faculty member makes it. But, frankly, I like administrative work (crazy as that sounds)—and I care about Rutgers. Being an administrator has allowed me to work on issues that are not "just" about the English department but involve the academic life of the university and colleagues in many departments. I had become involved in campus life and campus governance from the time I entered Rutgers College, probably because back then it was small and faculty meetings had substance. Whether focused on debates about ROTC on campus or conflicts over the direction of the university, these meetings mattered—and faculty attended. Now, even curriculum debates seldom inspire faculty passions or attendance.

As I look back on my administrative work, I have no doubt about which position I preferred: dean of humanities. Earlier I had been a successful department chair. I liked my colleagues (well, most of them); I enjoyed being able to work with them on new hires—and, in those days, we hired many. I also worked with faculty on the curriculum; and we instituted a requirement of a course in African-American writers that made our major more truly representative of English and American literatures. As chair, I strongly supported women faculty, getting raises for those whose salaries, I discovered, were lower than male faculty at the same level of distinction and years of service; and, importantly, instituting a pregnancy leave that gave women a semester off (with pay). I was amazed that a university so proud of its many programs for women's scholarship had antediluvian policies about this issue. I discovered early on as chair, and then as dean of humanities, that the battles for civil rights and women's rights may seem "over" to those looking at universities from the outside. They are not. "Historical" discrimination goes underground, in salaries, leave policies, promotion standards, and much else.

My nine years as dean of humanities have been my best ones at Rutgers outside the classroom; this position best enabled me to merge my academic and administrative interests. As area dean focusing on the humanities departments, I had the opportunity to work on the issues that bedeviled these programs that had once formed the center of liberal arts colleges. I saw the need to sustain the European languages—even as the enrollments of many were declining precipitously. I felt strongly about smaller departments like Religion, Classics, and American Studies and the importance of new hires to their vitality and to their role in the larger university. I saw that the Women's Studies program would wither unless the university made a strong commitment to it as a department with a PhD program—and it is now a nationally ranked department. Being an administrator gave me an opportunity to address academic issues that matter—and to build consensus with colleagues about what matters.

Building a career at Rutgers was, for me, building a career on a campus to which I have been devoted. I recognize fully that younger faculty do not have the options I have enjoyed, or at least cannot easily make the choices I made so readily and so early in my career. Building a career now involves securing a national reputation through publication and conference work. I worry that newer faculty will never be major voices in university governance because, amid professional and personal demands, they lack the time to attend to it. Or they do not develop a connection to the life of the campus early in their careers, and—when tenure is achieved—they rarely see an incentive to make commitments beyond their departments, if even there. For me, the future of a liberal arts university—and the humanities' role in a research university—depends on the articulate involvement of younger faculty. I have often wished that graduate training exposed graduate students to the realities of how a university operates—not just to complaints that it is now a corporate place.

My teaching and administrative work have allowed me to join many debates—most importantly those about the nature of the liberal arts in a large public research university: why does a liberal arts education matter? Will it survive outside of liberal arts colleges (and how many of them will survive)? How will the liberal arts continue to inform the work of undergraduates increasingly choosing education in the professional schools? How are they to be more than "stuffing" (a term one student used in questioning general education requirements) in the first two years of college? What, finally, does "liberal arts" mean in today's research university? I am convinced that these questions will get comprehensive action only if newer members of the university community join the debate—with passion.

For me, as I move toward retirement, it seems the greatest challenges to those who teach in the humanities are dual: how will younger scholar-teachers find positions, let alone build careers, in a world where part-time or non-tenured labor is becoming the norm? And how will we all make a cogent case and provide continuing redefinition for the meaning of a liberal arts education and for the place of the humanities within it? John Dewey wrote in *Democracy in America* (1916), "In the multitude of educations, education is forgotten."[1] Because of my re-education over four decades at Rutgers, I have long believed that the joy of education comes in encountering ideas far afield from where we are comfortable; and that the liberal arts urge us toward new fields, more ideas, and new alertness. They are finally the foundation of a vital democracy. I still believe this. If life in a research university is about the reality of certain limitations, it is also about the potential of certain opportunities. Research, teaching, and administration: conceived together, they give faculty in a research university the opportunities to make a difference—and always to remind our colleagues and the larger world why we chose the humanities.

NOTE

1. Dewey, J. *Democracy in America*, London: Macmillan, 1916. 289.

CHAPTER 4

TEACHING

Garrett A. Sullivan, Jr.

Throughout my career, a question has tugged at the hem of my consciousness: what is the value of teaching English? Which is to say, what is *my* value? What do my students gain from my classes? I have usually responded to my self-doubt by referencing critical thinking, close reading, and effective writing, but never to my complete satisfaction. Lately, though, I've come to recognize a mismatch between how I evaluate my own teaching and what I can hope to achieve in the classroom. Take the case of "effective writing." I can feel dispirited when I consider how *little* the writing of most of my students has improved after a semester; more often than not, final papers are only so much better than first ones, even when students produce multiple drafts. The development of robust skills in critical thinking and close reading can seem a similarly elusive goal. What, then, have my students *really* learned? How do I measure it and, thereby, demonstrate to the world and myself the validity of what I do?

But here's the thing: "critical thinking," "effective writing," and "close reading" aren't skills to be acquired in a single course; developing them is the work of years, even a lifetime, and the process requires the enthusiastic or at least dogged participation of the student. Whereas a college mid-term in Biology 101 might demonstrate the degree of student mastery of the material, essay assignments are records of what students have or haven't learned about reading, writing, and critical thinking since grade school. Consequently, humanities professors are in a peculiar position. On the one hand, we can legitimately claim we are attempting work of real social and cultural importance by helping to cultivate these skills in our students; on the other, this process of cultivation is a gradual one with deferred results that may remain hidden from us. In the meantime, many of us evaluate ourselves in terms of an impact that cannot possibly be realized in a semester or two.

There is an additional problem. As important to the workplace as they are, the skills I have just identified are not primarily vocational in nature, which means that their utility is not always immediately apparent. This has led to wrongheaded assertions about humanities degrees being a dead end for employment.[1] While these assertions wither under scrutiny—we've all had conversations with lawyers or advertising executives who stress how important their English or History majors have been for their professional development—spurious claims about the humanities remain culturally powerful. The reason for this is the ascendance of an attenuated, neoliberal model of education that depicts the educational process almost entirely in terms of jobs. The ambitions this model champions are vocational, or pre-professional in the narrowest sense of the word, and it scoffs at disciplines whose "outcomes" don't obviously conform to those ambitions. It interprets "worth" and "success" and "gain" through the lens of income achieved. And, without my becoming aware of it until recently, this model is a primary reason why I had doubts about the value of what I have been doing in the classroom. In other words, I have belatedly come to recognize the folly of letting the attenuated model determine my sense of pedagogical success or failure.

In the wake of this recognition, I've been contemplating what I find most valuable in a humanities education. I've started with a proposition that should be non-controversial, but which proponents of the neoliberal model deem scandalous: a humanities education is about more than jobs. The value of such an education doesn't take the sole form of a paycheck; our students feel its effects over the course of a lifetime, and it shapes the ways they exist in the world. For advocates of the attenuated model of education, this all sounds dangerously squishy, as if I'm urging students to "follow their bliss" or drop out and join the Occupy movement. My wish for my students is both more and less modest; it centers upon the basic philosophical question of how best to live. An education in the humanities doesn't settle that question for us, but it provides some of the raw materials we need to address it. By "raw materials," I mean more than intellectual content, as important as that is. At its best, a humanities education exemplifies a fruitful and enlivening way of being in and engaging the world.

With that principle in mind, I will devote the rest of this essay to three topics that inform my work in the undergraduate classroom, and that I no longer feel the impulse to apologize for: "embodied experience," "ethics," and "pleasure." These topics are not exclusive concerns of the humanities—ethics are obviously crucial to the study of medicine, embodied experience is central to human geography, and intellectual pleasure finds a home in all academic disciplines—but, taken together, they represent a significant part of what makes the humanities important.

EMBODIED EXPERIENCE

In April 2014, Eric Jain posted a short video on the blog *Quantified Self: Self Knowledge Through Numbers* that describes his efforts to test the effects of a full moon on sleep. The video describes data Jain accumulated on his own sleep habits, the tools he used to analyze it (most notably, a software called Zenobase), and the approach he took in doing so.[2] What interests me most, however, is the title of the presentation Jain delivers within his video: "Am I a Werewolf?" This is meant as a joke, but the disconnect between title and project exemplifies a phenomenon with which all devotees of *Freakonomics* are familiar: the application of a social scientific method to all dimensions of human experience. (The immodest subtitle of *Freakonomics* is *A Rogue Economist Explores the Hidden Side of Everything*.[3]) "Am I a Werewolf?": let me check my data.

As Bruce Feiler has recently pointed out, "We are awash in numbers. Data is everywhere...Unquantifiable arenas like history, literature, religion and the arts are receding from public life, replaced by technology, statistics, science and math...[Our culture's gurus] use research to tackle issues that were once the provenance of poets, theologians and philosophers."[4] One result of this is an impoverished sense of the world. The truths about sleep contained in Jain's data cannot hold a candle to those captured in John Dryden's translation of Virgil's *Aeneid*. At the end of Book 5, Palinurus tumbles to his death after "the soft God of Sleep, with easie flight, / Descends" upon him: "The God, insulting him with superiour Strength, / Fell heavy upon him, plung'd him in the Sea."[5] These lines seem quaintly archaic to my students, until they notice how wonderfully they capture sleep's compulsory dimension.

Am I implying that an ancient literary account of sleep is, in some way, as valid as the scientific data accumulated by Jain (in an admittedly DIY fashion)? Don't Virgil and Dryden traffic in *metaphor*—sleep as a god who falls heavily upon us—while science deals in *reality*? As I point out to my students, the opposition between the real and the metaphoric is an inadequate one. As Ann Game and Andrew Metcalfe put it, metaphor offers a "full-bodied and -emotioned way of knowing" that has the "ability to change the shape of the world."[6] Moreover, there is no arena of human activity that is not informed by metaphor, including, of course, the sciences. Consider, first, how cultural understandings of cancer have been affected by the notion that cancer is a foreign "invader" (rather than the internal growth and division of cells); and, second, how those cultural understandings have impacted both medicine and society. The "war" on that "invader" fuels charitable giving to fund important research; it also frames the way in which millions of patients understand and experience their own bodies while undergoing cancer treatment.[7]

Put simply, language is powerful and those of us trained to scrutinize its operations have a great deal to impart to our students. Much of literature's potency derives from its capacity to make students experience themselves in new ways (the same can be said of history, philosophy and the visual arts, among others). As teachers, we can facilitate this by introducing our students to experience-shaping language (the soft, inexorable descent of sleep) as well as by critically unpacking that language's implications (cancer as an invader). What is at stake in this? Just the way our students apprehend themselves in the world.

ETHICS

When it comes to Shakespeare's *Macbeth*, if there is one thing my students are certain of, it is this: Lady Macbeth is to blame. They recognize, of course, that husband and wife conspire to murder King Duncan. Nonetheless, they routinely simplify the ethics of this conspiracy. Lady Macbeth is the real villain because she viciously and vigorously goads her husband to take actions that he would never have taken on his own.

To complicate this view, I try out a different argument. The Weird Sisters tell Macbeth he will be king, but they don't say how. Nonetheless, he immediately intuits what he will do as well as its catastrophic effects: "My thought, whose murther yet is but fantastical, / Shakes so my single state of man, / That function is smother'd in surmise, / That nothing is, but what is not."[8] (Macbeth considers *not* killing the king—"Chance may crown me" [1.3.144]—but quickly drops the idea; he knows the road he will travel.) From the outset, Macbeth is aware, first, of his "black and deep desires" (1.4.51); second, that he will act upon them; and, third, that the consequences will be disastrous. At the same time, Macbeth is wedded enough to his scruples to resist doing what he knows he is going to do, as when he itemizes reasons for not killing Duncan (1.7.12–28). Lady Macbeth's role, then, is to override those scruples in the aid of her husband's ambitions. By goading him, Lady Macbeth helps Macbeth act upon his "black and deep desires." In playing the villain, then, Lady Macbeth serves her husband's aspirations.

My students don't need to accept this interpretation to see that scapegoating Lady Macbeth fails to capture the ethical complexity of the couple's relationship. In my reading, Lady Macbeth casts herself in the role of villain in order to coerce her husband into fulfilling his (and her) greatest, most terrifying desire. Thought of in this way, *Macbeth* suggests, first, the degree to which we are self-contradictory beings (Macbeth longs for and dreads the same thing); second, the extent to which our own desires and actions are inevitably bound up in those of others (Lady Macbeth embraces her villainy in the service of her husband's ambitions); third, the partial and qualified nature of our own agency (we cannot know the extent to which the Macbeths' actions are conditioned by those of the Weird Sisters); and, finally, the necessity of eschewing simplistic ethical valuations.

As humanities professors, we routinely work to estrange the familiar. The "familiar" *Macbeth* is a text marred by an ethical simplicity to which not only our students subscribe; today, Lady Macbeth serves as cultural shorthand for conniving, overpowering villainy. The "unfamiliar" *Macbeth*, however, presents us with a different set of possibilities, including the opportunity to come to grips with ethical complexity. To teach *Macbeth* this way is to pose some questions that unsettle our students: why are so many of us invested in the idea of Macbeth's comparative innocence and Lady Macbeth's near-total guilt? What precisely do "guilt" and "innocence" mean in this case? And, crucially, what role does gender play in arrogating them as we do? More broadly, why are we drawn to identify "good guys" and "bad guys" in complex ethical situations? Questions such as these obviously have a broader applicability—consider how the simplistic arrogation of guilt and innocence can inform and deform international politics—and addressing them thoughtfully is part and parcel of an education in the humanities.

Pleasure

I think of my classes in ecosystemic terms: each is a specific community of organisms that (hopefully) thrives for a period in the peculiar environment of a university classroom; and, over time, each generates its own distinctive ecology of ideas. When I am teaching multiple sections of the same course, there is significant overlap, but there is also noticeable discontinuity. Concepts or examples that flourish in one intellectual ecosystem wither in another; not all climates can sustain the same forms of life. While the discrepancy between classes can be frustrating, it is also a reminder to respect the peculiar integrity of each pedagogical environment.

I am overly fond of my ecology metaphor. To me, it implies a pedagogy both rooted in the soil of the classroom and, most importantly, predicated upon interdependence. Whatever their point of origin, ideas grow in the classroom in unpredictable and often inspiring ways, thanks to a collective commitment to intellectual activity. Where my metaphor is less useful, however, is in accounting for a specific element of that activity: pleasure.

While the pursuit of pleasure through collective intellectual activity was a familiar notion to the ancient Greeks and Romans, it is significantly less so today. The connection between "education" and "pleasure" is flimsier than ever. In the popular imagination, pleasure is what college students seek by skipping class or going to Fort Lauderdale for spring break. While we are exhorted by advertisers and self-help gurus to do what we love for a living, education facilitates that possibility in only the most functional of ways; it is sometimes the means, seldom the end. And yet, as many of our students recognize, a humanities education provides a powerful source of pleasure.

The conventional wisdom is that the number of students in humanities disciplines has been steadily shrinking for decades. However, the conventional wisdom is wrong. As Michael Bérubé has shown, "there was a decline in bachelor's degrees in English, just as there was a drop-off in humanities enrollments more generally. But it happened almost entirely between 1970 and 1980. It is old news." The crisis in the humanities, Bérubé argues, "is a crisis in graduate education, in prestige, in funds, and most broadly, in legitimation. But it is not a crisis of undergraduate enrollment."[9] That there is no such crisis is remarkable, given the steady drumbeat of dour reports on the folly of pursuing a humanities education. One is tempted to ask, then, why aren't things even *worse* for the humanities?

There are a number of possible reasons, of course, including the recognition among many students (and parents) that a humanities education *does* prepare them for the job market. Intellectual pleasure provides another reason. The classroom is an ecosystem; it's also a playground in which someone picks up an idea, tosses it from hand to hand to gauge its heft, and then lobs it to the next person to see what she can do with it; and, finally, the classroom is an incubator that nurtures insights that will mature over the course of a lifetime. The humanities classroom invites metaphor, because, like metaphor itself, it has the capacity to change the shape of the world for our students.

Of course, teaching is not always an unalloyed joy. There are times when I dread it, and other times when I'm certain I've forgotten how to do it. Teaching is an activity that, no matter how experienced I become, I am constantly learning (or re-learning) how to do, and perhaps with good reason: different ecosystems require different things of those who inhabit them. And yet, on days when teaching goes well—when the students are entirely present to the text, and our discussion sends little cognitive jolts throughout the room—it seems to resuscitate a culturally moribund conception of pleasure grounded in collective discourse:

> Humans, Aristotle wrote, are social animals: to realize one's nature as a human then was to participate in a group activity. And the activity of choice, for cultivated Romans, as for the Greeks before them, was discourse...Cicero does not want to present his thoughts to his readers as a tract composed after solitary reflection; he wants to present them as an exchange of views among social and intellectual equals, a conversation in which he himself plays only a small part and in which there will be no clear victor.[10]

Needless to say, this ancient vision of intellectual conversation is an elitist one, a cultivated form of leisure built upon significant social inequality. An education in the humanities (or the arts) is sometimes disparaged along similar lines: as a privileged frivolity suited to days gone by. Meanwhile, as so-called public universities grow unaffordable to many, the necessity of making practical, job-directed educational decisions seems greater than ever.

But, what happens *after* a student has secured a steady income (a prospect, once again, that is *not* antithetical to an education in the humanities)? Has her education provided her with the most useful raw materials for constructing a life? Has it exemplified fruitful ways of being in the world, of negotiating complex ethical situations, and of finding pleasure in the personal and collective investigation of ideas? In the past, when I've doubted my profession, it has been because capacities such as these (which are obviously as crucial to the workplace as they are to the home) have seemed vague and unquantifiable, not to mention impossible to inculcate in a semester. What I've finally learned, however, is that the problem lies less with my profession than with the metrics I've used to evaluate it. "Data is everywhere," and, when it comes to teaching in the humanities, what it cannot account for is of the greatest worth.

NOTES

1. Grasgreen, A. "Liberal Arts Grads Win Long Term." *Inside Higher Ed*, January 22, 2014, accessed August 11, 2014, https://www.insidehighered.com/news/2014/01/22/see-how-liberal-arts-grads-really-fare-report-examines-long-term-data.

2. "Eric Jain on Sleep and Moon Phases," *Quantified Self: Self Knowledge Through Numbers*, accessed August 6, 2014, http://quantifiedself.com/2014/04/eric-jain-sleep-moon-phases/.

3. Levitt, S. D. and S. J. Dubner. *Freakonomics: A Rogue Economist Explores the Hidden Side of Everything*, New York: Harper Collins, 2006.

4. Feiler, B. "The United States of Metrics," *New York Times*, May 16, 2014, accessed August 6, 2014, http://www.nytimes.com/2014/05/18/fashion/the-united-states-of-metrics.html. As Adam Kirsch puts it, "The problem for the humanities—the institutional and budgetary problem—is that changed minds and expanded spirits are not the kinds of things that can be tabulated on bureaucratic reports. In humanistic study, quantification hits its limits (even if quantifiers refuse to recognize them)." Kirsch, A. "Technology is Taking Over English Departments: The False Promise of the Digital Humanities," *New Republic*, May 2, 2014, accessed August 6, 2014, http://www.newrepublic.com/article/117428/limits-digital-humanities-adam-kirsch.

5. Dryden, J. trans. *Virgil's Aeneid*, F. M. Keener, ed., London: Penguin, 1997. 144–145.

6. Game, A. and A. Metcalfe. *Passionate Sociology*, London: Sage, 1996. 51.

7. Sontag, S. *Illness as Metaphor*, New York: Farrar, Straus & Giroux, 1978.

8. Shakespeare, W. *Macbeth*, K. Muir, ed., 1951; London and New York: Routledge, 1991. 1.3.139–142. Henceforth cited in the essay.

9. Bérubé, M. "The Humanities Declining? Not According to the Numbers," *The Chronicle of Higher Education*, July 1, 2013, accessed August 6, 2014, http://chronicle.com/article/The-Humanities-Declining-Not/140093/.

10. Greenblatt, S. *The Swerve: How the World Became Modern*, New York and London: W. W. Norton, 2011. 69.

CHAPTER 5

GRADING

Karen J. Renner

I don't know about you, but just seeing that word—grading—triggers a stress response: my shoulder muscles tense up, my breath catches in my throat, my heart races. Although my students submit their papers electronically now, the word still evokes some past nightmare image of mile-high piles of stapled essays tottering above me. "Grading" ruins weekends and curtails vacations. "Grading" is the reason we sit at our computers on sunny days while everyone else gets to play outside.

The most dreadful thing I have to do before each semester is construct a grading calendar, a schedule that ensures I strategically distribute the due dates of assignments. While the schedule guarantees that I won't get too many assignments at once, seeing a semester's worth of grading laid out before me like that inevitably plunges me into panic and despair.

Because we in the humanities know the pains it can cause, "grading" is an irreproachable excuse among colleagues for skipped departmental events, missed social engagements, and lapses in friendships. Say "Sorry I missed your wedding, but I had 43 papers to grade," and you are automatically forgiven.

Unfortunately, I don't have a magical remedy, a technological time-saver, or palliative rubric that will instantly end your grading ails. But if the word alone can conjure such intense negative feelings, perhaps it's time we neutralized its power.

It's interesting to me that we in the humanities use the word "grading" as it's not even an accurate term for what most of us do most of the time. In my mind, "grading" is what you do with multiple-choice questions, fill-in-the-blanks, and short, handwritten responses scrawled in the inch or two of blank space below a typewritten question. "Grading" involves Scantron forms and keys that slide right alongside a student's answers so that the grader can quickly gauge what's right and what's wrong.

In the humanities, what we mean by "grading" is, more often than not, responding to student writing. Sure, from time to time we give assignments that can be graded in the traditional sense, but they are not the assignments that cause us agony. The essay is our most cherished yardstick and also our albatross, and evaluating essays is far more involved and complicated than the word "grading" would imply.

First, "grading" implies an objective measurement of competence. A good grade signifies that material has been mastered. Literally: you may pass. But the evaluation of writing is necessarily subjective because good writing is, to cop a cliché, largely in the eye of the beholder. Even the most objective kinds of writing require the author to make some stylistic decisions, and whether or not a choice works is often a matter of personal preference. What is to one reader helpful reiteration is to another unnecessary repetition. What one person considers an amusing and illustrative opening anecdote, another finds inappropriate and juvenile.

Because writing is, therefore, creative and idiosyncratic to a certain degree, writers often develop a deeper and more protective relationship with their work. This connection in turn makes the process of grading a potentially emotional one. I know that when one of my students announces that he or she would like to discuss an essay grade, I steel myself for an encounter that may very well involve the citing of previous excellent marks in English and an implied questioning of my judgment, an insistence that copious amounts of time were spent on the essay, and—sometimes—outrage or tears. This relationship between writers and their written work is what makes grading in the humanities so unique. I used to teach math, and I can tell you that I never ended up with students crying in my office because they incorrectly solved for x, nor did they indict my method of grading; the answer was right or it was wrong, and it all had very little to do with me. I'm not saying that math majors don't get upset about bad grades, but they don't mourn misplotted parabolas in the same way that writers do unfavorably received essays. This emotional component of grading writing is an added drain.

Grading essays certainly isn't made any easier by the fact that the learning "curve" with writing is really a zigzag line. Rhetorical success is notoriously unpredictable. Each writing task makes different demands, and experience and expertise do not guarantee flawless execution for all of eternity. We know this ourselves: we'll nail one article easily only to find that the next one is infuriatingly elusive. We also know this from our students' work: who hasn't saved a prized pupil's essay for last, only to find it more time-consuming to respond to precisely because the student is trying to articulate an especially complex argument or is trying out a new rhetorical technique? The word "essay," which derives from the French *essayer* or "to try or attempt," is entirely appropriate, for every piece of writing is its own endeavor.

Writers are much like athletes. The gymnast knows he can perform a piked double Arabian, the snowboarder has landed a backside triple cork 1,440 more times than she can count, but whether or not they can pull it off on any given day is up for grabs. If it weren't, the Olympic Games would be a total bore. Like athletes, all that writers can do to increase their odds of landing the rhetorical equivalent of a triple lutz is practice.

What are we then—those of us who grade writing—but coaches, patiently watching our students practice, knowing that even the best-intentioned and most expert will not always nail the dismount, may not, in fact, be able to reach the bars in the first place? Yes, at some point, we actually assign grades to the papers we read, but that part typically takes only a minute and is hardly the most helpful feedback we give. Giving a baseball player his batting average or error percentage won't help him improve. Instead, what coaches do is try to explain why things went wrong and offer feedback to increase the likelihood of success in the future. For similar reasons, the bulk of our time is spent describing a way to connect a paragraph back to the thesis, illustrating how a writer could unpack a quotation to give an argument more impact, or perhaps merely explaining why exclamation points are not the best way to give emphasis.

And yet what do we call all this important, complicated work? Grading. Hardly a flattering term.

I have a friend who, when asked how her semester was going, would sarcastically reply, "Oh, you know, I'm touching minds, changing lives." On the one hand, she was pointing out the discrepancy between the cultural ideal of the teacher as a selfless, inspirational mentor, represented in films like *Dangerous Minds* and *Freedom Writers*, and the actual daily experience of teaching. On the other, however, she was mocking the idea that what happens in an actual classroom could be meaningful enough to touch minds and change lives. Perhaps doing so masked a desire, too often disappointed, for exactly those kinds of enlightening experiences, but even so, the result was a dig at both her students and herself.

We do something similar when we use the word "grading": we downplay the intellectual and emotional complexity as well as the significance of what we do. In addition, "grading," with all of its negative connotations, presumes a process that won't be rewarding or meaningful, at least not enough to compensate for the effort it took. Rather than employing an aggrandizing euphemism as we in academia are wont to do, we instead opt for a dysphemism, a kind of word that, as Steven Pinker explains in "The Seven Words You Can't Say on Television," focuses our and our listener's attention on the most disagreeable aspects of its referent. This type of term, as Pinker puts it, "kidnaps our attention and forces us to consider its unpleasant connotations."[1]

There are other words in our language capable of provoking dramatic emotional responses. They often have four letters.

"Grading" and expletives have more in common than we might at first realize once we consider their functions. Experts claim, for example, that swearing performs several positive emotional and social functions. One is to allow us to vent negative feelings; this is why we cuss when we stub a toe or when our computer blue-screens. In fact, in a fascinating study, researchers discovered that swearing actually helped people endure pain.[2] We use the word "grade" in similar fashion. Talking about "grading" helps us express in advance the mental strain we expect will come from reading stacks of our students' work. It's a sort of pre-emptive "ouch" in anticipation of the stress to come.

Expletives are also used for social bonding. I'm thinking here of how the word "bastard" can be a term of endearment or how friends sometimes affectionately tell each other to "piss off." "Grading" allows for comparable moments of connection:

"Would you like to come over for drinks?"

"Sorry, I've got 43 essays to grade."

"Ugh. Good luck."

We express anxiety over our coming plight, and our colleague responds with empathy and support, all via our shared understanding of "grading."

So much for the positive uses of expletives. More familiar, perhaps, are their negative functions. For one, expletives designate something taboo, impure, and generally icky. Doesn't "grading" accomplish the very same thing? Isn't that why a spontaneously uttered "ugh" is an acceptable response to our announcement that we have 43 essays to grade? We also use bad words to demean others. In fact, some of the most powerful expletives are derogatory names for people of a certain race, ethnicity, gender, or sexuality; others are degrading terms for body parts and processes. Sometimes, the two overlap.

The question is what or whom we degrade when we use the word "grading" and why we choose to do so.

The most obvious answer is our students.

One of the best things I ever did for my teaching was to become a student again when I enrolled in photography classes a few years ago. Not only did sitting on the other side of the desk allow me to see how students actually respond to the grades they receive, but the experience also reminded me of what it's like to be graded. Oh sure, as an academic, I'm graded all the time: students grade my teaching, department chairs and deans grade my employee performance, editors grade my research articles. But there's something different about being graded on a skill at which I'm a beginner desperately longing to be something more.

When handed back work, what was the first thing I did? Exactly the same thing I did as an undergraduate: scoured it for comments, somewhat desperately, I might add. Even if I received a good grade, I still felt disappointed if the professor said nothing about my clever pun on "depth of field" in paragraph three. In fact, I actually felt worse if I received a good grade and few comments. There is something tawdry about receiving an A on a paper you're not sure was really read. I would argue that it's worse than getting a low grade on a carefully marked-up essay. At least in the second case you know you were taken seriously.

And how did most of my classmates feel? Pretty much the same way.

Why did this surprise me? Why had I assumed that I was so much more discerning than my undergraduates?

Certainly, some students churn out work without much thought, but I don't believe they comprise the majority, and even if they did, would that general tendency be merely a matter of poor character among an entire generation? I think not. Our students know how we feel about grading their work. When we groan about grading, we send the message that most of our students can't write anything worth reading and, even when they have good ideas, their writing is a slog.

Imagine if parents treated the activities they had to do for the sake of their children this way. Imagine if "bus-stopping" were some degrading term that implied that the time spent walking one's children to the bus stop and waiting for them to be picked up was about as boring and as useless as watching grass grow. Imagine if parents said, with their children in earshot, "I've got to go to some parent–teacher conference" in the same tone of voice as we say, "I've got 43 essays to grade." What would be the effect?

Moreover, our students read the comments on their papers, and they read between the lines of those comments. If we're not engaged, they won't be engaged the next time they write for us and likely not the next time they write for someone else either. If they have no expectation of serious feedback, why would they not opt to spend their time on activities that promise to be more meaningful? Why shouldn't they expect that the effort they expend writing a paper be commensurate to the effort we spend responding?

We denigrate our students when we use "grading" like it's some swear word that designates dirty work. I don't think we do so simply because we're crotchety. I think we often have too many papers to grade at one time and struggle to find a way to balance our desire to be a good teacher with our desire to have a life. When we fail to achieve this balance, we look for someone to blame, and students are ready-made scapegoats, for they're the creators of all that supposed muck, aren't they?

The other group we demean when we reduce the intricate work of responding to writing to "grading" is ourselves. Why do we do such a thing?

Let's face it: responding to writing in meaningful ways is not an honored task. Oh, in a public setting, everyone from the president and the provost down to associate deans and department chairs will profess the importance of writing instruction. How could they not? Dismissing the teaching of writing is like saying you are opposed to puppies, small children, veterans, and the elderly. Certainly, it is a cardinal academic sin.

But the decisions administrators actually make tell another tale. The most writing-intensive courses serving the least experienced writers (e.g., freshman composition)—students who need the most one-on-one attention and detailed feedback—are typically taught by those lowest on the institutional totem pole (non-tenure-track faculty, adjuncts, graduate students), those with the biggest workloads and smallest salaries.

The message sent is that the teaching of writing is not very hard, not especially time-consuming, and certainly capable of being accomplished in a class or two, so that higher-up faculty need not sully their classrooms with grammar instruction or their desks with poorly written essays. If the teaching of writing is treated like the work of untouchables, then it is hardly surprising that the "grading" of writing would be also be seen as mindless, pointless, and thankless drudgery.

Although I know better, I find myself influenced by this kind of thinking all the time. The last month of each semester is taken up with student essays; research grinds to a halt, creative juices all but evaporate, my blog falls silent. I find myself saying to everyone how *long* it's been since I've done any writing.

But that isn't true: during that time, I've been writing oodles. Okay, so maybe my suggestions for revision on a student's essay about the gothic elements of *House of Cards* aren't exactly Faulknerian, but giving clear and directive feedback should count for something; we wouldn't appreciate good editors so much ourselves if that sort of communication were easy. So why don't we value this type of writing when we do it ourselves for our students?

Well, the easy answer is that our institutions don't value it or at least don't have mechanisms in place that assign it value. Where on my annual report can I write that I helped a student write a kick-ass paper on masculinity, class, and imperialism in the videogame *Luigi's Mansion*? Like syllabi, essay prompts, and handouts, our responses to students' papers are largely invisible labor that goes unacknowledged and uncelebrated. I'm not saying that things can and should be different, only that we should recognize that a considerable portion of our written work is not recognized as writing or as work.

It doesn't help that faculty members who do spend considerable time commenting on their students' writing are implicitly told that they are wasting that time. Frequently, this message is packaged as advice given in the best interest of the instructor's mental well-being: "You can't do everything, you know. Spend more time on your own work." The especially fortunate faculty member is also let in on some time-saving tricks of the trade, such as *Never spend more than 10–15 minutes per essay* (advice that never seems to adapt to the length of the assignment); or *Do more peer review!*; or (my personal favorite) *Don't put comments on final work because the students don't read them anyway*. The last is often accompanied by the suggestion that students who want comments on their final essays provide a self-addressed, stamped envelope (although I'm not sure how this gambit still works in the age of email).

Maybe some people have found ways to successfully put these suggestions into practice. If so, bravo. The only time I tried, it was a disaster. The quality of my relationships with students plummeted, and I enjoyed teaching less. What I realized is that I actually *like* grading when it involves more than grading. I don't especially enjoy the time it takes up or the stress it causes, but when I feel a return from the students—both that they benefited from and appreciated the feedback I gave—it's more than worth it.

What I realized is that what makes me miserable is not so much the time I spend responding to student writing but rather feeling like a sap for doing it.

So, what am I advocating? Certainly not that we join hands across the humanities and campaign for the censoring of the word "grading" or replace it with some other friendlier moniker. Changing our terminology won't alleviate the process. I'm sure I won't feel any better about having to *evaluate* or *respond to* or *comment on* 43 essays.

But, perhaps, it will help if we are mindful of the connotations that "grading" has accumulated over time and avoid falling victim to them ourselves—like the idea that grading is dirty work because we are handling the refuse of student writing. If we approach the papers we receive as best efforts instead of assuming that every error is the result of laziness or haste, we will respond more generously. And most of our students, in seeing us take their work more seriously, will very likely begin taking it more seriously as well.

More importantly, let's feel satisfaction, not shame, about the time and effort we put into grading. Let's accept that it is time-consuming because it is difficult and that although it is difficult, it's also worthwhile and perhaps even at times enjoyable.

In the film *The Gift,* a mother played by Cate Blanchett encounters the situation that all parents must find themselves in at some point: she is asked by her son what a swear word means, specifically "fuck." She deftly replies that it is "a bad word for something nice."[3]

Grading, I would argue, is also a bad word for something nice. At times, it might seem more like a nice word for something bloody awful (like when you have a stack of 43 papers awaiting you on your desk). But we know from experience that grading can range from grueling to gratifying. Let's at least start from the presumption that it will be the latter.

NOTES

1. Pinker, S. "The Seven Words You Can't Say on Television." In *The Stuff of Thought: Language as a Window into Human Nature*, New York: Penguin, 2007. 323–372, 339.
2. Joelving, F. "Why the #$%! Do We Swear? For Pain Relief," *Scientific American*, July 12, 2009, accessed August 15, 2014, http://www. scientificamerican.com/article/why-do-we-swear/.
3. *The Gift*, DVD, directed by Sam Raimi. 2000; Paramount Classics, 2001.

CHAPTER 6

DEPARTMENTAL AND UNIVERSITY CITIZENSHIP

Claire Bond Potter

Your first weeks on a new campus are exciting and confusing. Remembering names, finding your classroom, or learning how to download your class list are daily challenges. As if being the new kid were not enough, you will soon be invited to participate in institutional work that you have probably only observed from afar. Suddenly you are one of the people in charge, and you have new responsibilities. Hiring, creating curriculum, and participating in faculty governance are a few of the things that fall under the rubric of departmental, or university, citizenship. As a member of the faculty, you also have new authority over office staff, undergraduates, and graduate students and contingent faculty.

As that first week becomes a month, a semester, and more, be aware that becoming a good citizen is, in a sense, a final stage of your graduate education that occurs on the job. You are in transition and, at the same time, a member of a new community. How will you evolve into the departmental, and university, citizen you wish to be?

Let's start with who you are already. In addition to your training, you have a life. You may be—or hope to be—a parent; you may be childless, partnered or single. You may be differently abled. You have a gender, ethnic, regional, and a sexual identity. You may be confident about your insider status; or you may feel like an outsider to higher education, regardless of your accomplishments. For these reasons, some colleagues[1] with whom I discussed this chapter wondered if "citizenship" was not a loaded term for discussing ourselves in community with others. Although the term implies *inclusion*, citizenship also functions to *exclude.* Citizenship feels natural and legible to some; to others, citizenship is earned at a price to the self. As Deborah Gray White has observed, "the Ivory Tower can be an exhilarating, stimulating place. But it can also be isolating, debilitating, and lonely, especially for those who not only buck the status quo but whose very bodies stand in opposition to the conventional wisdom regarding academia."[2]

Regardless of who you are, you will need help from lots of people to learn how to function in your new institution. For this reason, some of the first allies to cultivate will be the staff whose work supports your labor: librarians, information technology support, administrative assistants, and janitors deserve your courtesy and frequent thanks. "Nurture and respect the staff members with whom you work most closely," says University of Colorado historian Paul Harvey. "Make friends with the receptionist in the Dean's office. Don't yell at your department administrator or secretary who may have forgotten to do something you needed them to do. Just gently remind them, make a joke about your own forgetfulness, and move on." Your time may feel more valuable than theirs, but it isn't. Don't make last-minute requests lightly because, sooner or later, there *is* something you will genuinely need at the last second and, when you do, don't forget to acknowledge that it is a favor, not your right.

Aside from its social and cultural context, university citizenship embraces activities and attitudes you bring to this new work. Even in your first year, you may be asked to serve on appointed or elected committees; participate in the creation and assessment of a new curriculum; advise student clubs; and brainstorm civic engagement projects. To be effective, you need to work with everyone, look out for other people's needs as well as your own, and meet your commitments. Some institutions will consider religious faith as a form of citizenship, something you should understand prior to accepting a job. Bob Jones University encourages its faculty and administrators "to commit to a church family," while Catholic University seeks faculty "who are not only professionally competent but who can also contribute to its Catholic, moral and cultural milieu." At other schools, particularly those funded with public dollars, public affirmations of faith may be viewed as inappropriate in a work context.

You will find that, even within a college or university, different departments nurture distinct expectations of what good university citizens do. "Learn your department's history," says historian Catherine

Kelly of the University of Oklahoma. David Mazella, a member of the English Department at the University of Houston, agrees. New faculty members need to listen to "what everyone is worried about, what everyone is proud of." Watch how your new colleagues conduct themselves in department meetings. Before suggesting changes, "ask why things are done in a particular way," Mazella urges. "The reasons will be more historical than logical, but they will help you make sense of what's going on." When committee assignments are distributed, "be selective, but be sure to follow through once [you have] committed."

Differences in collegial style are also worth understanding as you begin to navigate outside your home department or division. At one university where I worked, Department A was highly convivial; traditionally, it met once a month over drinks. Department B was well known as combative and factional, meeting weekly over brown bag lunches. Differences in departmental style pointed to serious political and philosophical divides as well: members of each department often pointed to the other as an object lesson on how things should *not* be done. And yet, members of both A and B were repeatedly elected to prestigious faculty committees, appointed as deans, and even asked to step in as provosts. In different ways, both departments were producing excellent university citizens who commanded respect from their peers in other departments.

You may wish to test your early impressions—again, in the form of questions rather than assertions that might make your new colleagues feel judged or criticized. It's worth remembering that the people who hired you have anxieties too: they want you to be happy and feel that you are in the right place. They are also trying to learn about you, and you should be as forthcoming as you can without breaching your own sense of privacy. For a few months, every conversation will be an *ad hoc* orientation. Colleagues will give you advice on the best doctors, home prices, and how to register students for classes. They will drop by to gossip about every hiring and tenure decision made at the institution since the Pleistocene Age. While being privy to political gossip can be an education, remember that opinions are often conveyed as facts and probably are not relevant to your own future at the institution. Try not to make exclusive alliances at the expense of relationships with a range of colleagues, and extend your connections across the university by attending events like talks and mini-conferences.

"As an assistant professor, meet and maintain relationships with people outside your unit," says historian Timothy Stewart-Winter at Rutgers University-Newark. Social and intellectual events can be a neutral space where you and your new colleagues can learn about each other informally, and where you can cultivate the skill of bridging real or perceived differences. These differences may be intellectual, political, or social. As Elaine Lewinnek, in American Studies at Cal State-Fullerton, recalls, "I was the only one in my department with young kids and a commute of over an hour. Other differences may involve race, sexuality, generation, or class origins. Going out for a beer with colleagues may be one of the most important things you do." It may also give you a low-risk space for understanding things that make little sense to you, since you will want to "take time to observe your new home before campaigning to change things," says historian Brian Ogilvie of the University of Massachusetts-Amherst.

A good departmental or university citizen does not have to *like* everyone, but does need to *work* with everyone. You may wish to remain politely distant from those who encourage you to identify with a faction, or who give you unwanted advice and information about your colleagues that may be delivered in a clumsy attempt to welcome you. On my first day at work as a publicly queer scholar, X dropped by. "Watch out for Y: he is very homophobic," this heterosexual full professor advised me about a departmental colleague. I can't even begin to convey how alarmed I was. I confided in another senior colleague who went out of her way to reassure me and introduce me to Y. If Y had negative views about homosexuality, he—quite properly—never shared them over the course of our relationship of almost two decades. Later, as chair of the department, he became a mentor, helping me run my first tenure case for a younger colleague.

Working through, and across, perceived differences does not have to be stressful. It will require developing skills like listening, diplomacy, and a capacity for principled compromise. However, it shouldn't require concealing legitimate viewpoints or, conversely, making yourself a target by taking rigid positions that put you in a minority position. You were hired to do a job—not fly under the radar until tenure, or change the world one department at a time. Instead, learn what kind of citizen you want to be by developing relevant commitments, and shopping them to the broadest possible audience. "Because I come from a performance background, I often say 'Play to the whole house,'" says Brian Herrera of Princeton University's Theater Department. "Make sure 'your performance' is legible to your hiring unit, to your division/college/university and to 'the profession' at large. Don't think you're solid just because the folks in the front row (or the balcony) think you're great," Hererra cautions. "And the only way to know these disparate audiences is by becoming, to the extent you are able, involved with each, and not over-involved with any one."

So, how might this work in practice? Let's look at three case studies.[3]

Marisol took her PhD in Art History at Prestigious University; she felt fortunate to have landed a tenure-track job at a liberal arts college. Her graduate mentors counseled her to avoid service, do the acceptable minimum in the classroom, and focus on her first book. As one advised, "No one ever got tenure for committee work or being a great teacher!" However, Marisol knew that faculty governance and teaching were important to her future colleagues. During the interview, she mentioned being excited about the many campus LGBT (lesbian, gay, bisexual, and transgender) events she had seen advertised, and she imagined herself working on a sexuality studies curriculum with other faculty she had met. However, she wondered if she would have to put off the other things she wanted from the job until after tenure.

Should Marisol lay low? Martha Jones, a professor of History and African American Studies at the University of Michigan might advise her to step up. "Everyone will do service, everyone should," Jones says. Marisol was correct about her colleagues' expectations, which match her own hopes for the job. "Doing the service that matters to you, and that you might even enjoy, is as good as it gets," Jones says. "Know something about what you'd prefer to do, what you're good at, what works for your overall lifestyle, and then seek it out." Hoping that you can evade service not only gives you a reputation for having to be forced into it, but can also produce "tasks that make you miserable."

What brought Marisol's mentors success several decades ago may not be appropriate or desirable for the career she will have. They may assume that research university standards for tenure are universal, when, in fact, their advice reflects standards by which relatively few scholars will be reviewed. Marisol needs to temper well-meaning advice with her own sense of where she is, what her new colleagues have communicated, and what she wants from the job. That said, Brian Ogilvie would urge her to ramp up her ambitions gradually. "Don't take on too much," he advises, "and make sure that what you take on is, as much as possible, aligned with your own longer-term goals. Teach a small number of courses and revise them carefully; don't develop a new course every year. If you do service outside your department, make sure that it involves something that you care about and in which you have expertise or want to develop it. If your plate is full, and your department head or chair asks you to take on something new, ask, 'OK, if I do that, which of my other responsibilities, X, Y, and Z, should I pass on to someone else?'"

Marisol will, of course, have to work to balance her commitments to the institution with a commitment to scholarship that meets her own, and her department's, standards. Ogilvie would counsel her to find time every day "for scholarly engagement" that leads to publication. While departmental citizenship and service to the profession are an important part of most tenure files, unfinished scholarship will be an obvious weakness at the time of a tenure review. Marisol would be wise to ask for advice as she expands her campus activities, and to evaluate it in context. At a research university like the one she attended, Marisol's scholarship and service to the department might have more of an impact on her career than university service, or even teaching. Brown University historian Matthew Pratt Guterl cautions that departmental colleagues may, consciously or unconsciously, prioritize what you have done for them over your impact on students, and that "over the long haul, you can't help students without tenure." However, seven years is a long time to put your light under a bushel. For Marisol to put off making contributions she knows are important, on the advice of outsiders to the liberal arts college, would probably be a mistake.

Akiko had just finished her first year in the Italian Department at Land Grant U. The department was congenial, she had been praised for her work on the majors' committee, and a paper she gave to the divisional seminar had been well received. Then, one day, a White colleague greeted her as "Mia," the name of another Asian-American woman who worked in the French Department. Akiko was stunned, hurt, and unable to respond. She went home and vented her feelings in a long, angry post on Facebook, where friends at other institutions responded sympathetically, some recounting their own experience with racial microaggressions.

Akiko's response to an unintentional, but callous, slight by a colleague was understandable. Being without words when upset is a common experience, particularly when a rude answer or an angry confrontation with a senior colleague seems unavoidable. Therefore, Akiko chose to vent in a way she believed was private and, she hoped, would help her process the event. A conversation with a second colleague would have been a better idea, however. Sympathy from friends certainly made Akiko feel less alone, but it may not have helped her put this incident in perspective or given her a strategy to process what she experienced as racist behavior. Worse, privacy settings did not guarantee that Akiko's words would not be broadcast beyond her intended audience: screen shots could be reposted elsewhere, she might have "friends" she has forgotten about, or a graduate mentor who believes he is helping could contact one of Akiko's new colleagues without her permission. One humanities professor recalls a *Social* similar situation: anonymous complaints about the department (like *media* "an angry Yelp review") on a job wiki came to light during a routine Google search by an administrative assistant. It was instantly clear who had written the post. When confronted, the writer removed it, but "it was impossible to take this back. No one senior ever forgot."

Being a good department or university citizen requires that we be thoughtful about what we communicate on the Internet as well as in person, not using social media to make a case against others even when we know we have been wronged. Good email etiquette is another habit worth cultivating. Knowing what level of formality each communication requires and learning to organize your email and answering it in a timely way are all important skills. Making a staff member, student, or faculty colleague hunt you down sends the unintentional message that their time is unimportant to you. When you are in the middle of a disagreement and feel yourself becoming frustrated or irritated, email can be risky and hard to interpret. Instead, pick up the telephone or walk down the hall to have a conversation with your correspondent or, if the miscommunication is a barrier to that, a sympathetic colleague. Above all else, police your copy line, and use "reply to all" sparingly, particularly if emotions are running high. Never spread the quarrel by adding people to the blind copy line, or forwarding emails without permission.

Consider that venting may make you feel better *or* worse, but unintended consequences attend the public airing of grievances: Akiko's legitimate concern was never discussed in her own workplace and she risked her behavior becoming the issue instead. "Behave respectfully toward everyone," counsels Brian Ogilvie. "Keep any negative thoughts about your colleagues to yourself, your therapist, or your diary." It might initially be a relief to discuss your experience on social media or in a blog post, but before you do ask yourself: would I say this directly to the person who has upset me? If not, don't write publicly about it either. To avoid crossed wires more generally (in 2014, a teaching assistant made national news when, instead of a study guide, she sent a naked selfie to students by mistake), Ogilvie advises establishing a private email account for personal business; archiving photographs on a cloud account or a personal computer; and encrypting personal documents.

Deon was thrilled with his tenure-track job at Impressive College. A previous postdoctoral fellowship, and the research package Impressive offered, meant that he was poised to finish a first book by the time of his reappointment. Normally, someone in his first year would not be asked to participate in a faculty search, but because another qualified person in the department was on leave, the department chair made an exception and asked Deon. It was a significant commitment, but he agreed. Although Deon was not able to get revised chapters to the press that spring, he learned that he liked, and was good at, committee service. Numerous colleagues, and the department secretary, made a point of dropping by to tell Deon how impressed they were with his work on the search. When he was asked to represent the department on a university committee, Deon was flattered and said yes, although it meant canceling summer plans to meet his new manuscript deadline.

Many people would have rightly counseled Deon to say no to the first committee, and certainly to the second. Canceling a vacation to do work for the department should not become a habit either: Deon needs a personal life, and he should plan downtime to recharge. And yet, he was eager to begin his career and enjoyed having an impact on campus. If he has also learned that he enjoys administrative work, and is realistic about his writing, why should Deon not say yes to a university committee? "Consider service beyond your department or program," Martha Jones counsels. "It can be a welcome relief from the smallness of some department dynamics, and it widens your circle of colleagues and allies." Deon may also be flirting with a leadership role at the university. He will need to finish his book and get tenure to do that, but spending time with "good leaders, administrators, and colleagues," Jones notes, will enrich Deon's career, whatever form it takes. Making relationships with successful administrators will give him an additional pool of mentors for understanding when to say no. Successful administrators have the experience of moving a research and teaching agenda forward while gaining administrative credentials, whereas many of Deon's departmental colleagues may not.

By saying yes to the university committee, Deon is also making an important contribution to the department that should be underscored. University service helps make a larger institutional case for the humanities, says English professor Brooke Conti of SUNY-Brockport. It is "a way of publicly representing and performing the value of your discipline and your department." People in other departments and divisions may have less sense than they should of what humanities professors do, "either in the classroom or in their research," Conti points out, and yet they are making decisions that have an impact on your department. "That's obviously not in itself a reason to do college-wide service," she reminds us. "But being a visible and respected contributor often has value beyond the actual work of whichever committee or task force you're on."

Being a good department and university citizen means making contributions, being perceptive about how they are received, understanding what you do best, and learning what you need to know. It means working with colleagues and staff effectively and kindly, even when they exasperate you. However, it does *not* mean being all things to all people; or doing everything you are asked to do, no matter how busy you are and regardless of who asks. While good citizens do sometimes take on an extra job, if you believe that you are doing too much university work, reach out to a senior colleague to help you withdraw from a few of these commitments. If you cannot, or if the work is what you were hired to do, try to negotiate for the resources you may need to do the job well, keep pace with your scholarship, and succeed in the classroom.

In other words, balance what you cannot control with the things you can try to control; know that the balancing act may occur over a longer time than one semester. Solicit and listen to advice. Be willing to accept someone else's authority while learning to establish your own. Be respectful of other people's work, and recognize what talents you need to develop.

And, above all, be yourself. This means, over time, that the job will teach you something about *you*, as well as about your colleagues and students. In learning what kind of university citizen you want to be, recognize your strengths and weaknesses. Be conscious of what ambitions you bring to that table as well as how your new job supports or hinders those ambitions. Learn what compromises open new doors and, conversely, whether you find yourself compromising in ways that create new problems. Good citizens are present. They listen; they speak up tactfully and respectfully; and they know when silence is productive too.

Remember, there is a life beyond the tenure process: that life, and many of the choices that make up a career, is yours.

Notes

1. Because it is easy to generalize from one's own experience, I posted a question about being a university citizen on two bulletin boards; colleagues of different ages, disciplines, and life stages provided their views. Some asked to be anonymous. Those who did agree to be acknowledged are Leslie Bary, Melissa Bruninga-Matteau, Brooke Conti, Matthew Pratt Guterl, Paul Harvey, Brian Herrera, Martha

Jones, Catherine Kelly, Elaine Lewinnek, David Mazella, Brian Ogilvie, Sean Williams, and Timothy Stewart Winter.

2. White, D. G. "A Telling History." In *Telling Histories: Black Women in the Ivory Tower*, D. G. White, ed., Chapel Hill: The University of North Carolina Press, 2008. 1–27, 21. See also McNaron, T. ed. *Poisoned Ivy: Lesbian and Gay Academics Confronting Homophobia*, Philadelphia, PA: Temple University Press, 1996; Agathangelou, A. M. and L. H. M. Ling. "An Unten(ur)able Position: The Politics of Teaching for Women of Color," *International Feminist Journal of Politics* 4 (2002): 368–398; and Gutiérrez y Muhs, G., Y. F. Niemann, C. G. González, and A. P. Harris, eds. *Presumed Incompetent: The Intersections of Race and Class for Women in Academia*, Boulder, CO: University of Colorado Press, 2012.

3. These experiences are fictional, and are not drawn from the lives of real people.

CHAPTER 7

RESEARCH AND THE PUBLIC: THE PERILS OF PUBLIC ENGAGEMENT

Brendan Kane

The email denouncing me as an apologist for genocide came at a particularly bad moment. Saturday morning, so my guard was down. Shouldn't I be watching cartoons with the kids and relaxing after a massive breakfast? Serves me right for checking work email on a weekend morning (although that is a different essay). The email arrived while I was still in the glow of what I felt was the greatest experience of my professional life, the opening of an exhibition that I had co-curated with my friend and colleague Tom Herron (English, East Carolina University) at the Folger Shakespeare Library (*Nobility and Newcomers in Renaissance Ireland*, which ran January through May 2013). The opening was a packed, gala event, presided over by the Irish ambassador and the director of the Folger, and attended by family, friends, colleagues, and hundreds of others. Tom and I gave opening addresses, welcomed guests, and reveled in an evening of excitement, support, *hors d'oeuvres*, and free booze. Seemingly, a fine time was had by all—certainly by my younger son Gavin, ten at the time, who ate his body weight in finger food—and compliments and kudos flowed as freely as the wine. And seemingly with the same effect, for on the following Saturday I was, as they say, fat and happy: relaxed, tired, and self-satisfied in the wake of what seemed a universally positive experience.

From such heady heights, the fall was fast and far. The message I received denouncing the exhibition as an offense to the tragedy suffered by the Irish people was copied to the Folger and to the Irish Embassy, and quickly made its way to the media. In short order, Tom and I found ourselves likened to Holocaust deniers in the Irish-American press—and that was only the worst of several unflattering comparisons. Having grown up in a large Irish-American family, and as an Irish historian and Gaelic speaker, I consider myself a part of that community, and the exhibition was, in part, intended to celebrate its past. To be painted an "apologist for genocide" by those I consider my own was devastating. As difficult as it was to read the articles themselves, reading the comments was worse. We all know that Internet comments can be an uncivil horror. Such knowledge hardly prepares you, however, for being the object of blogosphere wrath. After some initial forays in, I simply stopped reading the comments and hunkered down, ostriched away from comment threads, yet still nervous about what might start coming into my university email. The Folger, too, was bombarded with comments. Some were positive and seemingly made in ignorance of the controversy; others sought further information on early modern Ireland or asked follow-up questions related to the exhibition. However, many others were negative and prompted by the initial media attack, and the Folger's Facebook page lit up in what seemed a pile-on of outrage.

I had eagerly pursued the chance to curate the exhibition, keen to bring my interests, research, and ideas to a public audience. No one had to convince me of the potential joys and upsides of public engagement; they seemed self-evident and immensely attractive in a world otherwise confined to speaking with specialist peers or very non-specialist undergraduates. The perils of public engagement, however, I learned on my own. And a harsh lesson it was. Given to depression, I shut down. One week feeling fat and happy was followed by two months of mental paralysis, and a lingering blackness that trailed long in its wake.

My experience with the perils of public engagement was primarily driven by the politics of Ireland and its diaspora but, nonetheless, it has implications for any who seek to work in a professional capacity beyond the academy. Such work is increasingly popular among academics, as they undertake blogging, outreach, community partnerships, experiential learning initiatives, and myriad other forms of public intellectual life. My particular tale offers a point of departure for thinking about the unintended consequences of efforts to present in a public forum research that addresses complex and sensitive issues.

This last statement raises the obvious question of what I mean by public engagement. Not all forms of public engagement are the same, of course. Perhaps it is easiest to simply state what I am *not* concerned with, namely the conscious courting of controversy and/or the articulating of partisan positions that we typically associate with the "public intellectual." This particular individual sets out to stir debate and knows that criticism in the blogosphere, and in the press more generally, is not only part of the job, it is a *reward* of it—proof that the riding forth has been successful and worthwhile. Paul Krugman and Niall Ferguson—to take two examples from opposite ends of the ideological spectrum—know full well that people are going to be coming for them. They're fine with it; they expect it; they presumably would feel disappointed if pushback were not forthcoming. This essay is not for them.

Rather, I am addressing those academics thinking about presenting their work to an audience beyond their peers and students. This might mean giving a lecture to a local society or answering questions to the local media related to a public event. It might be a bit more complex, such as working with community groups toward some goal of mutual interest—a project that might even include the participation of students. It may even be connected to an issue that is controversial, say community rights or local politics or contested matters of remembrance. The point here is that, while public engagement can take many shapes and forms, so too can the perils that come with it. And that fact, regardless of the particular mode of engagement one endeavors to undertake, is worth reflecting on before venturing into uncharted territory.

To make a crude division, we might think of the *internal* and *external* perils associated with such endeavors. By "internal," I mean those originating within our own institutions. My own experience is at a research university, the University of Connecticut, which has a complicated relationship with public engagement. Outreach is a vital part of the University's character and mission, in part because it is the state's "flagship" public institution, and service to its citizens is a charge taken seriously and pursued quite passionately by some. My own department, History, hosts the Connecticut State Historian—an appointed position with duties including the promotion, preservation, and study of local history—and actively encourages the pursuit of public history by our students, many of whom are involved in projects ranging from advocacy work to the creation of local history digital humanities databases and museum displays. However, outreach and research require time and effort, and the more time we put into outreach the less we can devote to research and writing. Making the choice to do outreach work, then, can bring dire consequences, with failure to achieve promotion and/or merit increases being the two most obvious. No one in my department could dream of getting tenure or reaching full professor for curating an exhibition, no matter how prestigious the venue, and the person who published a monograph with an undistinguished press would best them in the merit pool every time.

There is a further, more interpersonal problem that may arise should you devote more energy to public engagement than to cranking out books and articles: your colleagues might perceive you as a less serious scholar. Undoubtedly, research institutions like the University of Connecticut support and encourage what we might think of broadly as the public humanities. The adverse effects of outreach on one's reputation and place in the pecking order should be, if not non-existent, at least negligible because outreach matches institutional objectives. However, we all know that talk by the departmental water cooler need not match administrators' pronouncements, and that there are those who feel firmly that public engagement is for the less talented and/or the lazy. A public intellectual may be one thing, but a "popular" one is another altogether. Whereas the former might be scoffed and sneered at by peers laboring in obscurity—the whiff of envy being frequently evident—the latter is more an object of open derision as a "sell-out" and traitor to the cause of specialist scholarship, the worth of which is measured in part by its inaccessibility to a general audience. Of course, many universities and colleges actively promote public engagement, even including it in the metrics for promotion and merit. Internal perils in those cases can arise as a consequence of *not* stepping outside of institutional walls. The question then becomes, how does one choose which type of work to pursue in the public sphere? Whether one works at a more research- or more service-focused institution, making that choice brings us face to face with certain external risks.

Given that the quantity and quality of such perils are largely unpredictable and unique to each circumstance, I wish here to focus on the greatest, and perhaps most obvious, of them: criticism that we might term "ugly." By the time we have completed graduate school, we all are used to, and, hopefully, somewhat inured to, harsh criticism. Perhaps we encountered it in comments on a seminar paper; or, more terrifyingly, around the seminar table or at a conference; or, worse still, after a job talk. Even if one has personally avoided the academic takedown (no such luck here; my two most harrowing intellectual

experiences came in job talks), we have witnessed it firsthand or heard
tell of some hair-raising savagery. The perils of criticism within the
profession are very real. Being the object of a peer's belittling wrath
can make one, especially early in one's career, feel as if the future has
gone dark: a reputation for being a careless, poor, or even unscrupu-
lous scholar can close doors to talks, conferences, publication, and
other opportunities. Unless the charges are based in proven mal-
feasance, however, the actual consequences rarely match the fevered
panic of the junior faculty dark night of the soul. The (in)famous
case of Michael Bellesiles—erstwhile tenured history professor and
winner of the Bancroft Prize who was run out of the profession—was
not driven solely by a gun lobby scorned but also by colleagues who
adjudged him to have committed mistakes of such number and gravity
that he was deemed (retroactively) untenurable. Although extraordinary in its *ad hominem* ferocity, the great English historian Lawrence
Stone's early career experience of criticism demonstrates that a peer's
takedown need not lead to professional death. Forty years after it
occurred, Stone still described his former tutor Hugh Trevor-Roper's
published destruction of his study of the rise of the gentry in early
modern England as "an article of vituperative denunciation which
connoisseurs of intellectual terrorism still cherish to this day."[1] Stone,
however, went on to a distinguished career at Princeton, evidence
that even the most egregious examples of viciously fought controversy
are enacted within a community that shares certain rules, albeit typically unwritten and unspoken, and generally seeks to maintain community harmony and order. Moreover, people who are gratuitously
brutal to others are often ostracized, or at least marginalized, in the
profession. Once you leave that community and start presenting your
work and trying to engage the public, however, all bets on civil discourse are off.

This is, perhaps, the most distressing aspect of controversies aris-
ing from public engagement: in the absence of norms or mechanisms
for adjudicating, or at least civilly managing, disputes, most academics just go quiet after the initial salvo and wait for their critics to tire.
Once criticism of my exhibition starting rolling in, my co-curator Tom
and I scrambled to figure out what to do. The staff of the Folger was
equally flummoxed, never before having faced such a situation. Mine
is a nature given to defensiveness, and I wrote numerous detailed
responses to people who had posted, typically anonymously, in opposition to our presentation. These responses never saw the light of day.
I circulated them only among friends and colleagues, who always
urged the caution of silence. Writing them offered some release and

Silence

catharsis—I at least got to "speak" my thoughts. But unsent, they did nothing to quiet my detractors, or bring civility to the disagreement. This quietism was not a unique strategy. I sought advice from people who had completed similar sorts of public projects, and to my dismay, the unanimous recommendation was to not engage. Doing so would only escalate matters, and I was treated to harrowing tales of how responses intended to be steps forward in reasoned debate served instead as fuel on the fire. "Disengage": I heard it like a communal mantra.

I should not have been surprised; the evidence was all there before me. More than once, I have taught the controversy over the proposed Enola Gay exhibition at the Smithsonian—a controversy so notable that it has been retraced in an article in the field-leading *The Journal of American History*.[2] Historians had hoped to mark the fiftieth anniversary of the dropping of the atomic bomb over Hiroshima with an exhibit that explored the costs to humanity of the atomic age. They were hounded by public groups and individuals who insisted on the celebratory "we won" narrative, and eventually the museum's director scrapped the scholars' proposal. In spite of having explored with students this controversy and its contexts, I had failed to reflect upon it as a symptom of more general problems of public discourse. Surely, one reason for rancorous public criticism is a widespread negativity toward academics in general, and tenure in particular. As Greg Semenza has blogged in *The Chronicle of Higher Education*, whereas people often decry the lack of public engagement by intellectuals, there is a countervailing cultural current of anger toward the professoriate.[3] In her recent (2014) commencement talk at Harvard Law school, Mindy Kaling pointed out to graduates the oddity that, while they should be proud of having worked so hard to attain their educations and degrees, they should understand that, if they enter politics or public service, they will spend their days distancing themselves from their Ivy League pasts. As she pointed out, Mitt Romney preferred to hit the campaign trail as "the Mormon guy" rather than the "Harvard guy." Talk radio and television are awash with criticism of academics, and education professionals are under attack from all points on the political spectrum. Tenure, as an institution that protects professionals at all levels of education, is constantly being challenged. Efforts at public engagement can tap into these anti-academic currents. The Internet, with its largely unmonitored comments spaces, also serves to ramp up negativity. For all of these reasons and others, I stumbled out of those first few months after the Folger exhibition with a dim view of the public and the media.

As we were preparing the exhibition, however, worrying about a potential negative reaction seemed a low priority. Job one was simply to finish the job: Tom and I spent seemingly countless hours selecting items to show, organizing case displays, prepping, writing gallery and catalog text, and so on. A museum installation, we quickly learned, requires a tremendous amount of work and a good deal of logistical acrobatics. What I learned more slowly, but quite intimately, is that consideration of how to deal with audience response—positive and negative—*is* part of the work of public engagement. Perhaps not as crucial as, say, choosing display items and writing case cards, but crucial all the same for making the experience rewarding for scholars and audience members alike. It must always be borne in mind.

In the end, therefore, part of my frustration stemmed from anger over my naïveté, or hubris. When we were creating the exhibition, Tom kept pointing out that we needed to speak to the tragic element in early modern Irish history: the massacres, the cultural destruction, the dislocations of colonization. We, of course, included materials that addressed these realities, and included explanatory text to bring them front and center. Yet, I remained insistent that we should move beyond the tragic and focus more on Irish agency in the world, thereby presenting a story about how the Irish (elites, anyway) were active players in shaping events in the age, even if, in the end, those efforts saw limited success. My justification for this—as I constantly told Tom—was that people understood the tragedy already and that it, therefore, made little sense to retell it: why confirm widely held beliefs when we had the chance to present new perspectives on, and details about, the Irish past and Irish–English relations? Tom, more sensible than I, was indeed correct. Had we not included the materials on massacre and loss he suggested, the rough edge of our public reception would have been rougher still. This is not to say that critical reaction—which came from a small, yet very vocal, group—arose entirely from unwillingness to engage with the Irish past in new ways. Undoubtedly, some people were excited to think more broadly about the Irish past, but simply happened to disagree with how we had done so. However, the pushback against our presentation did suggest limits on how controversial topics can be talked about in a public forum.

I don't mean to say that public engagement is all about peril. The benefits and joys are many and largely self-explanatory. In spite of myths that hold professors to be removed from the world in their ivory towers, many of us wish to engage widely about ideas, questions, and problems in the world. Indeed, that is why many go into this line of work, and teaching affords the first chance at such engagement: we

come to the syllabus with certain ideas; they get honed by presenting them to the non-specialist audience that is the undergrad class;
they are further refined through interactions with students. "Public
history"—as we call it in my discipline—can be seen as an extension
of that initial "outreach." Most of us remember the steep learning
curve to effective teaching, and wince thinking of scathing semes-
ter-end evaluations. We also remember when we finally "got it," and
teaching became a rewarding experience. The same trajectory holds
true for public engagement.

The memory of the exhibition's aftermath remains raw and painful.
However, doing the exhibition still counts among the greatest and
richest experiences of my professional life. It does, in part, because
it brought me into contact with so many wonderful new people—at
the Folger, in academia, and among the public—people with whom
I thought, learned, and enjoyed tremendous conversations and interactions. Much good has come from the project, too. On an institutional level, the University of Connecticut has now joined the Folger
Consortium—something the school has been wishing to do for
decades. Membership was not a result of the exhibition, but good
working relations established over the course of putting it on possibly helped. On a more personal level, I now have a wider network
of colleagues and, I dare to say, friends whom I met in the course
of this project. Finally, on a professional level, I have gained much
needed insight into the "perils" that might dampen the positives just
described. For these reasons, I most certainly would embark upon
such a project again and, indeed, am planning a number of them.

Nonetheless, I find myself reflecting on what I believe is the crucial weak spot in public engagement: the absence of means and modes
by which sensitive and complex topics can be discussed and debated
vigorously, yet still rationally and reasonably. That absence should
remind us of how wonderful a place the academy can be: its members
(typically) can argue passionately and unapologetically about ideas
and issues that matter, and do so without fear of character assassina-
tion and other forms of egregious abuse. Such dialogue and exploration should not be the sole preserve of the professoriate. Many of
the comments that came into the Folger about our exhibition, while
critical, grew out of a desire to debate in precisely the ways academics do among themselves. By all accounts, ours is a brutally divisive
age. All the more reason, then, for scholars not to retreat to their
towers. Rather, we and the public at large should think seriously and
collectively about how to make more intellectual activity public and
more public discourse intellectual, and about how to bring all of us

together around ideas and issues that interest and affect us. Not to do so carries the real peril.

NOTES

1. Beier, A. L., D. Carradine, and J. M. Rosenheim, eds. *The First Modern Society: Essays in English History in Honour of Lawrence Stone,* Cambridge: Cambridge University Press, 1989. 582.
2. Kohn, R. H. "History and the Cultural Wars: The Case of the Smithsonian Institution's *Enola Gay* Exhibit," *The Journal of American History* 82 (1995): 1036–1063.
3. Semenza, G. "Welcome to the Real World of Academe," *Vitae* (blog). In *The Chronicle of Higher Education,* June 12, 2014, accessed August 10, 2014, https://chroniclevitae.com/news/544-welcome-to-the-real-world-of-academe.

PART II

PERSONAL LIFE

CHAPTER 8

IMPOSTER PHENOMENON

Natalie M. Houston

At least a hundred times this morning, I wondered why the editors asked me to write this essay. I'm not an expert on this topic. What do I have to say that hasn't already been said? They will probably rescind my contract. Can't they see I'm an imposter?

I know I'm not alone in feeling this way. Maybe you've experienced some of these thoughts yourself. Do you suspect that other people have an inflated idea of your abilities? Do you worry that your success has just been due to luck? Or that if only people knew how little qualified you were for a particular project or job, they'd never want to work with you? When you read course evaluations or receive reader's reports on an article, do you focus only on the negative remarks and ignore the positive comments? Do you ever think, "I'll never know enough"? Welcome to The Imposter Club.[1]

Academia is filled with intelligent, successful people who are pursued by these doubts and fears, many of which are created or encouraged by the structures and conditions of our profession. These feelings often begin in the competitive arena of graduate school, and so understanding what the imposter phenomenon is and how to manage it is useful not only for us as individual scholars, but also as teachers of future generations. As my doubts while working on this essay suggest, imposterism never entirely goes away, but I have learned some effective approaches to understand and manage it, which I share below.

FEELING LIKE AN IMPOSTER

Research into this wide range of feelings and behaviors began in 1978 with the work of two clinical psychologists, Pauline Clance and Suzanne Imes, who interviewed 150 successful professional women who reported feeling like failures or imposters despite having received many external markers of achievement, such as advanced degrees, awards, promotions, and publications.[2] Since then, the growing clinical and self-help literature on imposter phenomenon has identified several key behaviors: the minimizing of one's successes, a focus on one's perceived failures or difficulties, and a pervasive sense of oneself as a fraud.[3] People with imposter phenomenon tend to compare their achievements negatively with those of others, to discount positive feedback they receive, and to feel that their own successes have been due to chance rather than skill. Such people frequently appear poised, confident, and highly competent to observers, but they do not feel that way internally. This mismatch between one's external and internal selves creates the feeling of being an imposter—someone who might be exposed at any moment as incompetent. These feelings can lead to perfectionism and habits of overwork that may lead to success in the short term, but are neither sustainable nor healthy over a long career.

If you're not sure whether the imposter phenomenon is relevant for you or your students, Clance's website offers a self-evaluation adapted from her 1985 book that includes statements like these:

> I can give the impression that I'm more competent than I really am.
>
> I tend to remember the incidents in which I have not done my best more than those times I have done my best.
>
> When I've succeeded at something and received recognition for my accomplishments, I have doubts that I can keep repeating that success.[4]

Rating how true these statements are for you provides a measure of how strongly you experience the imposter phenomenon. Many of us experience some of these feelings at least occasionally; the quiz can provide a simple means for assessing how pervasive or disruptive those attitudes are for you.

IMPOSTER PHENOMENON OR SYNDROME?

Although Clance and Imes originally wrote about the "imposter phenomenon," the term "imposter syndrome" adopted by some later writers has taken hold in popular culture. I follow Clance and Imes's decision not to use this phrase, because the word "syndrome," which describes disease symptoms, can become "one more way of pathologizing women."[5] Although Clance and Imes's early research focused on women, subsequent research and widespread anecdotal reports suggest that many men also experience feelings of imposterism.[6] Media coverage of imposter syndrome frequently reinforces the idea that this phenomenon is just about exceptional individuals by highlighting public figures and celebrities who admit to feeling like imposters.[7]

I choose to use the terms "imposterism" or "imposter phenomenon" rather than the medical term "syndrome" in order to highlight the larger structural contexts in which individuals are situated and the discursive frameworks through which they perceive their experience. In this essay, I'm interested in exploring how the professional structures of academia, and particularly of the humanities disciplines, might provoke the feeling of being an imposter. Examining the structures of our profession will, I hope, not only diminish the isolation and negative self-blame experienced by so many of its members, but also lead to positive changes within local institutions or national professional organizations.

I'm not a psychologist. I'm an English literature professor. I'm also a certified professional coach who works with academics and other professionals who want to move forward on the goals and projects that matter the most to them, and to create better work–life balance. Throughout graduate school and my early faculty years, I struggled with feeling like an imposter, and I still do, occasionally. After years of studying meditation, martial arts, productivity systems, and holistic self-development, I now have a greater awareness of how imposterism manifests for me, and I have acquired the tools to help me shift my mindset. Although I still notice myself feeling like an imposter sometimes, I have figured out strategies that help me create a happier and more sustainable approach to academic life—and, as a coach, I help others to do the same.

WHAT MAKES US FEEL LIKE IMPOSTERS?

Academia is a highly structured, hierarchical professional environment. Although the process of intellectual growth and professional development from one's first year as a graduate student to receiving tenure as a faculty member takes many long, slow years, the stages along the way are experienced as categorical shifts, usually contingent upon a stressful experience of evaluation: one sits for oral exams and then becomes ABD (all but dissertation); one defends a dissertation and receives a doctorate; one successfully undergoes review and gains tenure. Not only are those rituals of evaluation extremely stressful and likely to produce feelings of anxiety or inferiority, but also these abrupt shifts in external status may not match your internal self-understanding. For example, I defended my dissertation in June and taught my first graduate seminar in August of the same year, a rapid transition in status that caused me to feel like an imposter at times. Most academic institutions do little to assist students or faculty making these major shifts in status and responsibility, which can contribute to long delays in writing the dissertation, difficult adjustments to new teaching responsibilities, and post-tenure depression.

Graduate school not only fosters anxiety about one's intellectual abilities, but also extracts costs in other ways. The reduced economic power and likelihood of geographic relocation during graduate school and one's early years in the profession cause many in the humanities to delay some of the conventional cultural markers of adulthood, such as marriage, parenthood, or purchasing a car or house. It is not uncommon for recent PhDs to be very accomplished intellectually or professionally, but to feel behind their peers in other professions in terms of life stages. To have achieved faculty status but to feel like a beginner at adult life can encourage that tension between external and internal perceptions of accomplishment that is the hallmark of imposterism.

The structures of evaluation in academia can also promote the imposter phenomenon. Aside from those major, highly stressful assessment events that mark the transition from one rank to another, academics have relatively few opportunities to receive feedback on their performance. When we do, it is often attached to an abrupt and potentially career-altering decision: articles are accepted or rejected for publication, grant proposals are funded or denied, and job applications may be not only unsuccessful but even unacknowledged. When evaluation is relatively rare, the possibility of rejection becomes more intimidating and can lead to perfectionist behaviors, such as delaying the submission of publications.

Of course, most academics not only receive evaluations of their research or teaching performance, but also spend a lot of time evaluating the work of others. Such evaluations include not only numerous forms of teaching-related assessment, but also peer review of publications, proposal selection for conferences, and speaker selection for symposia. As academics in the humanities, we are trained to be highly discriminating. Our ability to analyze, to pick apart arguments, and to draw fine distinctions serves us well as scholars, but it can lead to a lot of self-directed criticism when we evaluate the work of peers and colleagues. Participation in hiring, tenure, and promotion reviews can frequently elicit comparisons (however unfounded) to our own CVs or dossiers. Even when serving on a hiring or evaluation committee far outside my own subfield, I experience not just admiration of another's publication record, but moments of despair about my own. Thus, these necessary contributions to the department, institution, or profession can also encourage feelings of imposterism.

One of the hallmarks of imposter phenomenon, according to Clance and Imes's original research, is the attribution of one's successes to luck or connections rather than one's qualifications. Yet, the brutal conditions of the current academic job market in the humanities mean that large numbers of qualified people do not find full-time employment. We are faced with a structure that claims to be about merit, but also involves so many factors beyond the credentials and publications listed on the CV that chance is actually a significant element in our profession. Sometimes there is no clear reason why one person is successful and another is not; that fundamental uncertainty and the high professional and personal stakes that ensue from it can contribute to the imposterism experienced by many new faculty, as well as produce feelings of guilt. Many graduate school friendships do not survive the job market intact. I felt tremendously lucky when I was hired into my first faculty position and, at the same time, terribly guilty that brilliant friends of mine did not get jobs that year.

Finally, the fact that many humanists do much of their work alone (rather than, say, in scientific laboratories or on collaborative research projects) can exacerbate the behaviors associated with the imposter phenomenon. In humanistic research, the end point is rarely clearly defined. You can always do a bit more research, and a book manuscript or article can always be further revised. It can be very difficult for scholars working alone to gain perspective and to be able to effectively decide when a project is done. Without the opportunity to closely observe other scholars' working habits, it becomes easy to assume that other people do everything with ease, and that you are the only one who struggles to prepare a new course, or to write an article. High-achieving people who feel like imposters tend to isolate themselves out of shame and to conceal what they perceive as their faults. This perpetuates the false perceptions we have and the assumptions we make about our own work and about that of others.

RECLAIMING YOUR AGENCY

When you feel like an imposter, you feel governed by what you perceive as the false external assessments of others. You give up your power to those who are evaluating you (in reality or in your imagination). Each of the strategies I discuss below depends upon cultivating a compassionate perspective from which to observe your own feelings and behavior and introduces ways to recognize your own agency. A willingness to entertain the possibility of telling a different story about yourself and your work connects to the deep curiosity and investment in narrative (whether cultural, social, personal, or literary) that I see as central to our work in the humanities.

MINDFUL AWARENESS

One of the challenges in dissolving imposterism is that your negative self-assessment presents itself as true in your mind. People with imposter phenomenon discount the positive feedback they receive from others, and primarily give themselves critical or negative evaluations. The first step in loosening the hold of these ideas is just to notice them as distinct from your observing awareness. Most of us have a fairly constant stream of self-talk running through our minds. Without judgment, just pay attention to when the imposter thoughts occur. What kinds of situations tend to provoke that inner critical voice that tells you that you're unqualified? Once you can distance yourself from that voice enough to notice a pattern, you can begin to choose how (or if) you want to respond.[8]

REALITY CHECK

The first strategy when feelings of imposterism come up is to focus on the present moment and ask yourself: "Am I OK right now?" The imposter phenomenon keeps us disconnected from the present because it fills our minds with anxiety about the future (the fear of being exposed) and with negative fixations on the past (magnifying past failures). Focusing on the present, minute to minute, helps dissolve that anxiety. The present moment is the only time in which we can act. Any practices that help you ground yourself in the present—such as breathwork, meditation, or physical movement—help release the anxious feelings of imposterism.[9]

REVERSE TO RELAX

A second powerful exercise when a self-critical thought comes up is to simply ask "Is it true?" If the answer is no, then just let the thought go. If the answer is yes (and the imposter mind will try to persuade you that it is, of course, true that you are a fraud), then you can ask yourself: "What if the opposite were true? How would I support that claim?" For every reason you come up with for thinking yourself a failure, come up with an argument for why you could be considered a success. For instance, if your self-critical thought says "You're a terrible writer," you could reverse it by asking "What if I were actually a good writer? What evidence is there to support that idea?" Reminding yourself of praise you've received or particularly effective documents you've written can help you see a different perspective. Exploring two different sides of the same statement helps relax the stranglehold of imposterism.[10]

THINK LIKE A CREATOR

Our specialized training as academics means that we are very good at researching things; we know how to survey a particular field of study, do a literature review, and prepare a course lecture on a topic we know little about. However, that well-honed ability can all too easily lead you to focus on what everyone else has said about a topic and to feel like you have nothing to contribute (or at least not until you've spent several years learning all there is to know about the subject). Research can become its own form of procrastination and perfectionism and, although it can temporarily soothe the anxiety of feeling like an imposter, it can also block you from moving forward with a project or course of study and ultimately cause more negative self-criticism. This tendency to over-research often accompanies the shifts in status mentioned earlier as well as the taking on of new responsibilities, like designing a new course or moving from the classroom to an administrative role.

The solution is to think like a creator, not like a sponge. Most of us were trained to be very good sponges: we can soak up information and absorb it so that it feels like it's our own. However, focusing on all that you don't know and on what other people are doing can easily overwhelm your own sense of agency. To think like a creator, however, is to always keep in mind what it is that you want to do, to build, to create in the world, whether that's through a course, an article, or a new administrative structure.

To practice thinking like a creator, simply ask yourself each day, in different personal and professional contexts: "What do I want to create here?" Focusing on what you choose to create can help you sort through a pile of teaching notes to outline a particular day's lecture; it helps you focus on a particular paragraph in the day's writing; and it helps at any moment when you start to feel that you don't know enough. Feelings of imposterism grow out of the many ways we get dislocated from our own agency and power; asking yourself what you want to create each day helps ground you in a place of conscious choice so that you can reclaim your power.

Integrating conscious choice and the power to create into your research practices can help you stay connected to your own questions, ideas, and potential contribution. I teach my students to take dialogic notes when conducting a literature review, so that they engage with the texts rather than only focusing on extracting key ideas from them. I also recommend keeping an idea notebook to capture ideas and to write about a major project as it develops.[11] When you're in the mindset of the creator, you can more accurately evaluate what it is that you still need to learn and what you can do to begin making your own contribution. Shifting your perspective from the passivity of the sponge to the activity of the creator helps you take clearer steps toward your important goals.

The strategies I've suggested in this essay are ones I practice weekly, even daily. They don't prevent me from ever feeling like an imposter, particularly at the beginning or end of a project, in situations of evaluation, or when taking on a new role. However, these practices help me shift into the present moment and anchor myself in my own creative power. Like returning to the breath in meditation, repeatedly coming back to the idea of being a creator is itself a practice that opens up a space of transformation.

NOTES

1. Parts of this essay are adapted from Houston, N. M. "Too Much Self Doubt? Try Thinking Like A Creator." *ProfHacker* (blog), *The Chronicle of Higher Education*, June 25, 2010, accessed August 6, 2014, http://chronicle.com/blogs/profhacker/too-much-self-doubt-try-thinking-like-a-creator/25071.
2. Clance, P. R. and S. Imes. "The Impostor Phenomenon in High Achieving Women: Dynamics and Therapeutic Intervention," *Psychotherapy: Theory, Research and Practice* 15 (1978): 241–247.

3. See, for example, Clance, P. R. *The Impostor Phenomenon: Overcoming the Fear that Haunts Your Success*, Atlanta: Peachtree, 1985; Jarrett, C. "Feeling like a Fraud," *Psychologist* 23 (2010): 380–383; and Young, V. *The Secret Thoughts of Successful Women*, New York: Crown, 2011.

4. See http://paulineroseclance.com/pdf/IPTestandscoring.pdf, accessed August 6, 2014.

5. Kaplan, K. "Unmasking the Imposter," *Nature* 459 (2009): 468–469.

6. Laursen, L. "No, You're Not an Impostor," *Science Careers* 15 (February 15 2008), accessed August 6, 2014, http://science-careers.sciencemag.org/career_magazine/previous_issues/articles/2008_02_15/caredit.a0800025.

7. See, for example, Pinker, S. "Field Guide to the Self-Doubter: Extra Credit," *Psychology Today*, November 1, 2009, accessed August 6, 2014, http://www.psychologytoday.com/articles/200911/field-guide-the-self-doubter-extra-credit.

8. A good introduction to mindfulness techniques is Kabat-Zinn, J. *Wherever You Go, There You Are: Mindfulness Meditation in Everyday Life*, New York: Hyperion, 1994.

9. Such practices are described in Houston, N. M. "Got a Minute? Relax." *ProfHacker* (blog). In *The Chronicle of Higher Education*, September 3, 2009, accessed August 6, 2014, http://chronicle.com/blogs/profhacker/got-a-minute-relax/22680; and Houston, N. M. "Got a Minute? Count Backwards," *ProfHacker* (blog). In *The Chronicle of Higher Education*, October 29, 2009, accessed August 6, 2014, http://chronicle.com/blogs/profhacker/got-a-minute-count-backwards/22801. I also recommend Neill, M. *Feel Happy Now!* Carlsbad: Hay House, 2008.

10. A fuller exploration of these simple but powerful questions can be found in Katie, B. *Loving What Is: How Four Questions Can Change Your Life*, New York: Harmony Books, 2002.

11. Houston, N. M. "Why I Keep an Idea Notebook," *ProfHacker* (blog). In *The Chronicle of Higher Education*, October 26, 2010, accessed August 6, 2014, http://chronicle.com/blogs/profhacker/why-i-keep-an-idea-notebook/28113.

CHAPTER 9

ACADEMIC GUILT

Giuseppina Iacono Lobo

Academic guilt plagues me whenever I am not working. In this profession, after all, there is always something to do: new publications to read, a book, article, proposal, conference paper, or even an annual update to write, grading, lesson plans, and course development—and that's only in between teaching, office hours, faculty meetings, and other on-campus obligations. The seemingly endless demands on my time blur the line between my professional and private lives. To say I take work home would be an understatement. Almost every room in my house bears the mark of my professional life, whether in the form of stacks of student essays on the dining room table, read and unread issues of *PMLA* on the television stand, or the pile of interlibrary loans in the foyer. Books I'm reading for fun (but really for a new course I'm teaching next semester) sit on my nightstand. These ever-present reminders of work undone fuel my academic guilt, acting as specters of my professional life even in the most private of settings.

Psychologists consider guilt—along with shame, embarrassment, and pride—a self-conscious emotion. Self-conscious emotions are those that force an individual to evaluate himself against socially constructed behavioral standards. Unlike basic emotions—anger, fear, and happiness—that are associated with physical survival and reproduction, self-conscious emotions are related to "social survival," meaning they are "useful in negotiating problems of cooperation, group living, and maintenance of social relationships."[1] For this reason, much research supports the idea that guilt can yield positive social outcomes.[2] However, excessive guilt can have the opposite effect, creating or exacerbating low self-esteem, anxiety, obsessive-compulsive disorder, and even depression.[3] It can also foster feelings of isolation and vulnerability.[4]

Academic guilt, too, is a self-conscious emotion. At its most innocuous level, academic guilt is a niggling feeling you get when you are not working, or when you failed to get work done. Perhaps you decided to indulge in a reality television marathon. Or you took a nap. Or spent too much time on social media. In cases such as these, some academics use guilt as a motivator. One blogger tells readers that she uses "bribes and guilt" as tools for writing, and suggests that her audience do the same: "So what if it's not healthy? You want to be emotionally balanced, swim with the dolphins. You want to write? Learn to deal with the sharks."[5]

Perhaps strategic bouts with academic guilt can be useful. However, it is not always deliberately self-imposed, nor does it always lead to productivity. Excessive academic guilt is, oftentimes, the product of an unrealistic perception of what it takes to be successful in academia, which, in turn, fosters unrealistic work expectations. A graduate student might wrongly think that the harder and longer she works, the more likely she will be to land an academic job; or an assistant professor tenure; or an associate or full professor—or all of the above—acclaim and recognition. Moreover, while distinct from moral guilt, academic guilt can have the same damaging psychological effects. Even the blogger's intentional use of guilt is, she admits, not emotionally healthy.

As I began preparing to write this essay, I found that many of my colleagues were unwilling or hesitant to discuss their experiences with academic guilt, while others denied its very existence. Just broaching the topic seemed to make some of them uncomfortable. The very nature of guilt is to make us feel unsure and exposed and, as one academic puts it, even "[t]hinking about guilt…makes me feel guilty."[6] For those of us suffering from academic guilt, what connection is there between this sometimes paralyzing feeling, our perceptions of ourselves, and our fears of how others might perceive us? And if we confess to feeling guilty, do we risk realizing those (mis)perceptions?

My focus in the remainder of this essay will be on academic guilt in all of its manifestations, ranging from guilt-as-motivator to guilt-as-inhibitor. In my experience, academic guilt exists along a continuum: the relatively innocuous and self-imposed guilt that the blogger described earlier can quickly transition into excess. Whether you live to swim another day, or get eaten, you're still swimming with the sharks.

I had my first brushes with academic guilt early on in graduate school. Truth be told, as a long-time sufferer from imposter syndrome, I was a prime candidate. Throughout my undergraduate years, I had coped with feelings of inadequacy by working harder, and I carried that habit with me to graduate school. The problem was that, in graduate school, my work was never done. So I slept less, made very few social commitments, and spent lots of time alone, poring over my books. Oftentimes, I would go a whole weekend without leaving my apartment, and I would look forward to Monday mornings so that I could venture out guilt-free.

The other problem was that, despite my loneliness, I was in good company. Academic guilt is all about social survival, after all, and academia is its very own society—complete with its own standards of behavior. Many of my peers fell along the academic guilt continuum as well, as our frequent discussions about productivity, procrastination, and the emotional roller coaster that is graduate school indicated. A dozen of us shared a basement office—an open room cluttered with desks and unused furniture from elsewhere in the building. Lacking cubicles, this space allowed us to survey each other's work habits, and to feel better or worse about ourselves depending on what those around us were accomplishing. While one of my good friends and mentors from graduate school told me early on that the key to survival in academia was always to follow the golden rule—"Thou shalt not compare thyself to others"—it seemed that comparing myself to my peers was the only way to know for sure that I was surviving. Together, we forged an academic conscience—a set of values against which we could measure our own successes and failures.

In between seminars or during our office hours, we would gripe about work done and undone, how sleep deprived we were, the last time we had cleaned our apartments or, in some cases, ourselves. In this way, academic guilt—whether feeling it, or inciting it in others to alleviate your own—is also performative. We took some pleasure in this communal suffering, as if it were a rite of passage into the academy. And the worse we felt—or, in some cases, the worse others thought we felt—the better suited we believed we were to our role as budding scholars.

I was always good at playing the martyr, shuffling around on Friday afternoons with stacks of library books and fresh photocopies, often turning down invitations to social gatherings. I only hoped that if others thought I was hardworking, perhaps I would believe it too. As it turns out, whatever impressions others had of my work habits, I was never able to stamp out that irrepressible feeling of guilt when

I wasn't working. More troublingly, the feeling of guilt became so prevalent that being without it seemed a worse alternative: if I could take time off without feeling guilty about it, what might that suggest about my dedication to academia?

In graduate school, faculty members often engender or exacerbate academic guilt in their students. Each semester, the English Graduate Organization would hold a series of coffee talks, informal gatherings with current faculty or former alumni with the goal of professionalization in mind. One of the most well-attended meetings was with the incoming department head, her topic of discussion being graduate student publication. As the state of the market worsened, those of us without a publication line on our CVs discovered new depths of academic guilt. Our new department head was a passionate scholar, known for her intensity in the classroom. Her talk quickly turned from publication to the profession itself. She told us that the work we were doing—our studies, our papers, our publications—was the very last bastion of culture. For that reason, she insisted, our dedication to it should be whole-hearted: if we did not wake up each morning thinking about the library and what discoveries we might make that day, we were in the wrong line of work. Further, if we did not commit our lives to our work, she threatened, we would be doomed to teaching at a 4–4 or even (gasp!) a 5–5 institution, out of which we'd never be able to publish ourselves.

As we sprinted up and down the guilt continuum for the duration of her talk, her words inspired three sorts of crises, all sustained by unrealistic perceptions of academia. The first was a personal crisis, upheld by the illusion that academia is a meritocracy: those who work the hardest get the most coveted jobs. Not working as much and as often as possible, then, would be a detriment to our immediate professional futures. The second was a crisis of expectations: our department head assumed that we were all hoping to land Research I jobs. Yet, for many of us, teaching at a 4–4 or 5–5 institution would have been a happy result, which was just another reason to feel guilty. The third was an existential crisis: if our work was indeed the last bastion of culture—a statement at once absurd and exhilarating—academic guilt took on an entirely new color. Not working compromised a project much larger than our careers.

Although I tried to make light of her remarks several days later, my conscience was still raw. Every day, I spent hours upon hours in front of a computer screen, at the library, or with my head buried in a book; now must I dedicate every waking moment to my professional life as well? Academia, it seemed, was all or nothing. How much more of my time and myself could I give in order to succeed? And what would success look like?: a well-placed publication? A well-defended dissertation? A tenure-track job? Tenure? Full professorship? An endowed chair? When, if ever, would I be allowed to rest on my laurels—even if only momentarily—and not feel so damn bad doing so?

My six years of graduate school were marked by long hours and a severe fear of failure because of my academic guilt. Although I wasn't always productive when sitting in front of my computer, or flipping through library books, maintaining the semblance of productivity seemed a better option than taking some time for myself. I brought my bad habits with me on the tenure track, although I've found that academic guilt as a faculty member differs from the graduate student variety. First, it is a much more isolated and isolating feeling. There is no cluttered basement office full of graduate students with whom I might commiserate and try to feel better (or worse) about myself. My community of guilt is now virtual rather than actual, relegated to email correspondences, Facebook statuses, or Twitter posts. My guilt is often provoked if one of my peers posts about a particularly productive day, a publication, or even a bout with procrastination. While I celebrate their successes and empathize with their failures, I also can't help but use their careers as a measuring stick for my own.

One of my favorite virtual instigators of academic guilt is the "Shouldn't You Be Writing?" meme. Started in support of National Novel Writing Month, November, this meme has been repurposed for academics year-round, with celebrities of all varieties censuring time-squanderers. Over the last several weeks, I signed in to Facebook only to find Darth Vader, the Queen Mother, and Grumpy Cat asking, "Shouldn't you be writing?" This concept, albeit silly, captures academic guilt quite accurately. Pictorial memes are all about rapid transmission and infinite textual possibilities: Grumpy Cat can say just about anything, as long as it's, well, grumpy. The "Shouldn't You Be Writing?" meme, to the dismay of the already guilt-prone academic, is textually static: Gandalf, Dr. Who, and David Beckham will tell you that you should be writing just the same. This reversal reduces every voice to one message, as if, no matter what time it is or where you are, you should always be writing.

In recent years, I've also coped with another form of academic guilt—survivor's guilt. While I and a handful of my graduate school peers were able to land tenure-track jobs, many of our brilliant colleagues were not so lucky. I even watched my husband go through several unsuccessful years on the market before deciding to leave academia, during which time I felt guilty when I wasn't working, when I was working, and every minute in between. In preparation for writing this piece, I polled a number of my colleagues regarding their experiences with academic guilt. One respondent told me that, because she got a tenure-track position, she often feels guilty about downtime because "so many of my friends have not been able to land this 'dream' job." She added that she often confuses leisure with slacking off, as if any time away from her desk is unjustifiable.

Being on the tenure track also raises more questions about the life-work balance than I ever experienced as a graduate student. I am constantly in the presence of colleagues who are tenured, have families, hobbies, and/or pastimes that occupy their time outside of academia. As one of two untenured faculty members in my department, I still find myself wondering how many hours of work each day are enough. How much of a life is it okay to have? Another respondent to my poll shared that, while her department discussed tenure requirements at a recent meeting, her chair said that tenure-track faculty can only have a life after tenure. For tenure-track faculty, is it less about establishing a life–work balance and more about achieving a work–work balance?

My quest for a work–life balance was reset last summer with the birth of my son. I suddenly have this wonderful and exceedingly demanding little person in my life who takes me away from work for hours or even days at a time. My department was supportive during my pregnancy, and even my dean insisted that no one expected me to work during my semester-long leave. Nonetheless, the prospect of putting work on hold for an entire semester seemed impossible. I churned out pages of my manuscript up until days before my son's birth, and I wrote my annual update while in labor. During my leave, and often with a sleeping baby nestled into my shoulder, I revised an article for publication, averaging a sentence a day.

I soon realized, however, that my son could not acquiesce to my hermit-like work–work lifestyle. I began taking him for walks in the afternoons, bringing him to music classes on weekday mornings, and story time at the public library on Saturdays. I was surprised to find that, after living in our home for three years, we have friendly neighbors (who knew?), a backyard that's particularly lovely on spring afternoons, and that the city of Baltimore is a fun and quirky place.

I would love to say that, while deep in maternal bliss, my conscience was clear. But that would be a lie. Old habits die hard. As I strolled along with my son toward the duck pond many an afternoon, that nagging voice was straining to be heard somewhere in the back of my mind. I have gotten so used to measuring days and time by work done and undone that letting go of the guilt has been quite a challenge. At this point in my career, academic guilt accompanies me like an old friend. I can count on it to be present at family gatherings and holiday celebrations; it joins me for the occasional evening off, or sleep-in session on a weekend; I bring it with me to conferences, into conversations with colleagues near and far, and, sometimes, even to the grocery store. It's no surprise, then, that it would also accompany me during this new journey in my life.

To a degree, I will always experience academic guilt. It's part of who I am, along with my fear of failure, feelings of inadequacy, and imposter syndrome. What I have learned over the last year is how better to manage my guilt so as to avoid its most crippling side effects.

I only realized how much my relationship with academic guilt has changed when I sat down to write this piece. In fact, now that I've gotten more accustomed to interruptions in my work schedule, I've begun to feel guilty about not feeling guilty enough anymore. Academic guilt, I have come to realize, had been my way of coping with the "life" part of the life–work balance: if I must set my work aside, at least I feel bad about doing so. If I no longer apologize for my private life, what might that suggest about my dedication to my professional life?

A career in academia brings with it lots of unstructured time, which is certainly an advantage of this line of work, but one that also leaves us susceptible to overworking, underworking, and guilt. What I'm still learning is that, just because there is always work to do, that doesn't mean we should always be working. I'm also learning that the only way to achieve a healthy work–life balance is to structure my unstructured time. Several of the respondents to my poll shared how they quit feeling guilty. One of my colleagues said that she had an intervention with herself after tenure, and imposed strict boundaries on her time. She neither grades nor prepares for class after six o'clock on weekdays, and takes Saturdays off entirely (except during grading season). Another colleague instituted a tradition of "Family Saturdays" in her household: "Family Saturday means no work, no chores, and no excuses."[7]

It seems that the best way to manage, or even eliminate, academic guilt is to establish a routine much like a nine-to-five work schedule. I no longer allow myself the luxury of holding vigil before my computer for hours at a time, waiting for inspiration, working on a lesson plan, and finding endless ways to distract myself during intermittent mental slumps. More importantly, I no longer consider all of my waking hours potential working hours. Yet, I find that my output differs little from what it was before. In many ways, I am *more* productive.

I have learned that my non-working hours are just as essential to my success as my working hours: even after the longest of days before my computer screen, my best ideas come while I am showering, stuck in traffic, or cooking dinner. These non-working hours help my mind to process what I've taken in during the day, allowing me to approach my working hours with a renewed focus, energy, and excitement.

A small part of me still admires the mythical academic who wakes each morning ready to hit the library stacks. And a bigger part of me still feels guilty for not being that person. But, as I later found out, even my former department head who touted this unachievable work ethic is an avid fly fisher and skilled musician. Embracing life outside of academia fosters excellence within the academy.

NOTES

1. Kim, S., R. S. Jorgensen, and R. Thibodeau. "Shame, Guilt, and Depressive Symptoms: A Meta-Analytic Review," *Psychological Bulletin* 137 (2011): 68–96, 69.
2. Kim, Jorgensen, and Thibodeau, "Shame," 71. See also de Hooge, I. E., R. M. A. Nelissen, S. M. Breugelmans, and M. Zeelenberg. "What is Moral About Guilt? Acting 'Prosocially' at the Disadvantage of Others," *Journal of Personality and Social Psychology* 100 (2011): 462–473, 462.
3. Blum, A. "Shame and Guilt, Misconceptions and Controversies: A Critical Review of the Literature," *Traumatology* 14 (2008): 91–102, 92, 100; Katchadourian, H. *Guilt: The Bite of Conscience*, Stanford: Stanford University Press, 2010. 23.
4. Katchadourian, *Guilt*, 23.
5. Barreca, G. "Bribes and Guilt as Tools for Writings." *The Chronicle of Higher Education*, May 23, 2011, accessed August 6, 2014, http://chronicle.com/blogs/brainstorm/bribes-and-guilt-as-tools-for-writing/35605.
6. Frank, A. "Some Affective Bases for Guilt: Tomkins, Freud, Object Relations," *English Studies in Canada*, 32 (2006): 11–25, 11.
7. Kale, V. "Family Saturday: Six Unexpected Benefits," *Richmond Family Magazine Online*, November 2013, accessed June 4, 2014, http://richmondfamilymagazine.com/article/family-saturday/.

CHAPTER 10

DEPRESSION: POST-TENURE AND BEYOND

Greg Colón Semenza

Two contradictory convictions inform my approach to this topic. The first is that an academic career is as likely as any to cause or exacerbate depression of various sorts. The other is that an academic career is as ideal as any for allowing one to confront and work through depression. I've suffered from depression, on and off, for longer and shorter periods, since childhood. My most recent depression occurred shortly after I received tenure in 2006, so this particular experience informs most of what follows.

Although my essay centers on "post-tenure" depression specifically, I hope it will be applicable to academics at various stages of their careers. So why narrow the topic at all? First, what I'll henceforth refer to as PTD is the only form of depression suffered by academics that has its own recognized nomenclature and, thus, its own literature—however small and contentious.[1] Associate professors are, on average, unhappier than other faculty members. In the Collaborative on Academic Careers in Higher Education conducted at Harvard University in 2012, nearly 14,000 professors were surveyed; in 9 of 11 categories related to research, associates were shown to be less happy than their peers; in five of seven categories related to service, associates expressed greater dissatisfaction than either assistant or full professors.[2] Second, because it is a transitional phase between an external incentives system and one based predominantly on internal rewards, the post-tenure moment allows reflection on what might be understood as the two halves of an academic career. Finally and most importantly, I focus on PTD because the concept is so damned counterintuitive; the very notion that one might become depressed at precisely the stage we all dream of reaching speaks in profound ways to the pervasiveness, perverseness, and peculiarities of depression.

I am not a cognitive therapist and, therefore, do not intend to offer any *solutions* for how I think individuals should handle their depressions. What I will do is share some of the scientific and personal information I've found to be most useful, analyze it in relation to my own experiences, and hope that you'll find it useful too. The purpose of this piece, in other words, is to create a space for contemplating an important, under-discussed issue.

I should say also that I delve only into those aspects of depression directly related to academic life. I suffer no illusions that my own depressions are tied exclusively to academic matters; past and current personal problems, personality traits, environmental factors of various sorts, and genetic ones as well, surely all contribute to depression. For the purposes of this essay, I'll take this point as axiomatic, avoid airing my dirty laundry, and stick to those matters that seem most appropriate to the aims and purposes of this volume.

Finally, I want to clarify up front that what I'm discussing in this essay is clinical depression, not sadness, work exhaustion, or professional crises of confidence. Depression among academics is often mocked by a small but loud group as a "first world" problem. Full or associate professors who suffer depression are told that they lack perspective; they should be more grateful for being tenured. Assistant professors who suffer depression are told they are selfish; at least they're not adjuncts. Adjuncts who suffer depression are told they deserve it; after all, they chose to be adjuncts. Graduate students who suffer depression are told to get over it; they should try living out there in the "real world." Such arguments extrapolate a hierarchy of happiness from one's occupation. They are scientifically erroneous even to the point of absurdity.

The fact is that depressed individuals, of all people, don't need to be told that their lives could be worse. Nor are they simply in need of a "reality" check. Their depression is probably more likely to be exacerbated by their thinking about the plight of adjuncts or starvation in the developing world than by not thinking about these things. Further, a common side effect of their depression is tremendous guilt about being depressed, especially since their lives may seem so terrific on the outside. Depression is not a rational illness, and it is not usually brought on by a single identifiable cause. When I have sunk into my own depressions, it wasn't because I failed to get the raise I'd been hoping for or finally realized a Mercedes was out of my price range. Rather, during certain periods of my life, I've been overwhelmed by the sudden onset of physical symptoms no different in their seemingly random and dramatic arrival than a seasonal flu episode: crushing feelings of listlessness, sadness, and self-loathing; difficulty concentrating, especially at work; intense physical pains, anxiety, and restlessness. Shall I go on? The point is that when individuals claim to be depressed post-tenure, they aren't claiming that tenure has made them depressed. Indeed, Rollo May's memorable description of depression as the "inability to construct a future" captures beautifully the fact that, while depression may be impacted by any number of events in one's past, the things that have already happened aren't necessarily the problem.[3]

Shortly after receiving tenure in 2006, I experienced a depression defined by hopeless indecision, fatigue, anger, and self-loathing. Four years later, when I felt confident I'd survived it, I had a completely different career trajectory, a new set of personal goals, and a plan for avoiding the same trap in the future. I say this, of course, as a man writing from the "other side." Although I *believe* I may have found a way to stay out of this hell, a voice somewhere in the back of my head tells me I'm deluded, saying "You'll be depressed again soon enough." This is one of my problems, my friends always tell me, that I tend to imagine the worst. My friend Hans once quipped that "Some people see the glass half full, some see it half empty, but Greg sees it in a million pieces." He was right, I'm embarrassed and frustrated to admit.

Hans died in 2008. A relatively young man who lost his fight against liver cancer, he was, to me, bafflingly optimistic, almost serene, right up until the end. In his final few days, a friend of ours asked him what he needed to do to feel at peace. "Nothing," he replied immediately. "I always did what I wanted to do. There's nothing I regret not having done." I was deeply affected by his words, realizing how differently I'd feel were I in his position. In the long term, those words, and Hans's death more generally, would cause me to reevaluate and reprioritize everything, and they would be crucial in guiding me out of my depression. In the short term, they increased the anxiety and self-loathing I'd already been experiencing.

On the surface, my life wasn't lacking in any way, personally or professionally. In the case of work, I'd actually been granted tenure a year early, and I felt like I was contributing positively to my department through the graduate directorship I'd taken on during my review year. I felt then, as I do now, lucky to work in a well-located, well-regarded, and well-run department with colleagues whom I consider to be impressive and amiable almost across the board. Generally speaking, my students are smart and hardworking, both at the undergraduate and graduate levels, and they get better every year. I make a decent enough salary. My office is spacious and private, and I can look out the windows at a beautiful campus.

So what was my problem?

Well, for one, look deeper into any situation and you'll see more clearly. Like everyone, I had my share of personal problems and past trauma. Professionally speaking, by earning tenure early I'd set expectations for myself I didn't feel capable of meeting. The graduate directorship meant being constantly focused on other people's problems rather than my own. In so many ways, my department seemed stuck in time, overly traditional, and resistant to change. Yes, most of my colleagues were great but, man, did I want to kill the handful who made everyone's lives so miserable and difficult. Students seemed harder to teach than ever. Less independent, less respectful, younger—or was that me getting older? My salary couldn't even begin to dent the massive debt I'd accrued in college and grad school. With all the knocking on the door and noise in the halls, my office felt like a prison (I started using the restroom on the third floor, Statistics, just to avoid running into colleagues).

An academic career, undoubtedly, can be wonderful when everything works out, but it also presents unique challenges no one teaches you about in graduate school. Academe is ripe for depression, mainly because all of the things that make it so wonderful—flexible schedules, isolation and extended periods of reflection, relative autonomy, being surrounded by high-achieving, intelligent people—can also make it unusually difficult and even intimidating. Because most of us don't have a boss breathing down our necks, or someone telling us we need to do our work in a certain place or at a certain time, the problems we experience with productivity, work–life balance, and so forth are easy to view as symptoms of our own flawed personalities. Our vulnerabilities and anxieties are amplified by the constant reminders that—no matter how impressive our achievements—there always will be people more productive, well-respected, and powerful than ourselves. And due largely to the peer review and student evaluation systems, an academic life is one defined by extreme ups and downs—regular cycles of "rejection" and "acceptance" that keep us from truly recognizing our accomplishments before we feel compelled to move on to the next project.

Then there's the myopia resulting from the extreme socialization process that occurs over the course of approximately 25 years of schooling, at least eight or nine of which typically are focused on a particular discipline, and then the so-called "probationary" period of the assistant professorship. Even ignoring the fact that the typical academic's entire childhood is one huge socialization process, his next dozen years look something like this: graduate from college with major in appropriate discipline. Earn admission to a competitive MA or PhD program or both. Take X number of credits' worth of the appropriate courses. Master languages. Learn to teach. Take comprehensive examinations. Take orals. Write dissertation proposal. Learn to publish. Defend dissertation proposal. Write dissertation. Conference. Defend dissertation. Publish. Get a job in an impossible market. Take on service obligations. Teach more. Publish more. Go up for tenure. Get tenure. From the moment one decides to pursue a PhD in the humanities, most of us are locked onto a single target: tenure. After all, tenure is the means to becoming the professor who—at some point along the way—we decided we wanted to be. And achieving tenure is so difficult, so immensely time-consuming, political, and stressful that it's hard to focus on much else until it's finally in our grasp. Earning tenure is nothing less than an obsession.

Of course, it's much more than that too. As conveyed in the "Statement of Principles on Academic Freedom and Tenure" (1940), "tenure" is defined by the American Association of University Professors (AAUP) and the Association of American Colleges and Universities (AACU) as follows: "Tenure is a means to certain ends; specifically: (1) freedom of teaching and research and of extramural activities, and (2) a sufficient degree of economic security to make the profession attractive to men and women of ability. Freedom and economic security, hence, tenure, are indispensable to the success of an institution in fulfilling its obligations to its students and to society." Tenure is neither a sinecure nor a personal reward. As the primary legal guarantor and protector of academic freedom, tenure is a fundamental necessity in any democratic society. Tenure is crucial also for what it allows us personally, which is job security, the ability to pursue our unique intellectual interests, and enough financial compensation to keep us away from better-paying but otherwise less attractive jobs. The convoluted process can make obtaining tenure itself seem like the goal, taking the emphasis off what tenure allows us to do and be. It becomes objectified, like a medal at the end of a marathon.

The fear among so many reactionaries is that tenure makes us lazy and unproductive. Too much job security will lead, they believe, to professors skipping out on work and heading to the beach during the week. In reality, there is no data to suggest that professors work less after tenure; in fact, the little research out there on faculty productivity suggests that workloads might increase over the course of one's career.[4] Although most of us probably would be healthier if we were to slow down a bit after earning tenure, we've grown so used to working obsessively that we find it nearly impossible to stop. We keep working in the same way, and often on the same things, as if we don't have a say about what we do and how we do it. The hoops we need to jump through are no longer in place, but we keep jumping.

Some might say, "But wait, there's still full professorship." Fair enough, but the word that comes to mind when I think of full professorship is "whoopee." At my institution, newly minted full professors are given a raise of about a thousand bucks and a congratulatory letter from some administrator they'll never meet. Nothing external really changes upon winning that distinction. If one feels satisfied at all, it's from being able to see the distinction itself as intrinsically rewarding. And the same with publishing a new book, teaching an amazing graduate seminar, or successfully revising the departmental merit system. Hopefully, one can experience real satisfaction, even joy, from such achievements. However, since the satisfaction and joy will be pretty much the *only* meaningful results of doing so, a great deal after tenure rides on how happy one actually is performing one's professional duties.[5] The Harvard Collaborative shows associates to be far "less satisfied with the accolades they receive for their work."[6] No longer sustainable after tenure is the illusion that one is working for anything other than one's own internal approval.

At precisely the same moment, one's duties become considerably more onerous. It's not like one graduates to some better workload upon receiving tenure. In fact, associate professors often do the lion's share of service in a typical department, especially in the way of administrative and advising (and graduate mentoring) tasks. Some might say this increased workload is itself the cause of depression, but I would qualify the point slightly, drawing on the research of Stanford neuroscientist Robert Sapolsky.[7] His groundbreaking work suggests that the two most significant catalysts for stress and depression are one's self-perceived position within a hierarchy and one's degree of disconnectedness from other humans. As the implications of the latter are relatively obvious, the former warrants more attention. Sapolsky's studies of non-human primates, for example, verify what the Whitehall studies of British civil servants show,[8] which is that our self-perceived rank within a hierarchy corresponds directly with the levels of stress hormone in our systems; low-rankers have higher blood pressure, more elevated heart rates, and, thus, a greater likelihood of such illnesses as depression and heart failure.

For me, the most important aspect of Sapolsky's work is the role self-perception plays in depression. He found that, because humans participate in multiple hierarchies at any given moment—work hierarchies, yes, but also family ones and those related to hobbies, etc—their self-perceived lowly position in any one hierarchy can be offset by their better position in another. The example often given is that if the lowliest worker at the EVIL Corporation is also captain of his local baseball team, he may never experience depression or regular stress. This insight also explains why it's problematic to assume tenured professors will be happy because of their rank. Because they often feel like they are doing more work than others, doing more work for others, and doing less work for themselves for fewer rewards, their higher rank does not translate neatly into greater happiness or lower stress. Sapolsky's research helped me to see that my professional identity had to a considerable degree come to subsume my other identities so that the pleasure I was experiencing in other realms wasn't enough to compensate for the frustrations I was experiencing at work. For me, this led to big adjustments, from increasing the amount of time I spent with my kids to signing up for an Ironman triathlon—one of my lifelong dreams—and devoting a guilt-free half year to training for it.

As importantly, I decided that I wasn't willing to accept that, just because I was doing *other* things, it was okay to feel frustrated at work. The plan here too was to figure out the causes of my frustration. The main problem was easy to see once I knew how to look: I was still working for external, not internal, approval. UConn had hired me in 2001 as a Renaissance specialist, but, over the years, my interest in film adaptations of literature had begun to surpass my interest in period-based literary study. The deeper I dove into adaptation study, the stronger became my conviction that proper work in the field demanded more thorough training and research in film history and theory. If I decided to pursue this training, however, I'd need to request more film-based teaching assignments and fewer Renaissance surveys; I'd need to publish less in my hiring field and more in the new one; and I'd need time to publish less while I acquired the skills and knowledge. So when I say I remained stuck after tenure in an external-rewards mindset, I mean I was choosing what to teach and research based on what I perceived to be others' expectations of me. Frankly, I was feeling guilty because the stereotypical path to academic success—publish the same book five times—had begun to feel more suffocating than empowering. In the end, because I hit rock bottom sometime around 2009, I decided to listen to my therapist for once, risk it, and make the clean break to film and adaptation studies. Wasn't this precisely the sort of move that tenure was in place to protect, even encourage? Suddenly, I was in a position to see tenure as the *solution* to PTD.

Once I decided to change my research focus, all the worrying about making that transition suddenly seemed silly. I had been feeling bored by my work for some time, and suddenly things felt fresh again. While I needed to begin establishing new professional ties and familiarizing myself with different materials and methods, it's not as if I'd entered an entirely new universe. The changes and the challenges proved as stimulating as the new material itself. Furthermore, no one really cared. Yes, a few friends inquired politely as to whether this new course "made sense," some even expressed concern about how it might set back my career, but most listened patiently to my explanation and claimed to understand the motivation perfectly well.

Regarding my professional life, I find myself wondering now why it took me so long to embrace change. All I'd really done, after all, was take advantage of what tenure is set up to encourage: the freedom—albeit within certain reasonable bounds—to teach and research the subjects we feel are most valuable and stimulating. Embracing this freedom has reminded me what I find most rewarding about an academic job, and my feelings of resentment about having to do so many tedious and unpleasant things has largely been overtaken by an appreciation for those things I love to do so much. We do have the power to affect such changes. They won't necessarily prevent the onset of clinical depression, nor will they terminate a depression one is already experiencing. Nonetheless, the power of seeing ourselves differently in the workplace can greatly reduce our feelings of stress and frustration, impacting dramatically our overall health. Experiencing more regularly and consciously the joys of academic work and, at the same time, lessening that work's defining centrality in my own life, has given me a greater chance to avoid the traps I've so often fallen into in the past. For the time being, at least, my glass seems half full.

Notes

1. Useful articles on the problem include Blanchard, K. D. "I've Got Tenure. How Depressing," *The Chronicle of Higher Education*, January 31, 2012, accessed August 10, 2014, http://chronicle.com/

article/Ive-Got-Tenure-How/130490/; Harper, L. "Grateful for Tenure, but…," *The Chronicle of Higher Education*, June 15, 2004, accessed August 10, 2014, http://chronicle.com/article/Grateful-for-Tenure-but-/44667/; Wilson, R. "Why are Associate Professors So Unhappy?" *The Chronicle of Higher Education*, June 3, 2012, accessed August 10, 2014, http://chronicle.com/article/Why-Are-Associate-Professors/132071/.

2. See Wilson, "Why are Associate Professors So Unhappy?"
3. May, R. *Love and Will*, New York: Norton, 1969. 243.
4. See Flaherty, C. "So Much to Do, So Little Time," *Inside Higher Ed*, April 9, 2014, accessed July 1, 2014, https://www.insidehigh-ered.com/news/2014/04/09/research-shows-professors-work-long-hours-and-spend-much-day-meetings.
5. I am speaking exclusively about rewards bestowed upon the faculty member as a result of his/her performance, in no way denying that the faculty member's work may have major external value for others (students, businesses, etc.).
6. Wilson, "Why are Associate Professors So Unhappy?"
7. See especially Sapolsky, R. M. *Why Zebras Don't Get Ulcers: An Updated Guide To Stress, Stress Related Diseases, and Coping.* 2nd ed. New York: W. H. Freeman, 1998.
8. See Marmot, M., et al. "Health Inequalities among British Civil Servants: the Whitehall II Study," *The Lancet* 337 (1991): 1387–1393.

CHAPTER 11

DOWNTIME

Christina M. Fitzgerald

When I was in graduate school, a friend of mine had her first child just as she was beginning her dissertation, when she was still working as a teaching assistant. She was married to a working professional, so financially she could handle this, but it seemed to me a lot to take on. I asked her how she managed teaching, writing, and being a new mom all at once. (Why I thought there could be any time that would be easier to handle these things can be chalked up to my youth and inexperience. Bear with me here.) She said to me that the key to balancing her academic life with her family life was one simple rule: never use the baby to take a break from the work, and never use the work to take a break from the baby; breaks must always be something else. I do not know why this conversation remained so memorable, especially since my single life at the time was pretty simple, but it did stick with me, and, to this day, it seems like wise advice. Even as a singleton renting an apartment, I had a "home life" that required the care and maintenance of that home, even if all that amounted to was cleaning the apartment regularly, paying the bills, and caring for my cat's needs. These days, although I do not have children, I do have a spouse, a rather high-maintenance canine companion, and an even higher-maintenance house, as well as certain responsibilities to our natal and extended families. As they say on the Internet, YMMV— your mileage may vary—but it is likely that all of us can distinguish between something we can identify as "home life" and its obligations and something else we call "work life." However, as academics who often work partly at home and well beyond the conventional workweek, and who strongly identify with our professions and disciplines, we sometimes let the lines blur and categories overlap so much that there is no room left for that something else—that "third thing" of true rest and relaxation.[1] We take breaks from writing to clean the bathroom. We put off doing the dishes because we simply must grade another paper. Time passes, and all we have done is what is necessary, what must get done.

That "third thing" (downtime, free time, personal time, "r & r," or whatever you want to call it) is not a luxury, but a necessity, and it needs to be a break from both work and other responsibilities. It needs to be true "recreation"—a time in which you re-create yourself, re-fuel your brain, body, or both. As cognitive science has begun to show, the brain may do additional creative and productive work while at rest, a benefit particularly useful to intellectual laborers. As Ferris Jabr reports in his *Scientific American* synthesis of studies of the effect of rest and relaxation on the brain, downtime is necessary for all kinds of mental functions and intellectual labor.[2] For example, scientists have shown that the brain at rest engages in coordinated communication among regions that are less active when a person is consciously concentrating on a task. This phenomenon, now called "default mode network," may be responsible for processing information and experiences that help forge our identities, develop our understanding of human behavior, and develop ethical values.[3] Other studies show that the brain learns and remembers more effectively after both sleep and also waking rest and relaxation.[4] Moreover, additional studies have shown that more numerous, shorter vacations and time off each day are more beneficial to productivity and morale than one long vacation a year—a finding that academics, in particular, would do well to take note of.[5] In short, as Jabr writes:

> Downtime replenishes the brain's stores of attention and motivation, encourages productivity and creativity, and is essential to both achieve our highest levels of performance and simply form stable memories in everyday life. A wandering mind unsticks us in time so that we can learn from the past and plan for the future.[6]

However, we are not disembodied brains. The body, too, needs recreation, and it has become relatively common wisdom that even mild forms of exercise can produce health benefits—both physical and mental. Physical recreation provides additional benefits to the mind by helping to reduce stress, anxiety, and depression.[7] Even merely recalling recreational activities can increase positive moods and lower rates of depression.[8] Thus, not only does the brain engage in necessary processes that occur only while at rest, and derive immediate benefits from that rest, but also, just as importantly, downtime produces long-term benefits that can mean both better productivity and a better life.

It is clear, then, that you need a "third thing." But, how you go about that is up to you. Whether practiced alone or in company, your third thing should be something that relaxes and recharges you, not drains you, and it should be something that is not an obligation or feels burdensome. For example, although eating is a necessity of life, cooking can still be a recreational activity if you like to do it and want to take time to get better at it or to try new things. However, if you find this task obligatory or even stressful—as I often do, actually—it is probably not a good "downtime" activity. It belongs to the "home life obligations" category. Moreover, for me, online social networks have started to become enervating rather than energizing. They add to the buzz in my head, instead of calming it. If that is true for you, too, your downtime should not be spent reading Facebook, Twitter, or blogs. My own blog, for example, has started to feel a bit like a work-related obligation, although I enjoy writing it, so it does not count as true "downtime." Whatever you choose, it does not necessarily have to be something you could categorize as a "hobby"; it could be as simple as making time to read for pleasure, or drinking a ritual cup of quality tea as you free your mind of work and home obligations, or listening to an album from start to finish with real concentration. Intellectual and aesthetic pursuits that do not immediately relate to your work count. Think deeply about them and discuss them energetically with like-minded people, but try not to convert them into lines on your CV. That is how you turn your "third thing" into a work thing, and that is not necessarily good for you in the long run.

Your third thing could be a regular social event—a weekly dinner party or potluck dinner (if you need to share the costs or labor), a bowling night, a movie night, etc—or it could be a scheduled solitary practice. It can be many things, a different thing each day of the week, at different times of day, but it should be a regular part of your life. Ideally, each day should have at least some downtime, but daily activities could be short and simple, whereas a weekly one could be something more ambitious or one that takes more time. If you have to schedule it in order to make sure it happens, then do so. Schedules have always helped me make room for recreation, and, lately, I have been using timers to help me stay focused on work tasks for concentrated bouts (this is especially useful for keeping grading from expanding to fill all of the time you have). That said, do not let that scheduling then turn the activity into an obligation or an anxiety, or make you too rigid. In my experience, being overscheduled can add to stress and anxiety.[9]

If all of this sounds hopelessly privileged, keep in mind that the Universal Declaration of Human Rights, Article 24, declares that "Everyone has the right to rest and leisure."[10] Seize that right and do not feel guilty about it. Yes, you could be writing your dissertation, book, article, grant, or class notes instead of what you are doing for recreation, but you could also be taking a real break instead of mucking around on Facebook or doing the dishes right at that moment. Your work will expand to fill the time you give it; do not let it do so. You will produce better work if you are rested and recharged. If you are financially stressed, your leisure does not have to cost money. If you are strapped for time, it does not have to take up large chunks of time; it can be eked out of the busiest lives.

My downtime has evolved over the course of my career, and there are numerous ways I have spent it—reading, watching television and movies, volunteering for the dog rescue group from whom we adopted our dog, taking classes on non-work-related subjects (drawing classes at the museum; "Animal Behavior in Zoos" through UCLA Extension and the Los Angeles Zoo), teaching myself Italian, playing sous-chef to my foodie spouse at dinner parties we throw, and so on. However, I have had the most complex relationship with long-distance running, and so I want to use it as an example of both how to do and also how not to do downtime. If you find long-distance running an incomprehensibly freakish activity performed only by masochists—and really, who can blame you?—just substitute some other activity in your head as I describe what running did and did not do for me.

I began running in 1999, when I was a dissertating PhD student at UCLA, and I took up the sport for a number of reasons. Some of them had to do with fitness, but a lot of them had to do with mental health and socializing. I had a friend who wanted a running partner and was relentlessly supportive of my running; once I was able to run 30 minutes or more at a time, we would plan weekend days around our runs and do things afterwards where we did not mind being sweaty (mostly outdoor activities in the Los Angeles sunshine). She also wanted some social time with a female friend, as she spent almost all of the rest of her time with her male partner. I just wanted to get out of my lonely apartment and take a break from writing the dissertation. Once I built up the stamina to run for an hour with ease, she suggested I join the LA Road Runners, a training group for the LA Marathon. While I thought that actually running a marathon sounded like lunacy, the training plan the Road Runners provided helped me stick to running, making it my clear "third thing."

Moreover, I was in desperate need of a wider social group. I was feeling acutely the isolation of dissertation writing and being on fellowship. In addition, many of my friends had coupled up and were spending more time with their partners and less time with single friends, and I was suffering from low-grade depression, as well. A big training group that emphasized running at a conversational pace turned out to be just what I needed to get out of my head and into the wider world. Every Sunday morning, I got up at some absolutely ridiculous pre-dawn hour to take two busses from midtown LA to Venice Beach (because I did not have a car at the time) to join the group long run. On other days of the week, I ran by myself, following the handy training schedule. What motivated me to get to the group run was not so much the running itself—clearly, I could do that on my own—as it was the opportunity to talk to people, to be outside, to see the ocean, and to enjoy one, two, or three hours just passing the time. Those of you who do not run probably think "passing the time" is an odd way to describe a three-hour run, but if you are building up your endurance, not trying to set a time goal, running at a conversational pace, and talking to people, that is really what it amounts to.

I did not have a lot in common with the people in my pace group, but they were still good company on a run. You cannot have very complicated conversations on a long run, especially on the crowded paths in the communities along the Santa Monica Bay, so topics were often light. Moreover, the differences between us were good for me, as they got me out of the bubble of academia and dissertation writing. I explained to them the loneliness that graduate school can induce or exacerbate, and they were kind and sympathetic. There is nothing like a group of people literally cheering each other on to one big goal to help figuratively cheer you toward other life goals. Further, my friends in this group were relentlessly positive, never competitive. Even when they hit a wall or somehow disappointed themselves in one of the many races we did as we built up to the marathon, they still celebrated others' victories. This was different from graduate school culture, where even allies and friends would sometimes take one person's success as a comment on their own perceived failures. This is, unfortunately, one of the terrible effects that academic culture can have on a person's outlook and just one reason why having a "third thing" that takes you away from that culture is so important.

Particularly when stable, tenure-track jobs are scarce, it is hard not to feel either survivor's guilt or envy and bitterness, depending on your position. However, in running, at least at the non-elite level, you are mostly competing against yourself, if you are competing at all; sometimes, the goal is just to finish.

Over time, however, running became more goal-oriented for me, and more competitive. I discovered that I was naturally good at it, that without much effort I could reach modest milestone goals: sub-four-hour marathons were a piece of cake and qualifying for the Boston Marathon was not much more difficult. After I moved to Toledo, Ohio, I also started winning or coming in second in my age group in shorter races. (The competition had been much fiercer in LA, especially when I was still in my early 30s, a peak age for runners.) I was not so driven that I wanted to work hard at running, but even with the modest goals I set for myself, the competitiveness started to take over and eventually soured running for me. Making it so goal-oriented set me up for disappointment and frustration when I missed those goals, which then made it seem like work, which also meant it no longer served its purpose as an escape and outlet. I remember even breaking down in tears in one marathon when I realized I did not have it in me to keep up my desired pace in the last quarter of the race.

I think it is safe to say that, if your "third thing" is making you cry, then it is probably no longer doing you any restorative good. That is why I have not run a marathon since the 2007 Boston Marathon. I have also let up on running in general, as other interests and commitments have taken up its time. I have not replaced running with a single thing as time-consuming, but maybe that is a good thing. Keeping a variety of interests and activities in rotation might prevent me from getting burnt out on any of them. However, although I do not do anything as spectacular now, I do set aside time to unwind, to leave work and other obligations behind. My spouse and I both try to finish all work by 7 p.m. each weeknight and to leave weekends open—partly to take care of household responsibilities, but partly to relax—except under extraordinary circumstances (and even then, we try to work only half days). On weeknights, we cook (well, he does), watch television, read, and play with the dog. On weekends, we do a variety of things that we enjoy, together and separately. We have even occasionally managed a short vacation during the school year, over a fall or spring break (our academic calendar has both); we do not save it all for summer, which can be just as busy as the school year with conferences, research trips, writing, and administrative duties. It may be a little hectic to get away during the semester, but it is often to our benefit to take a short break, so that we are not steamrolled by the passing semester, only to find ourselves collapsing unproductively over winter break or for the first part of the summer. As noted earlier, some research shows that more frequent short breaks are more beneficial than single long ones, and I personally find that a short break mid-semester refuels me for the second half, just as it is intended to do for our students.

My friends with children often have this kind of management of downtime worked out, in large part, because they have to schedule everything or else the system falls apart and important tasks or events are forgotten. In some ways, single people and couples without children need to be more conscious of making time for recreation, to make sure that they are setting aside relaxation time for themselves, although they may seemingly have fewer family responsibilities. Remember, work will fill the time you allot to it and, in my experience, we single and child-free folks are especially prone to letting it do so. Such behavior does not always mean higher or better productivity in our scholarship or more effective teaching, either. Do not let yourself believe the myth that you always need to be working. Sure, Chaucer tells us in the opening line of *Parliament of Fowls* about "The lyf so short, the craft so longe to lerne," but "the craft" could be woodworking as well as continental philosophy. Some of the most productive and influential scholars I know are the ones who have families and also pastimes as time-consuming as running marathons. How do they manage it all? They schedule and they work in concentrated bouts; they do not waste time. That is why, in my household, we have the 7 p.m. rule (which is not to say we always succeed at making that cutoff, but we try), and why I try to stay conscious of the time I let slip away in ephemeralities. I am still working on giving more time to real relaxation and less to time wasting—I'm not perfect at it—but simply knowing I need to make time for a "third thing" helps me do so.

After all, what is the prize for always working in academia (or worse, always seeming to work)? In some workaholic departmental climates, you may have to keep your downtime on the down low, but that does not mean you cannot have it. You will, of course, have to do what is necessary to get a job and to earn tenure. And you will likely want to be promoted to full professor and have to reach certain levels of accomplishment for that. I have done those things and I am here to tell you they can be done while still having a life. And a life worth living really does need recreation, relaxation, play, and rest. Take that time. It is your human right.

NOTES

1. My idea of a "third thing" is somewhat parallel to Ray Oldenburg's concept of a "third place," as developed in his book, *The Great Good Place: Cafes, Coffee Shops, Community Centers, Beauty Parlors, General Stores, Bars, Hangouts, and How They Get You Through the Day*, New York: Paragon House, 1989.
2. Jabr, F. "Why Your Brain Needs More Downtime," *Scientific American*, October 15, 2013, accessed June 15, 2014, http://www.scientificamerican.com/article/mental-downtime/
3. Jabr, "Why Your Brain Needs More Downtime."
4. Jabr, "Why Your Brain Needs More Downtime."
5. Jabr, "Why Your Brain Needs More Downtime."
6. Jabr, "Why Your Brain Needs More Downtime."
7. This recent meta-study reviews the current findings: Mammen, G. and G. Faulkner. "Physical Activity and the Prevention of Depression," *American Journal of Preventive Medicine* 45 (2013): 649–657, accessed June 25, 2014, doi: http://dx.doi.org/10.1016/j.amepre.2013.08.001.
8. California State Parks. "The Health and Social Benefits of Recreation: An Element of the California Outdoor Recreation Planning Program," 2005, accessed June 15, 2014, http://www.parks.ca.gov/pages/795/files/benefits%20final%20online%20v6-1-05.pdf.
9. My quick search of databases for psychology and cognitive science studies on overscheduling showed that much of the research is being done on children and adolescents; therefore, it is not immediately pertinent here. However, I also noticed that a number of the most recent studies (after 2010) were PhD dissertations. Perhaps it is telling that young-in-the-field academics are studying the phenomenon of being over-scheduled?
10. "Universal Declaration of Human Rights," *Wikisource*, http://en.wikisource.org/wiki/Universal_Declaration_of_Human_Rights, last modified September 24, 2013, accessed June 15, 2014.

CHAPTER 12

MATERNITY

Kristen Ghodsee

Exhaustion. Bone-marrow-sucking, soul-crushing, never-ending exhaustion. No matter how many hours of sleep I stole from the time demanded from me by my baby, my students, my immediate colleagues, and my colleagues further afield, I never felt rested. I could not sleep for more than an hour before I jolted awake in the middle of the night recalling some paper I forgot to grade, some assignment I had not written, some pressing email that remained unanswered, or some letter of recommendation undrafted and now long overdue. There were long days of teaching and advising when I would pick up my daughter from daycare, feed her, bathe her, and then put her in bed in the blur of being on autopilot. I would return downstairs to a partner hoping to share some "couple time," and fall asleep after the first few sentences were exchanged. I became a single mom not long after that.

My daughter was four years old when I had my most desperate moment as a mother on the tenure track. I was up against a hard deadline for copyedits on my first book—the book that would hopefully earn me the all-coveted tenure. I needed just a few uninterrupted hours, but it was almost impossible to take a break from my daughter, who demanded constant attention. I flew out to stay with my mother and grandmother who had both offered to help with the child. It was no use. My daughter wanted mama and no one else.

One morning, I locked myself in the bathroom with my laptop. Kneeling on the tile floor, I hoped to answer the last of the author queries. I had about 20 minutes before my daughter started pounding on the door for me to come out. Then I heard my mother's voice trying to coax my daughter away to play a game, and a few minutes later my grandmother started chastising my mother, in Spanish, about how spoiled my daughter was and how parents these days didn't know how to properly raise children. My mother started yelling at my grandmother (in Spanish) to be quiet and help her. Then she cooed at my daughter (in English) about how fun it would be to do a puzzle together. So there I was, my legs folded under and falling asleep, with tears streaming, while I tapped away at my keyboard. There was a thin door separating me from my screaming daughter, my code-switching mother, and my sanctimonious Puerto Rican grandmother. I don't know how long it took, but I did not succumb to the cacophony. I met the deadline.

I am haunted by that experience. My daughter enjoyed the attentions of both her grandmother and great grandmother—two women who loved her with the collective force of a category one hurricane—but she wanted her mama. The editors of this volume asked me to write a chapter on "maternity." I was not asked to write about "managing parenthood in academe," and I think that there is a critical difference. As much as we want to institutionalize equal benefits for mothers and fathers, there are some burdens that fall disproportionately on those who possess the biological equipment to conceive, gestate, deliver, and nurse human babies—at the current moment, those who are assigned female at birth. Moreover, social constructions of motherhood are far more rigid and oppressive to women pursuing careers than social constructions of fatherhood. Fathers are expected to be in the workforce, and if they choose to spend time with their young children, they are rewarded for their still relatively atypical affective labors. Mothers enjoy no such rewards.

A few years ago, a colleague of mine agreed to write me a letter of recommendation for a fellowship for which I was applying. She was in her early 40s and had waited until she earned tenure before getting pregnant. The due date of my fellowship application coincided with her expected date of delivery. She had a normal pregnancy and all of the prenatal tests showed that the baby was healthy. The due date for my letter came and went. The due date for her baby came and went, and I heard no word from her. Fearing the worst, I was hesitant to email, until I got a notification from the fellowship committee that my application would be disqualified if my colleague did not produce a letter.

So I finally wrote to her. "Dear X, I am really hoping that my message does not come at a terrible time. I was hoping for some good news from you, but your silence has unnerved me." I tentatively inquired after her health, and asked if I should seek another letter writer. I was happy to do that, but I would need her to email the foundation to explain that she was unable to write for me for medical reasons.

I received this reply: "I just gave birth a week ago. Had some significant complications. Spent several days in hospital and 18 of last 36 hours in emergency. Still dealing w/medical consults, etc...Pretty exhausted and overwhelmed."

I wrote her back. "Is everything okay now? Is the baby okay?"

She replied, "Yeah...very tough pregnancy and delivery...I'm left w/herniated disk, compressed nerves, major bladder damage and a mass in my uterus that they are trying to figure out. Pretty much hell right now."

A few days later, she wrote to me again. "I have lots of recovery—apparently, having a herniated disk caused endless problems (just discovered on MRI finally). It is going to be a while before I'm myself again but I'm feeling better. I'm going to work on your letter due mid-Nov. this weekend. Should be able to take care of the ones you originally asked for. My apologies for all the hassle. Usually I'm so on top of things, but this pregnancy really did me in."

I closed my eyes when I got her last message and thanked the Ob-Gyn gods that I ended up having a C-Section. I didn't really care about the letter of recommendation anymore. I figured that my application was already dead in the water. Then, a thought crossed my mind. It was just for a moment, but it was long enough that it still bothers me many years later. I thought: *If I had asked a male colleague to write for me, this wouldn't have happened.*

I immediately caught myself. Oh god, if I thought this—a mother and a professor of gender studies—how could I not expect that others would think the same? Parenthood could not really be shared equally between men and women, and everyone knew it, no matter how politically correct it was to pretend otherwise. My male colleagues might become fathers and lose endless nights of sleep, but they were unlikely to end up in the emergency room with a herniated disk, compressed nerves, and major bladder damage from the arrival of their child.

As much as we try to legislate gender equality and the equal responsibility between mothers and fathers, there is a brutal biological reality that cannot be ignored. As someone with liberal intellectual sympathies, I am completely willing to believe that both sex and gender are socially constructed categories, and I am a strong advocate for the idea that all parents should be equally involved in the raising of their children. Despite this, I would be a self-deluding idiot to ignore the fact that (at least as of 2015) the human beings who are physiologically capable of manufacturing babies are those of us who were assigned female at birth and in possession of a uterus. This biological reality creates a fundamental inequality between the MAABs (male-assigned at birth) and the FAABs (female-assigned at birth).

In addition to the differential physical effects of maternity and paternity, women face other specific biological challenges related to timing. The stresses of the tenure track often coincide with a woman's peak years of fertility. Fecundity declines for even well-nourished, healthy women by age 30 and plummets after age 35. Yes, many women are able to have children through their early 40s, some with medical intervention, but there is no guarantee. Many women feel compelled to wait until they achieve tenure before getting pregnant, but by the time they are ready to start their families, their bodies are no longer cooperating. Depending on the circumstances, in vitro fertilization (IVF) can be expensive and many insurance plans don't cover it. Further, the hormone injections required for IVF to work can be psychologically debilitating.

Back in 2006–2007, I was a residential member at the Institute for Advanced Study in Princeton, New Jersey. The Institute had a small gym, and I spent about 30 minutes on the treadmill each morning. One day, I went to the bathroom and heard the heavy sobbing of a woman in the stall beside mine.

"Is everything okay?" I said, not knowing whom it was.

A long groan emanated from the stall.

I waited by the sinks, until one of my senior colleagues emerged. She was an art historian from the School of Historical Studies, and she explained to me that she and her husband were trying to have a baby. They had waited until both of them had tenure, and now she was in her early 40s.

"The shots are killing me," she explained. Both my colleague and her husband had fellowships at the Institute that year. She complained that while he effortlessly plowed along on his book project, she was riding a wild roller coaster of hormone injections.

"I can't concentrate. I can't think. I can't get anything done," she said to me. "It is so unfair."

As many researchers have pointed out, the timing of the tenure track coincides perfectly with male (assigned at birth) biology. For aspiring academics (and members of other professions), the 30s represent what Sylvia Ann Hewlett calls "the unforgiving decade."[1] Women must fight to establish themselves professionally at the exact moment when their fertility is declining. Both my colleague in the bathroom at the Institute for Advanced Study and my colleague with the major bladder damage were women in their 40s who waited until after they had job security to have a child. Men simply do not have to face this challenge.

Even if a woman conceives naturally and survives her pregnancy unscathed, there is little discussion about the physical and psychological costs of breastfeeding. A 2013 article in the *Journal of Human Lactation* argued that women are disproportionately paying the price for the public benefits associated with exclusively breastfed children.[2] The authors argue that exclusive breastfeeding is "time intensive," and that this labor is a significant drain on the women who provide this service. Although colleges and universities have tried to accommodate lactating women, the responsibility for breastfeeding still falls overwhelmingly on those of us with breasts capable of lactation. The biological costs of childbearing and childrearing continue to put humans that were female-assigned at birth at a significant disadvantage compared to their peers who were male-assigned at birth.

One obvious solution for the discerning academic is simply not to have any children. Refusing to reproduce is perhaps the most elegant way to ensure the equality of the sexes, and in fact, we have good evidence that the gender wage gap almost completely disappears when you disaggregate the data and look at women with no children. As Ann Crittenden argued in *The Price of Motherhood*, educated women pay a massive pecuniary penalty for having children.[3] The gender wage gap is really a maternal wage gap, because American women find it almost impossible to juggle work and family responsibilities (particularly since the United States has no paid maternity leave). In our no-holds-barred, dog-eat-dog, late capitalist economy, anyone who ends up in the emergency room with major bladder damage because of something she elected to do (i.e., having a baby) is falling down on the job.

While I respect the decision of some of my colleagues to forego children, I personally find great joy and satisfaction in my own daughter. And as her social security number reminds me, I know that my daughter will be a contributor to our collective society, at the very least because her future wages will be taxed to pay for other people's retirement benefits. I did not wait until I had tenure to get pregnant. I got pregnant while I was still in graduate school, and then I worked my butt off to make sure that I made the tenure cut. I was leaning in well before there were circles to support aspiring leaners.

Back in 2011, the labor economist Rachel Connelly and I decided to write a handbook for women trying to combine motherhood with academic careers.[4] To our great and continuing delight, the book has found a wide audience among aspiring graduate students and junior professors, both male and female. However, one of the early criticisms of the book was that we reinforced the gender binary by targeting our book to women. By addressing the challenges and difficulties of "maternity," some feared that we were undermining the intellectual justifications for the widespread policy of parental leave.

I believe that it is essential that we separate these two issues. Having a child has huge ramifications on any couple, but it will have larger ramifications for the member of that couple who has the physical job of conceiving, gestating, birthing, and breastfeeding the child. This does not matter whether childbearing happens within a same-sex couple, among a polyamorous conglomeration, or within a garden-variety heterosexual pairing. She who gets pregnant may suffer tooth decay, sciatica, swollen extremities, hemorrhoids, varicosities, irregular facial pigmentations, and a variety of other possible ailments that afflict the gestating female. Add to these biological indignities the various social expectations of motherhood, and there is a perfect storm.

Women who have children do face significant disadvantages in the labor force, and particularly in academia, and these must be acknowledged. Acknowledging them does not mean that we deny the very important role that non-gestating partners have to play in child raising, but we should not blind ourselves to the nature of the inequality for the sake of political expedience.

How then do we manage maternity in the academy? How can you make a life in the humanities while being a mother? I wish I had the perfect answer, but the truth is that everyone will manage it differently. The key thing is that it can, and that it must, be managed. Women who have children in graduate school or on the tenure track will pave the way for the women (and hopefully someday men) coming up behind them. There are also important policy changes that must be implemented both nationally and institutionally so that women do not continue to be disadvantaged by their biology. There are many men and women in the academy who are fighting for these changes. At the individual level, the key thing is to recognize the challenges, and to face them head on. Maternity (like mischief) can always be managed.

NOTES

1. Hewlett, S. A. "Executive Women and the Myth of Having it All," *Harvard Business Review* 80 (2002): 66–73.
2. Smith, J. P. and R. Forrester. "Who Pays for the Health Benefits of Exclusive Breastfeeding? An Analysis of Maternal Time Costs," *Journal of Human Lactation* 29 (2013): 547–555.
3. Crittendon, A. *The Price of Motherhood: Why the Most Important Job in the World is Still the Least Valued*, New York: Macmillan, 2002.
4. Connelly, R. and K. Ghodsee. *Professor Mommy: Finding Work/Family Balance in Academia*, Baltimore: Rowman & Littlefield, 2011.

CHAPTER 13

LIFE WITH CHILDREN: CHILDREN ON CAMPUS

Michael Bérubé

If I hadn't had a child at the age of 24, toward the end of my third year in graduate school, I probably would never have gotten my PhD. I know this sounds counterintuitive; that is why I open with it. However, it also happens to be true.

It was the summer of 1985, and I had taken an incomplete in Richard Rorty's Heidegger seminar the previous spring. But the summer festered and I dithered, wallowing in the conviction that there was nothing I could possibly tell Rorty about Heidegger. Now, this was a problem, not only for the obvious reasons but also because, after two years of graduate school, I had completed only nine courses; Virginia expected its graduate students in English to take three per term for their first two years, and then dial it back to one per term for year three, when students began teaching a 2–1 load that dropped to 1–1 in years four, five, and beyond. Therefore, I was gradually backing myself into a situation in which I would have to take *five* courses while teaching three (very clearly impossible), or extend my coursework into a fourth year (a very bad sign). However, summer continued to fester, and I continued to dither, and....

Then, one day in August, my then-girlfriend Janet Lyon took an EPT and it was unambiguously positive. We were pregnant! Yay? And by the end of September, we were married. I wrote my paper for Rorty in mid-late August, longhand—the last paper I would ever write with a pen. It came to approximately 50 pages, and I had turned into the

Graduate Student from Hell—the one who takes a self-indulgent incomplete and then turns in a behemoth essay just before the new semester starts.

But from that point on, I never experienced another period of dithering or wallowing. The stakes were just too high: I now had a baby to take care of. And when Nick became a toddler, and developed severe asthma that almost took his life at two, the stakes became still higher: I now needed a job with really good health coverage. My anxiety over what Richard Rorty would think of my work had been obliterated by my anxiety over becoming a parent; now my anxiety about completing a dissertation was obliterated by my anxiety over my child's health. And I learned something interesting about how my anxiety works: it flows freely from one subject to another, but there is only a fixed amount to go around.

Of course, having children meant spending many of my waking hours taking care of children—and losing many of my sleeping hours. During my first year on the tenure track at the University of Illinois at Urbana-Champaign, Nick's bouts of asthma were so bad that he routinely woke up at 2 or 3 a.m. needing to use the nebulizer. Not until he began using Vanceril, aerosol steroids, in 1990 did he begin to stabilize. And then, just as Janet joined me on the tenure track in 1991, we had another baby, James. Now we were untenured professors with two babies. And this second baby had Down syndrome; Jamie required 3 weeks of intensive care followed by almost ten months of high-intensity parenting that included an apnea monitor (which would go off repeatedly during the night) and nasal feedings with a gavage tube (which we inserted with the help of some Vaseline). For this operation, Janet's training as a nurse was invaluable.

Those were not happy times. They were suffused with anxiety and dread, and even a little resentment too: my childless colleagues had no idea that we had to do our work (preparing our classes, pursuing our research) in short intense bursts, sometimes no longer than 15 or 20 minutes. But here (already!) I am treading on highly contested ground. Academics have all kinds of reasons to resent each other, and often when they can't find a reason, they make one up. However, the "children on campus" question is legitimately resentment-inducing for many people, and for many good reasons. Professors with young children can resent their childless colleagues, straight or gay, on the grounds that nothing makes sane work–life balance harder than children—and because professors can be "working" (i.e., thinking) for all their waking hours (and some of their sleeping hours), work–life balance is for many academics an exceptionally difficult thing to achieve.

At the same time, childless professors, straight or gay, can resent the professor/parents who always go home promptly at 5 p.m. (or earlier) and whose conversations and social practices are (a) centered firmly on their children's soccer leagues, ballet classes, school adventures, creative achievements, bowel movements, piano recitals, zoo visits, and science experiments, and (b) sanctioned always and everywhere by the full weight of the apparatus of reproductive heterosexuality. Which is really heavy, as it happens, and can be quite oppressive.

Then again, academe can also be one of those rare places where the apparatus of reproductive heterosexuality doesn't always function to full capacity: you will, if you are a reproductive heterosexual (or an adoptive parent, gay or straight) find that academe is full of people who believe that *serious* professors should not have children at all, and that anyone who has more than two children (or more than one?) is obviously unserious. Most of the time, this is old-school snobbery at work—the beliefs of people who think that the life of the mind requires unwavering dedication to Scholarship with no petty distractions involving soccer leagues, ballet classes, school adventures, creative achievements, bowel movements, piano recitals, zoo visits, and science experiments. Further, the old-school snobbery, being old school, falls far more heavily on mothers than on fathers. But sometimes, it touches on matters of university policy, and this is where things get very complicated very fast.

Let us say that a university has a policy on voluntary leaves with pay and rollbacks of the tenure clock (as well it should). Now let us say that in the interest of gender equity, untenured female faculty who give birth should be entitled not only to a standard amount of maternity leave (as well they should) but also to a one-year rollback of the tenure clock, on the grounds that new mothers inevitably wind up doing most of the work of child care, especially with regard to infants.

So far, so good: this is, I think, a reasonable base from which to start. Paid paternity leave would be even better, six to eight weeks, or paid partner leave in the case of same-sex couples. When Jamie was born in September 1991, Janet was, in fact, granted a one-year rollback of the tenure clock, and rightly so, in light of the degree of care Jamie required during his first year of life. Illinois had no maternity or paternity leave, however; all faculty were granted five weeks of annual sick leave, but Janet took only two weeks after Jamie was discharged from the neonatal intensive care unit (ICU), in the well-grounded belief that we didn't know whether we might need to use the other three at some later point in the semester. (We did not.)

But should the same accommodations be made for adoptive parents, even if they are adopting a child who is already past the infant or toddler stage? I do not see why not. Child care is child care, and adoptive children often require forms of assimilation and acculturation that are every bit as challenging as the trials of infant care. But then why should these provisions be extended only to faculty members who have children by birth or adoption? Isn't that inevitably discriminatory, pursuing gender equity while discriminating against childless faculty, gay and straight? (Yes, it is.) And what about people with aging parents who require various forms of eldercare? What about people who may become responsible for siblings or other family members requiring care for medical emergencies or mental illness? What, indeed, about every other possible relation of care we can imagine?

Furthermore, what about the untenured faculty member who might need a second leave, or a second one-year rollback of the tenure clock, prior to his or her promotion-and-tenure review? Should children with special needs or chronic health conditions, and their parents, be granted extra time as well? And what about the possibility that a second rollback might be construed as a form of infantilization, unduly extending a faculty member's probationary period, or as creating a "mommy track" (whether occupied by mommies or not) for certain faculty members? And to return to where we started, aren't these last two objections—about infantilization and a mommy track—testimony to the way in which the tenure system discriminates against women?

The proposition that starts off with a relatively simple matter of gender equity quickly spirals into serious complexity. As I write this, I am serving on a faculty senate subcommittee at Penn State, one of whose charges is to devise an equitable leave policy, and this is more or less how the deliberations have gone down. I don't know where they will wind up, but for my part, I tend to err on the side of inclusiveness and the most humane possible workplace: everyone who requires a semester leave, or a rollback of the tenure clock, *for any of the reasons I have enumerated earlier*, should receive one. A second semester of leave, or a second rollback, should be granted to faculty members whose lives have become severely complicated for any of the reasons I have enumerated earlier. And prior to tenure, I am not sure there is a case for a *third* leave or rollback. Post-tenure, a university committee on leaves and absences should handle every application on a case-by-case basis. It is just impossible to imagine ahead of time all the complications of our lives.

So much for policy. Now back to the personal, where the policy is lived. On a day-to-day basis, a professor's life can be wonderfully flexible, depending on his or her teaching schedule; accommodating one's children's needs in the middle of the day, for doctors' appointments or sudden emergencies, is rather easier on a campus schedule than on your usual 9-to-5 (or your 11–7, 7–3, or 3–11). And, of course, campuses are full of potential babysitters (although when Jamie became a teenager we began using the term "companions"), whom we generally pay $12 per hour. But a semester or a quarter is not so easily finessed. When my mother broke her hip in the fall of 2006, she clearly needed someone to help her get around (and to do something about her house, which would not have made it into the finals of the Hoarders' League but would very likely have qualified for the playoffs). I was able to visit her for two weeks in Virginia Beach, making up a medication chart, straightening out matters with her doctors and attorneys (she had been inadvertently knocked down by a Home Depot employee), and cleaning the house. However, I was not able to make that visit until the end of finals week. By contrast, my children's diurnal needs can usually be accommodated with some creative parenting—and a constant awareness that Janet and I should not schedule our classes for the same days.

We learned that elementary lesson the hard way. When we arrived at Illinois in 1989, when I began my first year as an assistant professor and Janet taught two classes at graduate-student wages as an ABD, we were assigned two courses each. Janet taught MWF at 9 and 11; I taught MWF at 10 and 12. However, Illinois had no campus daycare for our three-year-old; the most the university would do, back then, was offer us a referral to a municipal agency that would offer us five referrals to daycare providers. To make things even more baroquely Illinoisian, we could not be given those five referrals in person when we applied to the municipal agency; we were informed that we would have to return home and receive a phone call. The result of all this finely reticulated nonsense is that we eventually found a place for Nick at which we could afford half-day care. This was not ideal for Nick because, when we dropped him off at 1, he found himself on a schedule that mandated early-afternoon naps. Partly because of his asthma medications, partly because of his body's interpretation of its own circadian rhythms, Nick did not take naps. And it was not ideal for us, because it meant that Janet and I would meet in the hallways of the English Building between classes to hand him off to each other during the ten-minute intervals between 50-minute classes. Janet likes to tell people that we simply threw him across the hall—me to her at 11, her to me at 12 (Nick and I would grab a lunch at the Illini Union), me to her at 1, whereupon she would drive him to Kinder Cassel—but we almost never did this. Although it is true that I once realized, while waiting for the 9:30 bus with Nick, that I had managed to lock the house while leaving my house keys in the living room, and shocked Nick by breaking a plexiglass window in order to retrieve my keys, make the bus, and hand him off to Janet in time for my 10 a.m. class.

That experience is why, although my children are adults, I still care about the state of campus daycare—including the Penn State controversy you probably haven't heard about, the dispute over the campus's Bennett Family Center. In the summer of 2013, Penn State announced (without consulting anyone beforehand) that it would turn over the management of the Bennett Center to an organization called Hildebrandt Learning Centers. No reason was given for the decision, but it was clear to all concerned that this move would deprive all Bennett Center employees of Penn State benefits. The decision was met with strenuous and vocal opposition (including demonstrations), as well it should have been, and as I write, the prospects for the Bennett Center look reasonably good: a task force was formed in response to parents' protests, and the report of the task force largely validated parents' concerns; so I am hopeful.

I suppose I should close by checking my privilege, because no speech act in academe should be exempt from a privilege check and a trigger alert. I enjoy two distinct layers of privilege, on top of all the innumerable layers of privilege I enjoy as a white man in an advanced industrial nation. Layer number one: I get to travel a lot. Although I rarely attend conferences other than the MLA, I accept five or six speaking engagements per year and, during my service on the International Advisory Board of the Consortium of Humanities Centers and Institutes, I have gone to meetings in China, Australia, England, and South Africa. Especially when Jamie was younger, my travels had the potential to put serious strains on our marriage, leaving Janet with long stretches of solo care for a special-needs child. For that reason, and to broaden Jamie's horizons and enhance his living skills, I began taking Jamie with me on some of my travels when he became mature enough to sit through his father's lectures and seminars. I tried this as early as 1998, when he was seven, hiring a local graduate student to accompany him for the two hours during which I would be occupied; but not until 2005 did I have the confidence that he could be left to his own devices during the business hours of my various campus visits. I have done long-term solo Jamie care a number of times: four one-month stints while Janet taught in Ireland, and two three-month stints (summer 1996, fall 2012) when she lived on her own to concentrate on writing free from family distractions. In return, Janet has held down the fort for three of my extended absences—a month-long fellowship in 2006, a month-long summer teaching gig in 2011, and a six-week School of Criticism and Theory seminar in 2013.

Which brings me to layer two. The world being what it is, academic women usually get penalized professionally for doing child care—whereas men, *mirabile dictu*, get extra credit for it. People who might object to a mother taking her child along on a speaking engagement tend to think it's just great that I do it. The rule holds *a fortiori* for children with disabilities, because men are so rare in the field of special-needs care, and the gendering of child care is far more emphatic when the child in question has special needs. Because I am the beneficiary of that social inequity, it is obviously my job to overcompensate, to balance the scales as best I can. Work–life balance is elusive, and is a matter of mental and psychological health. Life–life balance, between partners, is still more elusive, and is a matter of reciprocity and justice. For now, and for the rest of Jamie's adult life, our division of labor runs as follows: I do the legal things (his relationship to state and federal bureaucracy, his special-needs trust), and Janet does the medical things. I joke that on a day-to-day basis, this amounts to a 90–10 split; but, of course, a medical emergency can come out of nowhere, and there will always be the need for thyroid checkups, eye exams, physicals for Special Olympics, and so forth. And that's how we'll go about balancing life and work, and life and life: by making stuff up as we go along, and by trying, in the immortal words of Bill and Ted, to be excellent to one another.

CHAPTER 14

LIFE WITHOUT CHILDREN

Sean Grass and Iris V. Rivero

When the editors of this volume approached us to write an essay on what it means to be "childless" in the academy, we were intrigued. Over the years, we have heard any number of presentations wholly or partly about the complications of having children: whether and how to stop your tenure clock, what rights you have under the Family and Medical Leave Act, and what tuition discounts you receive for dependents. It's not that we don't appreciate the information. For one thing, we have both contemplated a future career path in administration, where knowledge of these things is crucial. For another, policies associated with medical leave can be every bit as crucial for faculty facing serious illness as for those expecting a child. But for the childless, these programs often seem to imply, however subtly, that faculty without children have it easy—that we don't have personal obligations or complications and, instead, spend our time at culinary clubs, or traveling Europe, or otherwise making luxurious use of endless expanses of free time. If only it were so. The fact is that being childless in the academy can pose its own complications. By writing this essay, we hope to help the childless know what to expect, and to give their colleagues, chairs, and deans a sense of the issues that perturb these modern-day Sphinxes—inscrutable to the parenting majority—who can't or won't have a child.

In the interest of full disclosure, we should say two things up front: (a) we are childfree by choice, having determined long ago that our temperaments, backgrounds, and career goals are not suited to child-rearing; and (b) because we don't have children, and because we are

writing about the challenges of childlessness—some of which, naturally, are posed by our colleagues with children—we run the risk of
offending every parent who reads this essay. Although we discuss here
the thoughtless behaviors of some colleagues with children, we do so
under the assumption that these behaviors would frustrate *any* con-
scientious academic professional, with or without children. In fact,
we know that they do. As we prepared to write this essay, we spoke
with colleagues in our departments and elsewhere in our university
and with academics we know at other schools. Some were childless,
and others were parents. We have also drawn from Iris's participation
in ADVANCE grants and professional development workshops, some
of them funded partly by the National Science Foundation and many
of them designed to promote the careers of women in higher education. As we considered our own experiences and gathered anecdotes
and opinions, we were struck by the extent to which other childless
academics have had experiences like ours. Meanwhile, talking with
academic parents often opened our eyes and theirs: some parents we
spoke with had no idea how their actions look to the childless, while
others turned out to be as bothered in some respects as we are. In
short, academic parents aren't all thoughtless, selfish ogres, nor are
the childless all models for professional conduct. Having admitted
as much at the start, this essay can move on to the work of creating
greater sympathy among responsible professionals from both groups
by identifying the challenges that the childless often encounter in
the academy and explaining how these challenges become sources
of inequity and frustration. If you're childless in the academy—or if
you're a colleague or administrator who wants to know what childless
faculty might be thinking—here are some things you should know.

Probably the most consistent source of irritation for childless faculty is the assumption, often explicit, that childless faculty are available for a greater array of departmental and university obligations
than parents, especially when those obligations happen outside of
normal business hours. If you're childless, you never need a sitter and
don't have children to get ready for school; therefore, it's no imposi-
tion for you to take the campus interviewee to dinner, rush the visiting speaker to his early morning flight, or spend three hours on a
Saturday talking with pre-teens as part of the "Science, It's a Girl
Thing" initiative. It's not the case that your colleagues with children
will never shoulder this work; many do, because they are conscien-
tious professionals who believe in sharing the burden and creating a
vibrant campus community. And it's not necessarily that we, or any
childless academics, are more inclined than parents to volunteer for

such tasks. However, we have each had more than one exchange with a colleague who has said, sometimes verbatim, "Well, you can attend this, right? You don't have a family." Our standard response now: we *are* a family, albeit a family of two. To suggest otherwise—to imply that it's less important to us to have dinner together, to talk about each other's days, and to have time for sympathy and affection than it is to "real" families—is thoughtless and hurtful. Some academic parents immediately beg off such events by remarking that they have a program at their son's school or a game to watch for their daughter's soccer team, and no one questions the excuse. What can a childless academic say that carries the same weight?

Along similar lines, you might find yourself puzzled, as we often are, by a strange inflexibility on the part of colleagues who are parents. At Texas Tech, Sean served five years as the director of graduate studies, and he once heard an elected member of the graduate studies committee insist that she could not attend any meeting that ended after 2:30 p.m. because she had to pick up her children from school. On the surface, this seems reasonable: her children were young, and the limitation still left two-thirds of a business day when the committee might meet. However, the committee was large, and by the time each member's teaching schedule and standing department, college, and university obligations were taken into account, it became clear that meetings would have to begin after 2 p.m. or the committee could never meet at all. Iris has had similar experiences, sometimes involving early meetings (the children must be taken to school) and sometimes late ones (they must also be picked up). In such cases, we have been surprised by the positive unwillingness of some colleagues with children to pay for an hour of babysitting, put the child on the bus, or make arrangements with the parent of a schoolmate who might help to chauffeur. What amazes us most, perhaps, is that we have seen otherwise thoughtful colleagues who write eloquently of gender or class stand in front of underpaid support staff—many of whom, in our experience, are women with children—and exclaim loudly that they *cannot* be on campus at this or that time, because they have kids. Meanwhile the staffers, who make less than half of a faculty member's salary, somehow manage to arrange it although they must be at their desks eight hours each day. One person we spoke with noted that a colleague with children who was especially loud about his unavailability for large swaths of the work day was also—to no one's surprise—the first to gripe if an administrative assistant was away from her desk when he needed something, even if, as sometimes happened, she was off picking up a sick child from school.

What we have found particularly worrisome, however, is that some chairs and deans seem to condone the behavior, or at least to ignore it, although doing so can create inequities in the workplace and undercut professional expectations. Perhaps this is because our department chairs have tended to be parents themselves. Together, we combine for nearly 30 years in the academy and have had six chairs, only one of whom was childless. Considering the remarkable petulance of many faculty, having a chair who is used to dealing with children may make sense. However, it has seemed to us that some of our chairs—perhaps subconsciously, perhaps even reasonably— have often shown a sympathy for parental responsibilities that they have not extended to other kinds of obligations, even when those are professional rather than personal. Iris was once asked to cancel a time-sensitive research meeting with her graduate students so that she could attend a hastily scheduled faculty meeting; this was not a "legitimate conflict," but she rescheduled the meeting late in the evening when neither she nor her laboratory group had the energy to work. She later learned that a male colleague who skipped the faculty meeting got a free pass because he had a "sick child." Sean had a similar experience when collaborators on a grant sent him their parts later than expected, leaving him to work frantically on the final day to pull it all together. In the process, he missed a faculty meeting at which a committee was presenting its report—a committee he served on, and a report he helped to write. Although he told the committee's chair and his department chair early in the day about his dilemma and let them know he couldn't attend, he was scolded by both. He discovered later that another colleague who had a "family obligation" had not been scolded at all. Many childless academics, we learned, have stories of this kind.

To be clear, the issue is not whether parents ought to care for their children. Of course, they should. However, it is strange that begging off a meeting to meet a research deadline seems to be regarded—by some at least—as a failure of time management, whereas begging off to meet a personal obligation is okay. To the childless, this looks and smells like a double standard. To parents, our apparently unforgiving attitude probably looks selfish: after all, it's easy for us to downplay familial obligations, precisely because we don't have children. We are prepared to admit that we *are* selfish, and that in great measure it is our selfishness, by which I mean our unwillingness to take full responsibility for lives other than our own, that has kept us from having kids. However, that concession ought to be met with an equal one on the other side, for parents are often selfish, too, particularly when their efforts to juggle work and family have negative effects on the rest of us who inhabit their professional world. As part of his standard first-day-of-class lecture, Sean now tells students, "It's perfectly okay, and sometimes admirable, to take care of personal obligations—to attend this wedding, go home for that birthday, or spend extra hours waiting tables because your service team is short-staffed. Doing these things might make you an excellent friend, a beloved grandchild, or a fantastic employee. But they will not make you an excellent student in my class, and that's what I'm here to judge." Being an excellent parent does not make you an excellent member of your academic department.

We suspect that department chairs often act inconsistently because their position is more difficult than that of the classroom teacher. Charged with governing and evaluating faculty who have complex personal obligations, they err on the eminently human side. Childless faculty need to understand this, because it's unlikely to change. However, chairs need to understand that they walk a dangerous line when they don't expect faculty with children to make reasonable arrangements for childcare, or when they don't hold all faculty to the same professional standards. Parents ought not to be patted on the back too strongly for getting their book out "even though they have kids"; the childless ought not to be told, however good-naturedly, "I wish I had your free time. I'd have published three books by now!" Neither sentiment helps to make a happier workplace. At bottom, I suppose that our philosophy is this: if we have chosen childlessness so that we need not structure our lives around *our* children, we certainly don't expect to structure them around our colleagues' children; we don't expect to spend more time at evening events, don't expect to have meetings only between 9 a.m. and 3 p.m., and don't expect to encounter higher expectations for our research. When we're asked to take on more than our fair share of such activities, we get frustrated, and a little resentful. Like parents, we have other and better things to do. They just don't happen to involve raising kids.

Naturally, administrators ought to try hard to accommodate faculty and staff with children. As graduate director, Sean always helped faculty with children to get manageable teaching schedules, whether that meant an evening class (after a spouse had come home from work), a midday class (to accommodate chauffeuring), or teaching online (for a colleague with an infant). His administrative assistant, too, worked a flexible schedule. Yes, she needed to work 40 hours, but he hardly cared when she did it. It's when faculty are subjected to differential expectations that problems arise. From what we can tell, the problem seems even more acute for those who are childless and partnerless: what could you possibly be doing with your time? Never mind that you may have an aging parent to care for, that you volunteer to shelter homeless animals, or that you spend much of your time trying to find a partner—no mean feat in a college town, if one is averse to dating in the workplace—so that you can settle down and have children of your own. When we were graduate students, we saw young faculty struggle mightily to find personal happiness in a college town if they weren't already partnered up when they arrived, and we have seen that also at Texas Tech and Iowa State, neither of which is surrounded by a sizeable professional community. If you are both childless and partnerless, you may find that your department's expectations of you differ subtly even from its expectations of young childless faculty with partners, particularly if the latter are objects of sympathy for having run the gauntlet of graduate school and *finally* arrived at a place where they can start having children.

One bit of good news for childless faculty is that many academic parents—and, not coincidentally, many of the ones we like best—feel pretty much as we do. As a current colleague told Sean, "I get steamed when some parents say they can't meet after 3, or that they can't go to something, because they have kids. It drove me nuts before I had kids. So now I try to behave better. We have kids, we both work. We get babysitters and arrange for daycare. If you're getting a paycheck, parenting is what you do outside of work, not instead of it." Former colleagues of ours at Texas Tech, married and tenured in the same department, made many concessions while their son was young. They brought him to their offices and, occasionally, to faculty meetings; they taught on opposite days so that one would always be "off" to be at home with the child. If plans went haywire and they needed to bring their son to campus when one was teaching and the other had been summoned to a meeting, they paid a graduate or undergraduate student to sit with him for the hour. Meanwhile, both have published books, earned tenure and promotion, and gone on to administrative positions. We have never heard anyone complain that this couple's obligations as parents conflicted with their obligations to their jobs. They're such consummate professionals, in fact, that we envy everything about them—everything, that is, except having a child.

At the many professional development workshops, ADVANCE and otherwise, that Iris has attended, where she has met female faculty from universities all over the country, she has often been struck by the gap between two very different narratives: one that says schools are adopting humane policies designed to allow women to "have it all," a family and a career; and another that shows that only a small proportion of women of color move on from earning a PhD in engineering or one of the hard sciences to attaining promotion to full professor. When Iris started at Texas Tech, she was the only female faculty member in her department. Sure, her colleagues could "have it all": they were men, all but one of them with a stay-at-home wife. But, then there were successful women in other engineering departments who were publishing aggressively, getting grants, and earning their promotions. These women, Iris reasoned, were potential mentors and models, although she didn't want to have children. Yet, as Iris sought them out and got to know them, she found that every one of them had either a stay-at-home husband or kids who were already grown and for whom she had, or her husband had, at some point put a career on hold. The situation may be less dire for parents in the humanities. However, it's hard to imagine that, even there, *something* doesn't have to give in the professional lives of parents, at least for a time.

For good reasons, Iris has, thus, come to resent the narrative that says women (or men) can, with little trouble and aided by enlightened university policies, have their family and their career. She resents it partly because—as every reader of *The Chronicle of Higher Education* or even *Time* magazine knows—this can be a destructive narrative for women who end up feeling like failures when they try to juggle too much. But she also believes, as does Sean, that the power of this narrative, or at least the desire that it be true, helps to drive some of the problems we have been outlining. Any enlightened workplace should want its employees to be happy and fulfilled, and we're all familiar with the truism that happy employees make productive employees. Yet, what if "happy" in this context means spending more time reading bedtime stories than reading student essays, more time sitting at dance recitals than sitting at committee meetings, or more time producing bake-sale goods than producing peer-reviewed scholarly work? If workplace policies send the implicit message that personal obligations trump professional expectations that one teach well and produce scholarship actively, whose interests are being served? Not those of the students in our classes—who are, after all, also somebody's children. Nor those, we would argue, of the faculty *en masse*, because perceived deficiencies in research and teaching can become excuses for a university administration to take a financial cudgel to a department or look upon its borderline tenure cases cynically.

Finally, as we learned only recently by changing jobs, it turns out that being childless can have unexpected personal implications, and these too have the potential to create minor discontent. When we arrived at Texas Tech fresh from our doctoral programs in 2001, we were lucky to be part of a campus-wide hiring surge; consequently, we were surrounded by other young faculty from many departments. Making friends was easy, and few of them had kids. That changed as we pushed into our mid-30s and many of these friends started families. All 30-somethings go through this, of course, but friendships that are formed over several years aren't necessarily much changed even by having children. Moving halfway across the country at age 40 was different. Arriving at Iowa State as tenured associate professors, we found we were in no-man's land: too old (and tenured) to befriend anxious junior faculty, too young to attract the notice of senior colleagues headed for retirement, and too childless to find a social circle our own age. The other 40-somethings have lives centered on their kids. Their sons and daughters don't go to school with ours, don't play baseball or ice skate with ours, and don't have the same homeroom teachers or go to the same dances. Our new colleagues haven't been unpleasant or neglectful; far from it, they're fantastic, and we don't regret the move. However, their lives are different from ours, and we don't have years of friendship already banked to make up the difference.

This essay probably won't win us more friends. On the contrary, it will likely irritate those who see themselves in our anecdotes, and it could annoy our chairs and deans who have acted so often in good faith but, sometimes, with greater sensitivity to personal obligations they can sympathize with than with the professional ones they ought to require. In this context, the best advice we can give is simply to be a good colleague, whether or not you have kids. And to the childless, particularly, we would say: shoulder your share, volunteer for the occasional inconvenient event, but don't be a martyr, and don't demand less of any of your colleagues just because they have children. If push comes to shove and our experiences sound like yours, show a copy of this essay to your chair or dean. Ours will probably be annoyed with us anyway, and it's only a small extra burden for us to have yours annoyed at us, too. As it happens, we've gotten pretty used to small extra burdens.

CHAPTER 15

AGING: "WHY SHOULD NOT OLD MEN BE MAD?"

Eric Lorentzen

Some think it a matter of course that chance
Should starve good men and bad advance,
That if their neighbors figured plain,
As though upon a lighted screen,
No single story would they find
Of an unbroken happy mind,
A finish worthy of the start.

—W. B. Yeats, "Why Should Not Old Men Be Mad?"[1]

Come, my friends,
'Tis not too late to seek a newer world.
Push off, and sitting well in order smite
The sounding furrows; for my purpose holds
To sail beyond the sunset, and the baths
Of all the western stars, until I die.
It may be that the gulfs will wash us down;
It may be we shall touch the Happy Isles,
And see the great Achilles, whom we knew.
Though much is taken, much abides; and though
We are not now that strength which in old days
Moved earth and heaven, that which we are, we are –
One equal temper of heroic hearts,
Made weak by time and fate, but strong in will
To strive, to seek, to find, and not to yield.

—Alfred, Lord Tennyson, "Ulysses"

The two epigraphs above represent significantly disparate musings on the benefits or pitfalls of the experience of aging. From as early in my postsecondary education as I can remember, I have tended to gravitate toward the former, less sympathetic mindset about getting old. While I was still a teenaged undergraduate, I was keenly aware that I would invariably feel the effects of time in a painful way, and I routinely entertained fears that I would, someday, cease to be. I wasn't sure about why I had these anxieties, or whether others shared similar fears, but I was aware of the shaping influence they had on my life. I suffered my first full-blown "midlife" crisis at 25, and spent a considerable amount of time negotiating the ways in which art, literature, music, film, and other humanistic endeavors engaged ideas of both growing up and growing old.

Happily, there were fields of study at the university that were also, at least in part, preoccupied with such concerns, as well as some of the other things about which young people are frequently passionate: love and human intimacy, beauty and the search for "truth," social justice, democracy, and everything else that I might pursue to help make the world a better place. Indeed, I found a humanities curriculum that was not only willing to assist me in exploring these burning issues, but I made friends with fellow humanities students who had similar interests, passions, and fears. Predictably, I became an English major.

Throughout my undergraduate years, I was introduced to a multitude of great writers, of both poetry and prose, but I have always kept a special place in my heart for those who echoed my fears and anxieties about getting old—Yeats, Thomas Hardy, T. S. Eliot, and others who also lamented that one would (if lucky) wrinkle up, gray over, and slowly lose the things that seemed most vital to a young reader. I remember the shivers I would get in reading Yeats's final lines from "Politics":

> And maybe what they say is true
> Of war and war's alarms,
> But O that I were young again
> And held her in my arms.[2]

I fondly recall how, after nights of drinking and other youthful debaucheries, my friends and I would gather in candlelit dorm rooms to recite "The Love Song of J. Alfred Prufrock," and how I would, when it was my turn to read, often have difficulty in holding back the tears, regardless of my perhaps imperfect understanding of what it would really mean to part my hair behind, or for what reasons eating a peach might prove to be daring. Reading Hardy was comparably gloomy in novel or poetic form (as it still is), either in recognizing that Jude Fawley was only 30 at the end of *Jude the Obscure*, or perusing Hardy's crushing lyrics:

> But Time, to make me grieve,
> Part steals, lets part abide;
> And shakes this fragile frame at eve
> With throbbings of noontide.[3]

Although most of these great writers did not seem to be offering any solutions to the "problem" of aging, it was a relief to know that others wrestled (and suffered) with these larger facets of being human. The humanities offered a discursive community in which it was acceptable to consider these overwhelming questions with dignity and grace.

Although now, years later, I'm an associate professor of British literature who specializes in the nineteenth-century novel at a liberal arts university in Virginia, my concerns have only grown more complex. Notwithstanding my crisis at 25, I find myself properly middle-aged, in my 40s, and working with students who seem to get younger and younger each year.[4] My purpose in the remainder of this essay is to examine the unique conditions which those of us who work in the humanities face in our daily (and yearly) lives, as workers, teachers, and public intellectuals. Life in academe poses both great challenges and great possibilities for coming to terms with the ubiquity of human aging. By scrutinizing my own experiences with aging, both in the academy and in the classroom, I hope to open up a topic that is under-discussed in professional settings.[5] My goal is not to be prescriptive in offering solutions to the "aging problem," but rather to explore some useful strategies for recognizing and contemplating the force that aging has in university life, by detailing some of the ways that I have incorporated these issues into my own academic thinking. This conversation is crucially important, especially because "many of us also feel strongly that the later years of life should be more than merely an evasion of dying."[6]

Negative attitudes about growing older dominate our cultural landscape, and it is difficult to escape the typical age-as-loss paradigm.[7] As aging professors ourselves, it's easy to get caught up in such constructs, especially when our subject matter fosters putatively constant contemplation of heavy topics in the classroom. Our curriculum positions us to think deeply about a number of dark matters

on a daily basis; from illness and tragedy to death and grieving, from
slavery and genocide to suicide and murder, we deal quite a bit in the
kinds of "humanities" that seem profoundly inhumane, the kind that
can keep one up at night. As a result, our intellectual communities
of professors and students tend to share the kind of psychic baggage
that both leads to and results from study in the humanities. Aging is
just one of the areas in which this variety of connection is possible in
academe, but it is an extremely powerful one, fraught with anxiety
and "irrational" fears.

In fact, one of the most significant challenges I face each year is
negotiating how I interact with students who feel just like I felt when
I was an undergraduate (prematurely?) worrying about getting older.
As Leni Marshall has astutely argued, the age-as-loss conception of
aging is not one that exclusively affects middle-aged professors:

> Most students arrive at college with a set of stereotypes about aging
> firmly but unconsciously embedded. Humans internalize age ste-
> reotypes about the same age as they do race and gender stereotypes,
> around four to six years of age, and their prejudices strengthen with
> age. Students associate being old with illness, physical decline, insti-
> tutionalization, negative and rigid attitudes, poor personal hygiene,
> senility, unattractive physical features, mobility impairment, victim-
> ization, loneliness, poverty, anger, and death.[8]

Indeed, given this comprehensive catalog of infirmities commonly
associated with aging, fears about growing older begin to appear
more rational than irrational. In the classroom, I frequently encounter moments during discussion that reveal some of the profound anxieties my students have about aging. Whether we are examining aging
characters in important works of fiction, like Ebenezer Scrooge, Silas
Marner, Edward Casaubon, or even Colonel Brandon (with his flan-
nel waistcoats and rheumatism), or poems that take the topic itself
for its focal point, such as Hopkins's "Spring and Fall" or Tennyson's
"Ulysses," some of my students are clearly disturbed by the prospects
of becoming older, while simultaneously betraying a number of the
prejudices that Marshall mentions above. They often see these char-
acteristics of aging as inevitable biological stages, at the same time
that they can recognize ways in which their active agency can help
them avoid becoming Scrooge-like, lonely, or curmudgeonly. They
"understand the paradox that aging is both within their control and
beyond their control."[9]

One of the poems I teach on a regular basis is William Wordsworth's
profound "Ode: Intimations of Immortality." In his ode, Wordsworth

(or his poetic persona, if you prefer) contemplates the negative changes he has suffered in getting older, and laments particularly the gradual loss of vision that he has experienced from childhood onward. He characterizes these "[f]allings from us, vanishings"[10] in terms of absence; he now lacks the ability not only to see manifestations of the divine in the natural world, but also to appreciate the wonder in the familiar that, for him, represents the freshness of youth. The poem proves to be remarkably complex, working on a number of different levels, but students invariably recognize that a primary theme is the hazards of aging. At the end of the central fourth stanza, he asks the poignant climactic questions "Whither is fled the visionary gleam? / Where is it now, the glory and the dream?"[11] Regardless of a multitude of other thematic concerns we may take up in reading these lines, my student readers always pose the question, and I'm paraphrasing here: "Why doesn't it only suck to get old?" They want to know, as Wordsworth did before them, if there are compensations for all the things you (supposedly) lose when you age. The discussion frequently revolves around the poet's grief over this loss, his obvious despondency about growing old, and whether there are any "pros" to add to the overwhelming list of "cons." Our discussions inevitably get beyond the poem itself, as our class tries to apply this question to their own lives, with most students not being remarkably impressed with Wordsworth's evaluation of abundant compensation: the solace of his memories of a happy youth, his past connection with a divine force, and the assurance of an afterlife that such a connection would appear to guarantee. Instead, they want to know what the speaker is supposed to do with all the years that remain on this side of the grave. While celestial rewards are all well and good, what kind of mundane consolations can we expect in our "declining years?"

These moments in class can be rather poignant and, at times like these, I am thankful for all of the angst that I experienced when I was a student. I don't get rattled when my students begin to ask provocative questions about aging, or when I notice their voices catch with emotion as they posit that they have already, even at their young ages, begun to feel the loss of the wonder in the familiar, or in the natural world. One student remarks that if you are ever around young children when they play outside, with their visceral appetites for joy, you already feel the loss; another declares that her little sister gets more excited about a chocolate chip cookie than she gets about most things in life. When I tell them that I feel essentially the same in my 40s as I did when I was their age, dispelling the myth that when you're older you'll automatically feel differently in terms of a basic identity or subjectivity, an entirely different line of inquiry opens up, as they contemplate the ways in which age is represented in their everyday lives. And this is the point at which the great challenges of dealing with aging in the academy can become great possibilities instead, not just for struggling students, but for struggling instructors as well.

For many years, I found that it was getting increasingly difficult to teach poems like Wordsworth's "Ode," but working in the humanities and the academy forces you to come to terms with issues you might otherwise attempt to ignore. As a result of my recurrent exposure to the literature of aging, my goal became to take on the subject unflinchingly; I was determined that life in the academy, rather than being a psychological burden, would instead become an opportunity to theorize aging in ways that might offer me my own abundant compensation. Moments in the classroom, such as the Wordsworth lessons discussed earlier, became transformative for me as well as my students, as soon as we made the final intellectual move of considering the representation of aging in society.

My own epiphany came when I started to reconsider the part those great authors of my youth played when they supposedly echoed my fears about aging. In fact, I started wondering to what degree those great literary voices had helped to *construct* my fears and anxieties about aging, rather than merely echoing something that was reputedly universal in me. From a practical standpoint, the process meant finding a way to use my academic position to "make a way" toward a better understanding of the role of aging in our lives. I had spent years theorizing, both in class and in print, categories of being like race, gender, class, and sexuality, but somehow I had missed out on age as a similar construct! I had been aware of it in terms of media representation, advertising, and other discourses I had taught in past rhetoric and composition courses, but somehow, I hadn't theorized aging the way I had other subjects.

Of course, and perhaps ironically here, one of the wonderful benefits of getting older in the academy is the increased sense of academic freedom we have to pursue intellectual callings outside the area of specialization for which we were originally hired. Many scholars develop new areas of interest, both professionally and pedagogically, as they age. Therefore, I began to incorporate, slowly, but steadily, discussions of aging into my literature classes, and made it a part of my professional research as well. My new objective was to "examine both the ways in which the humanities have contributed to the construction of stereotypic images of aging in our society and the ways in which the humanities can be employed to deconstruct these images."[12] This unique methodology has helped both me and my students to recon-figure our conceptions of aging, and to recontextualize the ways in which age is narrated in literature, popular culture, media, and our own humanities spheres. One result is that the subject itself has become less intimidating, and our discussions now focus ultimately upon the ways in which our fears about aging have come to be what they are, and how we might reimagine them. For students, the "more clearly they see that context—the inequalities structured into our current ways of aging, for example—the less an irrational fear of aging will grip them."[13] Not only have I noticed that they are less fearful in thinking about their aging processes, but also they have a more nuanced grasp of the issues older persons and the elderly face in general, whether they occur in literary narratives or their daily interactions.

Thus, for me, the first step in coming to terms with the ways aging functions—both within and beyond the academy—was to introduce the topic in a more self-reflexive and critical way in my nineteenth-century British literature courses. My second step was to undertake the research that culminated in my chapter for this volume. I wanted to find out how widespread this preoccupation with aging is among academics, particularly those teaching in the humanities, and the strategic tactics they were engaging to help their students and them-selves. The research, while by no means comprehensive, was substan-tial enough to offer remarkable insights about a topic of concern to many scholars, although it also suggested that most of us have a dif-ficult time talking about aging in our respective institutions, with our flesh-and-blood colleagues.[14] My third step was to secure institutional funding for this new line of inquiry, by authoring a grant proposal to establish a new cultural studies course in my department that would include a more interdisciplinary unit on aging, in order to combine representations from across the humanities and social sciences, and even some material from scientific disciplines like gerontology.[15] My university approved my proposal and expressed significant inter-est in the outcome; the new course is scheduled to run during the fall semester of 2015. A final move might be to construct a specialty course on age studies theory—a subject that would make a splendid first-year seminar offering, or a period course that took aging as a primary focal point ("Aging in British Victorian Literature").[16]

These academic opportunities to engage the phenomenon of aging in critical, meaningful ways have been a real source of personal and professional growth for me. I am not suggesting that they have helped me fully eradicate all negative thoughts and feelings about growing older; when I get up from this desk at the end of my writing session and my joints pop like popcorn, or when I lament my seeming inability to restore my metabolic rate to what it once was, or even when I "sit and wonder of every love that could have been,"[17] I might still experience a sense of melancholy. However, my increased awareness of the social constructedness of aging, all the benefits that I derive from my scholarship on aging, and the real advantages that a career in academe offers as we age have become more than a mere mitigating force. Throughout my research, I have learned that science often presents a rosier picture about the quality of our lives when we age than do our humanities discourses.[18]

From an institutional perspective, in addition to increased academic freedom, age brings other tangible benefits that make an academic life in the humanities increasingly rewarding. In terms of a professional life, we have the flexibility to take on only the projects that really mean something to us, rather than feeling an obligation to work up every angle that promises potential publication. We tend to become more selective as far as conferences go—both in terms of content and location—making professional work more enjoyable and less perfunctory. In terms of service, we find ourselves in a better position to affect a shaping influence on the identity and praxes of our departments, and their places within the larger institution. In terms of teaching, we simply get better with age, becoming more flexible and knowledgeable resources for our students, more connective practitioners of multiple disciplines, and more polished readers and evaluators of student writing. If we are fortunate enough to work at a university that appreciates our teaching a variety of courses, the chance to find, develop, and implement new sources of inspiration is truly unique, with an opportunity for repeated personal and professional re-vision that would not be an option in most professions. Certainly, one of the invaluable benefits of a life in academe, in addition to our work being also what we love, is the better-than-average chance we all have of achieving a "finish worthy of the start."[19]

Notes

1. Yeats, W. B. *Selected Poems and Three Plays*, M. L. Rosenthal, ed., New York: Macmillan Publishing Company, 1986. 182.
2. Ibid., 200.
3. Hardy, T. "I Look Into My Glass." In *The Complete Poems*, J. Gibson, ed., New York: Macmillan Publishing Company, 1986. 81.
4. See Westervelt, L. A. *Beyond Innocence, or the Altersroman in Modern Fiction*, Columbia: University of Missouri Press, 1997. 1.

5. See Marshall, L. "Teaching Ripening: Including Age When Teaching the Body," *Transformations* 19 (2008–2009): 55–80, 55–56; Cruikshank, M. "Beyond Ageism: Teaching Feminist Gerontology," *Radical Teacher* 76 (2006) 39–40; and Daly, B. "Dancing Revolution: A Meditation on Teaching and Aging." In *The Teacher's Body: Embodiment, Authority, and Identity in the Academy*, D. P. Freedman and M. S. Holmes, eds., Albany: SUNY Press, 2003. 123–43, 129.

6. Deats, S. M. and L. T. Lenker. *Aging and Identity: A Humanities Perspective*, Westport, CT: Praeger Publishers, 1999. 20.

7. See Heath, K. "In the Eye of the Beholder: Victorian Age Construction and the Specular Self," *Victorian Literature and Culture* 34 (2006): 27–45, 28; and Kirkwood, T. "The Art and Science of Ageing." In *The Art of Ageing: Textualising the Phases of Life*, B. J. Worsfold, ed., Lleida, Spain: DEDAL-LIT, 2005, vii.

8. Marshall, "Teaching Ripening," 57.

9. Cruikshank, "Beyond Ageism," 40.

10. Wordsworth, W. "Ode: Intimations of Immortality." In *The Norton Anthology of English Literature*, S. Greenblatt and M. H. Abrams, eds., 8th ed. New York: W. W. Norton and Company, 2006. 311.

11. Ibid., 309.

12. See Deats and Lenker, *Aging and Identity*, 1.

13. Cruikshank, "Beyond Ageism," 40. See also Marshall, "Teaching Ripening," 56; and Deats and Lenker, *Aging and Identity*, 8.

14. See Sokoloff, J. *The Margin that Remains: A Study of Aging in Literature*, New York: Peter Lang Publishing, 1987. 1–5.

15. See Combe, K. and K. Schmader. "Shakespeare Teaching Geriatrics: Case Studies in Aged Heterogeneity," *Journal of Aging and Identity* 1 (1996): 99–116.

16. See Cruikshank, "Beyond Ageism." 30; and Marshall, "Teaching Ripening," 69–72.

17. Gibbard, "The Sound of Settling."

18. See Deats and Lenker, *Aging and Identity*, 4; and Combe and Schmader, "Shakespeare Teaching Geriatrics," 99–116.

19. Yeats, *Selected Poems and Three Plays*, 182.

PART III

DIVERSE LIVES

CHAPTER 16

CLASS

Simon Yarrow

Only a wall—but what a wall!

—Thomas Hardy, *Jude the Obscure*[1]

I don't mind there being some medievalists around for ornamental purposes, but there is no reason for the state to pay for them.

—Charles Clarke, from *The Guardian*[2]

The quotations above are basic to the predicament I want to explore in this chapter. In the first, Jude stands before a college wall. It is formidable but not as impregnable as the wall of elite social prejudice Thomas Hardy figuratively intends us to see him facing, which Jude could never surmount in his quest to study Classics at Christminster. The second quote, an ugly incitement to philistinism attributed to the then Labour minister for education, assumes a populist appeal to social prejudice against "esoteric" disciplines such as medieval studies as a cover for public spending cuts. This assumption, that humanities scholarship is an exclusive occupation, an ornament for those who can afford it, reinforces perceptions of class that are implicated in the way humanities is practiced and who gets to practice it in the United Kingdom. Such views have failed to send undergraduate recruitment to the humanities into terminal decline. However, they dangerously linger at a time of transformation in the sector very much along the lines of higher education in the United States. I have worked in both America and Britain, but shall concentrate my comments upon the latter, which I know more intimately. Although I suspect a major pastime and way of avoiding doing anything about social inequality in the United Kingdom is to debate class (perhaps as Americans would race), I do think class discrimination, although distasteful for Americans to discuss, has a greater relevance to professions in the humanities than is customarily admitted—not only in terms of the prevailing political and economic environments in which the humanities now operate, but also in terms of the personal and social problems that it raises. The character of humanities research in the United Kingdom is endangered by competition from sub-prime education providers, private high-end establishments, and popular entertainment media. One way its practitioners might demonstrate its relevance to government and the state is by reinvigorating it intellectually through the recruitment of academics from socially diverse and excluded backgrounds.

My parents did not go to university. My Dad was one of 11 children, none of whom went to university. He left school without any qualifications at the age of 15. At my school, I was one of those children the local authority provided with free school meals. We fit descriptors like "disadvantaged," and "low participation background" (i.e., someone whose family has rarely, if ever, accessed higher education). Now, as a parent on a comfortable salary teaching and researching medieval history, and knowing what a pittance my Dad took home in pay at the height of his earning power, I can hardly begin to imagine how my parents managed to support their three children. Mine is the conventional success story, although if I were asked to narrate it I would draw attention to the scars it leaves, and play down the "self-made" topos others commonly adopt. This is a modest exercise in witnessing to the missing Judes and Judesses left out in the cold despite their talents and potential.

There is inequality of opportunity in England's system of higher education, and it results in a terrible waste of talent, particularly in the humanities. It has always been like this, although there are ebbs and flows in the broad trends. From the Labour government's expansion of higher education in the wake of the Robbins Report of 1963 until the late 1980s and the removal of academic tenure from the profession, the nation saw, according to Richard Hoggart, "an intelligent...and humane expansion of higher education" involving "generous provision for those in need...research in an atmosphere of teaching, teaching in an atmosphere of research, and...the task of turning a disciplined eye on society itself."[3] This post-war modernization was not thoroughgoing social democratization. It colonized the newer universities with Oxbridge faculty and their values, preserving the old school tie networks within this larger framework. An unspoken hierarchy has since endured in the sector. A majority of universities, trading as polytechnics until invited to rebrand as universities in the 1990s, concentrate on STEM (science, technology, engineering, and math) subject research, vocational training, and teaching, with the humanities disciplines being rarely (but sometimes excellently) represented. The "Russell Group" universities, an association of 24 research-intensive institutions, several of which were beneficiaries of the 1960s expansion, regard themselves as the powerhouse of research-led training in the humanities, and they historically catered for those burgeoning postwar middle classes who benefited from the grammar schools introduced by the Education Act of 1944. At its apex sit Oxford and Cambridge, two towering gatehouses to the United Kingdom's ruling institutions. An official government report produced in August 2014 by the Social Mobility and Child Poverty Commission (SMCPC) concluded from its analysis of the social background of those who run the country that "elitism is so embedded in Britain that it could be called social engineering."[4] Whereas Oxbridge graduates comprise less than 1 percent of the population, they number 75 percent of senior judges, 59 percent of cabinet ministers, 57 percent of permanent secretaries, 50 percent of diplomats, 47 percent of newspaper columnists, and 33 percent of BBC executives.[5]

I had a typical comprehensive (state) school education. My school was ethnically, religiously, and socially diverse. There were African Caribbeans, Poles, South Asians, Jews, Sikhs, Muslims, Catholics, suburban middle-class professionals, and working-class girls and boys such as myself. Comprehensives were not academic hothousing facilities, but they did improve provision for some working-class communities. Further, they were inspiring examples of cooperation and cultural and racial mixing in challenging conditions. At my school, there were pregnant 15-year olds, attempted suicides, an honor killing, and behaviors indicative of social deprivation and sexual or mental abuse (one filthily clothed bear of a young man had a habit of poking glue-pens up his asshole and then smearing them on the faces of fellow pupils; he would also shit into wastepaper baskets in the corridor during class changes). During the great controversy over the *fatwa* issued (on St. Valentine's Day 1989) against Salman Rushdie, author of *The Satanic Verses*, I was asked by a Muslim pupil if I might remove a copy placed in his locker by a Sikh class mate. Had I been as politically and religiously savvy as the Sikh, I probably would have put it there myself "for a laugh." Hogwarts it was not. I was one of three people in my year to apply to Oxbridge.

The Sutton Trust, a UK think tank supporting social mobility through education, recently reported "a persistent gap in application and entry rates between advantaged and disadvantaged students."[6] Approximately 45 percent of Oxbridge undergraduates are consistently recruited from the 7 percent of the school population who are privately educated. These schools often share centuries-old connections with an Oxbridge college through a common founding patron, and traditions of undergraduate recruitment that reflect this. Over the period 2007–2009, four of these schools and a sixth-form college sent more students to Oxbridge than nearly 2000 state schools (approximately two thirds of the state sector).[7]

Some Oxbridge admissions tutors take very seriously the task of judging the relative merits of vast numbers of highly talented applicants, and certain colleges are known for their outreach efforts. The government currently requires universities to undertake such work if they are to be allowed to charge full tuition fees. However, the aggregate statistics always show "room for improvement," a recurring phrase that sounds suspiciously like the leitmotif of an underlying culture of elite bias. This year, private school pupils make up 39 percent of Cambridge undergraduates and 43 percent of Oxford undergraduates. State schools have always prepared for university young people from disadvantaged backgrounds who never make it there even when they have the qualifications to go. The Higher Education Funding Council reported a "missing 3000" every year between 1997 and 2003 who had the right qualifications and were from disadvantaged backgrounds but who failed to access any of the United Kingdom's 13 leading universities. In its own report of 2005, the Sutton Trust concluded that the factors requiring attention included "aspirations, distance from home, inter-personal skills, and aversion to debt."[8]

Aged 17, I stayed overnight in a Cambridge college to be interviewed for an undergraduate place. The other applicants spoke with confidence (and without my urban West Yorkshire accent), and seemed very grown up. They had a curiously stiff familiarity I'd not previously encountered. Their expert mutual whittling down of degrees of separation soon established a shared cultural capital. Annabella had a cousin who'd been head boy at Barnaby's school. Josh knew Toby's brother from playing "rugger" at county level. For the first time in my life, I met a section of society I'd never thought really existed outside of Merchant-Ivory films. It was as if they'd all been there before, which of course, in a sense, they all had done—vicariously through uncles, older brothers, and parents, who had "gone up" to Oxbridge before them. They quickly and tacitly understood that I wasn't one of them and, therefore, there was no need to speak with me. I wasn't accepted to Cambridge University. My entrance exam was a mediocre pass and the comment on my performance at interview was uncomplimentary. "He had looked so much better on paper, he disappointed in person," they fed back to my teacher.

The near silence in public debate that repeatedly greets the above statistics proves the problem is more profound than mere conspiracy. It is a culture of denial based upon institutional solipsism, a failure of imagination and social insensitivity—in short, all the qualities one might attain through an expensive boarding school education. Why would the media, the civil service, and the law courts line their acute analytical sights up on themselves rather than collectively bathe in a marinade of their own distinction? The danger of such a culture for the humanities, let alone the nation, is an intellectually sterile and conformist outlook that results from the confusion of elite sociability with academic excellence ("he disappointed in person").

It would be risible to call this culture a closed elite. However, for those few who make the journey, the obstacles are stacked high. The capacity to withstand extended periods of material insecurity by falling back on family resources is often regarded as a given by those who enjoy it. Figures for the recruitment of junior research fellows (JRFs) at Oxbridge, that vital first step out of doctoral diapers, are difficult to collate given the dispersed nature of its administration across colleges. As a doctoral candidate well advanced in my research at Oxford, it was made clear to me that, having not been educated as an undergraduate there, I should not expect opportunities to tutor within college. I spent five postdoctoral years living off loans, grants, and teaching gigs here and there before I got a permanent job. The competition among postgraduates and postdoctorals has only gotten fiercer since then. A steady reduction in research funding and its concentration upon university consortia, largely of elite universities like my own, means even the most talented graduates can't build a career in the humanities unless they have private means to fund it. It is all the more disarming to hear that, when asked to comment on hiring processes in 2010 for JRFs, one Cambridge professor observed, "Obviously there will be the odd bit of patronage, but when candidates are interviewed there will be others on the panel and special pleading can't necessarily fix anything."[9] Financial resilience and cultural capital are clearly mutually reinforcing factors that limit social inclusion in the humanities.

In the last 50 years, the participation rate across the UK higher education sector has risen from 4 percent to over 40 percent. Most of that expansion has taken place in the last 15 years as part of government policy to position the United Kingdom in a "global knowledge economy." Since 2010, the sector has started being transformed by an ideologically motivated marketization of higher education under the guise of prudent public spending cuts by the government. The Robbins idea of the university is being dismantled as universities are forced to improvise responses to the controls, constraints, and opportunities opened up by the new partially marketized environment. A student loan system and increased managerialism driven by a public auditing mania generate plenty of highly nuanced league table data and marketing material for student consumers and their parents to pore over. The need for new marketing and revenue streams in the form of massive open online courses (MOOCs), distance learning, research grants, and collaborations with the private sector, and an increased emphasis on the production of research outputs and impact, all distract from the traditional emphasis placed on research-led teaching in which staff and students are engaged in a genuinely collective and creative effort of intellectual discovery.

Higher education has moved from an elite to a mass system, and is moving from a unified model to a pluralist and consumer model along US lines. Social inclusion is even more under threat in these new conditions. Among the 50,000 fewer applicants in 2012, the first year of the new (capped) hike in tuition fees, there are likely to have been many from low-income families for whom debt signals potential catastrophe rather than enterprising outlay. For those applicants from low participation backgrounds who take the plunge in the future, the for-profit education providers (a well-established feature of the US sector) are circling, with their newly acquired higher education licenses won on the back of business models that put the marketing of a "unique student experience" before education. Families with little experience of higher education are most vulnerable to such sub-prime products. One fear is that the United Kingdom will see the rate of failure to complete degrees increase from 20 percent to the 50 percent rate that exists currently in the United States. At the high end of the sector are those Russell Group universities, confident of the world-class education they offer, and pleading for liberation from the tuition-fee cap. The rumor that Oxford and Cambridge might even go private in order to protect their international standards against those of the US Ivy League recurs with greater frequency in the news. Meanwhile, the New College of Humanities, founded in 2012, is a private liberal arts college in a central London location promising an education to trounce the league table leaders—for double the price.

I have made an academic career in the humanities. How on Earth did I manage it? And how does "class" help to make sense of the experience? Starting out, I had no idea what building a professional career would involve, having had no examples to look to from among my immediate or extended family members. I guess I must have had some talent, although too little to regard my tentative progress as evidence of providence. I have progressed through the support of very generous-spirited people who turned a blind eye to my frailties, heard past the accent, made allowances for the rough edges, and pitched me a lifeline at crucial moments either by writing me references or speaking up for me on bursary or scholarship committees. From these positive experiences, I have learned to see that structural and conflictual notions of class alone won't make sense of my journey.

That journey has been a precarious and often painful experience that I'm still learning to live with. I'm suspicious of those who truck in trite anecdotes about possessive individualism and self-making in order to explain their similar journeys. My journey has been gradual and halting; at times, the ground has given way underneath me, and I've found myself tracing circles back to points of departure I thought I'd left far behind. Class discrimination proceeds more often from ignorance and habit than hatred. It flows through those pervasive capillaries of discourse that diffuse into the emotions, embodied practices, and thoughts that constitute everyday institutional practices. Its mystifying effects render it invisible even to its victims, for as Foucault has taught us, power has its perverse pleasures and rewards.

I have a comfortable life enriched by the people I've worked with and the opportunities a career in the humanities has given me. However, the scars remain in the feelings of engrained deference and deracination, in my "chippiness" and in memories of relative poverty, or "financial embarrassment" as my Mum always called it (a reminder that lack of money might well encourage thrift, but it certainly teaches one deep shame too).

It is easy for the socially disadvantaged to get swept up in the romance of humanities academia, and acculturation represents a pathway to a more empowered self that replaces deferential habits with new ones of entitlement. The temptation to imitate elite social behaviors, and the seductions of the environment, confuse and contort identity. My mental hat doffing, the reverence I offer my "betters" reflexively, lies in tension with the Bridesheadian fantasy of being like one of those dons condescending to college retainers as if they were favorite pets. This tug of loyalties to different identities is a constant site of personal ambush. I feel displaced and left to hold the line between where I came from and where I am now. Old friends and family notice, or imagine, a change in you, a pretentious, self-congratulatory manner, a smugness bordering on bullying, and a refusal to remember one's place or honor one's roots. One person's wide-eyed, enquiring Jude at the wall is another's barbarian at the gate is another's sell-out and class traitor.

When I arrived in my current post about a decade ago, I was one of four state-school-educated members of the History department, which numbered approximately 30 staff. I have a grievance for "the missing" that I sometimes find difficult to get beyond. I bristle easily. I am perceived to be "chippy." Like paranoia and hypochondria, chippiness is one of those afflictions for which being wrong most of the time is no consolation for being absolutely right some of the time. Chippiness is to the socially disadvantaged as hysteria is to the feminist, or as "high-spiritedness" is to colonial subjects (starting with the Irish), a snub *de haut en bas*; it serves as a rhetorical foil for the self-mastery displayed by the white English male. Similarly, although I digress, Americans are "vulgar" for the way they so openly pursue and celebrate victory, for, of course, proper English conduct is to be stoical in defeat *and* victory.

This sense of conflicted, brittle identity—and of being open to the easy dismissal deserving of the chippy—inhibited me for a long time from writing. My feeling of being entitled to a voice was predicated for me on gaining membership and acceptance from those I feared could spot me a mile away. I have found only recently that I am entitled to a voice, and that my best efforts at scholarship, no matter how limited they may be, have validity and contribute to an ongoing discussion and open-ended debate that is vital and enriched by their presence.

CONCLUSION

I seem to have made it through all the obstacles, an inconvenient truth for someone attempting to make the claims I have in this chapter. Is my denial of personal success a form of self-hatred? Perhaps. But the truth is, I am convinced that people more talented than me have failed to make a career in the humanities through no fault of their own, people from whose abilities the humanities disciplines would have benefited.

In the current academic climate, in a Mexican stand-off between social inclusivity, intellectual elitism, and marketization, I would make an old-fashioned plea for intellectual elitism for the masses. Oxbridge and our other elite universities should be wary not of dumbing down but of dumbing up. If Oxbridge were to go private, it would be in danger of resembling a theme park even more than it does now. Socially deprived students are not broken and they are not failures. They have often succeeded against adversity and shown more commitment, faced more challenges, and had to make more difficult decisions than those "to the manor born." They are an insurance policy against the short-termism of the market and the dead hand of entrenched wealth. They have a greater willingness and capacity for creative thought because their views and emotions have not been molded and hardwired from an early age by the institutionalizing effects of the average public school.

In 2012, the government obliged those universities that wished to charge maximum fees to operate outreach policies. It assigned, but later withdrew, money to support such policies. No university I know of is in the business of social engineering. However, it is worth making the point that outreach and widening participation programs give students from lower socioeconomic groups an invaluable sense of inclusion and a raised awareness of what is possible in studying the humanities.[10] However, the use of fee waivers and bursaries to mitigate debt worries is woefully undeveloped when compared with the financial packages based upon finely contextualized application data that are offered by US universities. We must look to these to help overcome the financial as well as the social stigma with which socially disadvantaged groups are burdened. The study of the humanities is a crucial public activity where "the task of turning a disciplined eye on society itself" might best be defended and expanded by a combination of intellectual elitism minus the snobbery, and social inclusivity without the sub-prime commoditizing of education.

NOTES

1. Hardy, T. *Jude the Obscure*, New York and London: Harper, 1905. 98.
2. Woodward, W. and R. Smithers. "Clarke Dismisses Medieval Historians," *Guardian.com*, May 9, 2013, accessed July 30, 2014, http://www.theguardian.com/uk/2003/may/09/highereducation. politics.
3. Hoggart, R. *The Way We Live Now*, London: Pimlico, 1996. 40–47.
4. Social Mobility and Child Poverty Commission. "Elitist Britain?," www.gov.uk, August 28, 2014, accessed July 29, 2014, https://www.

gov.uk/government/uploads/system/uploads/attachment_data/
file/347915/Elitist_Britain_-_Final.pdf. See page 10.

5. Ibid., p.10.

6. http://www.suttontrust.com/news/news/access-gap-at-top-unis-is-still-ten-fold-as-poll-shows-support/

7. Sutton Trust. "Degrees of Success, University Chances by Individual School," July 2011, accessed July 31, 2014, http://www.suttontrust.com/wp-content/uploads/2011/07/sutton-trust-he-destination-report-final.pdf.

8. Sutton Trust. "State School Admissions to our Leading Universities, an Update to the Missing 3000," March, 2005, accessed July 31, 2014, http://www.suttontrust.com/?s=Missing+3000.

9. Grove, J. "Junior Researchers Led a Merry Dance as Up to 300 Circle Each Post," *timeshighereducation.co.uk* April 12, 2012, accessed July 30, 2014 http://www.timeshighereducation.co.uk/419602.article.

10. I am pleased to say that my own institution has a very healthy outreach policy, including residential academic enrichment courses that instill precisely the kind of confidence one needs to negotiate academic culture.

CHAPTER 17

RELIGION: FAITH IN ACADEMICS

Kristen Poole

Religion is such a deeply personal concern, and so I'd sooner ask someone how much money she makes (the great American taboo) than whether or not she believes in God. I almost never discuss my religion in an academic context; I worry that people will think I'm a Jesus freak about to hand them pamphlets, or that the fact I believe in God somehow discredits my scholarship, which focuses on early modern religious culture. And, until very recently, I have refused to bring up my faith in the classroom; it is too intimate and, because I teach at a state university, it feels like a violation of the separation of church and state.

This reticence puts me in a bit of a pickle for writing this essay. When I was asked to contribute something on religion for this volume, I imagined I could present some fact-based account of The State of Religion in Higher Education Today, full of statistics, while keeping my own religious beliefs at a comfortable remove. However, draft after unsuccessful draft made me realize how strange it is to read a commentary on religion when one has no idea of the author's religious subject position.

Therefore, at the risk of being confessional, here comes my confession. Fortunately, there are templates for such things, so I'll just borrow from the Nicene Creed as it appears in the Episcopal Book of Common Prayer.

"I believe in one God, the Father, the Almighty, maker of heaven and earth, of all that is, seen and unseen." One thing that amuses me about the Nicene Creed is that the other bits (about Christ and the

Holy Spirit) have lots of explanations and qualifications, since those concepts lacked consensus at the time the Creed was written in the fourth century. The Creed really is a committee document, trying to establish definitions yet giving people enough wiggle room that they can sign on in good conscience. However, this first sentence, the only one about God in the whole text, is short, sweet, and to the point. I imagine that when they came up with that sentence everyone just said, "Yup, that's pretty much it" and had a hopeful moment of thinking that they could hammer out the rest before lunch. Fundamentally, the sentence expresses the idea that there is something larger than us in this mind-blowingly enormous universe that our little puny human brains can't possibly comprehend. I don't think of this something as a being who controls all—a great puppet-master in the sky—but, unfortunately, our culture seems to have had a semantic contraction of the word "God" so that this has become the dominant under-standing of the term. It's too bad, because this narrowing of signifi-cation eliminates the semantic crisis of "God" that, to me, is part of the point of the incomprehensibility and inexpressibility of the divine. As we need a noun to communicate to each other, I still use "God," although I like how Marcus Borg refers to God as just "the More."[1] Therefore, when I say "God," I am really thinking "The More." (In a way, I also like Barbara Brown Taylor's definition of God as the glue that holds everything together,[2] but "I believe in The Glue" just sounds weird.)

"I believe in one Lord, Jesus Christ, the only Son of God...." Hmmmm, well, yes, sort of. In all honesty, this is the most difficult part of the Creed for me. I very much consider myself a Christian (another term that now has assumed a popular meaning that doesn't really apply to me). I know that I am a Christian and not a Jew, Muslim, Hindu, transcendentalist, or practitioner of yoga. I go to church, pledge money, and—proof that I'm really in—even serve on committees. However, I am, in truth, a pretty bad Trinitarian. Fortunately, I have discovered the contemporary theologian Kathryn Tanner, who thinks of Trinitarianism not in terms of ontology, but as an expression of different modes of relationship.[3] For me, the important point here is that it's one thing to be easily impressed by The More in the vast abstracted cosmos or in the stunning beauty of nature, but another to recognize that The More is also in the annoying colleague, student, or neighbor. (Although it's very easy to see The More in babies.) Thus, for me, Jesus as a person, as a teacher, and as a myth, is about how to work at understanding God in humanity.

"I believe in the Holy Spirit, the giver of life...." This is a no-brainer. Even my atheist friends recognize this one, although they don't call it the Holy Spirit. Augustine defined the Holy Spirit as the love that streams between the Father and the Son. My translation: the love and energy that streams from The More through the people. This is experienced in many ways: you can feel it at a marathon, at the symphony, during office hours, while drinking wine with spouse and/or friends, when reading to your kids, or even when reading alone. I sometimes think I don't *believe* in God, I *experience* God, and the Holy Spirit is the name for the experiencing.

"I believe in one holy catholic and apostolic Church...." Sad to say, when it comes to exercise—either physical or spiritual—I am not very disciplined. In fact, I'm downright lazy. I need the structure of the church, with its calendar, liturgy, and people, to keep me in touch with The More. I need the weekly prompting to get me out of my head and my stressful calendar to put things in perspective. I also need the community to get me outside of academic myopia and, yes, arrogance. Academics can believe that they are the only ones who are thinking, and that intellectual pursuits are unquestionably the highest ones. Church communities, in my experience, are full of humbling surprises: the boring accountant turns out to have been a philosophy major at Princeton and reads Hannah Arendt for fun; the smiling sexton (i.e., the caretaker) who doesn't speak much was a Sherpa porter on Mount Everest. Churches also temper the ego by folding you into their historical palimpsesting: just read the footnotes in the hymnal, with their centuries of adaptations, and you are reminded that yours is but a fleeting moment in the larger scheme of time. Most fundamentally, I suppose, the value of churches for me is that they give human (read: flawed; beautiful) expression and structure to The More. I certainly have moments of doubt—an integral part of the long Christian tradition—but listening to the choir sing some William Byrd or Thomas Tallis reminds me that we're just trying to give voice to the numinous.

Therefore, bracketing my anti-Trinitarian heresy, my spiritual laziness, and my resistance to a term that has been co-opted by the religious Right, I am actually a devout Christian. More specifically, I am a liberal, social-justice Episcopalian who attends a big urban church in Philadelphia, studies theology, and finds it all incredibly powerful, but also, thankfully, a source of humor.

So, that was embarrassing. And I didn't even confess anything terribly personal, like my sins or dark nights of the soul. It is this embarrassment—my own and perhaps yours—that I want to explore in this essay. Had I written about my other subject positions—my class, gender, or race, say—that would have been more normative for academic discourse. However, somewhere along the line the taboos flipped, and discussing one's religion, even if it is just mainstream Protestantism, breaks a code. Just to be clear, I am certainly not advocating that we return anything to taboo status; I simply find it odd that personal religion has become conversationally off limits, at least in the Northeast academic environments where I have spent my career.

I have been observing the professional discursive habits which surround religion for years. By "profession," I mean the corner of it that I inhabit, or rather the corners—Shakespeare studies, Milton studies, and early modern religious studies. I have noticed a sort of split discourse. On the one hand, it seems socially and professionally acceptable to speak openly about one's disbelief, or to make jokes that presume a room of nonbelievers. I became aware of how prevalent this is when I first started (secretly) going back to church in my mid-30s, having previously dropped out of organized religion for all of the traditional reasons in college. I also started noticing the genre of the anti-creed, or the disavowal of an author's faith that is a preface to many books on religious history. I think that this public, sometimes even in-your-face, antipathy toward religion is generationally tagged. There was a generation for whom trashing religion (Christianity in particular), and/or belief in God, was a strong countercultural statement. My graduate students today seem interested in religion, but usually in a more neutral way; they don't associate it with a bourgeois establishment and the cultural norms they are trying to overthrow. My generation (born in the mid-1960s) is somewhere between these positions.

On the other hand, while the public anti-religiosity can give the impression of an ardently secular academic community, there are a surprisingly large number of academics who practice some kind of faith. This isn't generally something that's publicly announced, but I have gathered this through private conversations at conferences. For instance, I was once very surprised to learn that a leading scholar in my field, and a New Yorker no less, is a Baptist. (Because Judaism is both a cultural and a religious identity, it is less of a surprise to learn that someone is Jewish. But there is no telling who might be, say, a Presbyterian or a Buddhist.) I am not sure if other people who listen to the anti-religion jokes (the latest I heard was during the plenary lecture at a large conference this year) are as secretly embarrassed as I am, or if it is just considered good academic taste to keep our faith to ourselves. Whatever the case, it seems to me that, for most academics I know, there is a strong social contract that stipulates separation of one's faith life and one's professional life.

As I'm not evangelical, and because I like to keep my personal business separate from my workplace anyway, that's generally fine by me. In everyday departmental labor, I just try to bring my religion into my work life in quiet ways: before I turn on my computer in my office, I take a few minutes to center myself; when I find myself in a contentious situation, I try really hard (sometimes *really* hard) to remember our shared humanity and The More; when I am in a dysfunctional faculty meeting, I chuckle to remember that St. Paul, trying to herd the cats of the disparate groups that would form Christianity, had to address conflict about vegetarianism (Romans 14:1–3). Mostly, I try to remind myself of the monastic connection of labor and devotion as I engage in the tedious tasks that are part of the job (email, book orders, email, committee reports, email, etc). Those are all a necessary part of moving along a mission in which I firmly believe: teaching the humanities.

It is in my interactions with students, then, that I find it most difficult to maintain the separation of my work and my religion. Part of the problem is that it is entirely unclear to me what that division should be, or if there should be a division at all. The academic model in which I was raised (not counting Catholic high school) was one that entailed an informal ban on expressing personal religious beliefs in the classroom. I remember clearly, in my hippie-ish Midwestern liberal arts college, a professor stopping a student who started to give a definition of "grace" that he had learned in confirmation class; the student was gently reprimanded and told that type of information was inappropriate in the classroom setting. In another class, by contrast, I remember a student "sharing" a personal sexual experience as a gloss on a poem by Wordsworth; that comment was not shut down. Those are, perhaps, extreme classroom examples, but throughout college, personal comments about religion seemed out-of-bounds in a way that other personal information was not. In graduate school, this continued to be the case. I only learned that my beloved dissertation director was a practicing Christian years after I had graduated, and then only at second hand. My director and I both work on religion, but our personal subject positions vis à vis questions of personal faith never came up; I was in my secular humanist phase, but still desired the conversation.

This silence might be all right except for the fact that most of what I teach has to do with faith, as religion is in the bones and marrow of early modern literature. When I am teaching Shakespeare's *King Lear*, or Donne's Holy Sonnets, or Milton's *Paradise Lost*—all of which address the speaker's or characters' relationship with God—it seems disingenuous not to talk about, well, God. Of course, I can lecture or steer the conversation in other directions—say, economics or politics—but that leaves a very large elephant sitting in the room. Students, I find, are curious and want to talk about the literature in the context of their own religious backgrounds. For some students, this might mean noting all of the biblical references they recognize; for others, this might mean a curiosity about Christianity, as they had a completely secular upbringing. And for still others, this might mean making some sort of a testimonial.

The testimonial is the type of comment I find most worrisome because, as I've said, it makes me embarrassed—although the students usually seem to find it an interesting classroom moment. They perk up their ears, and sometimes get into a productive debate. I once taught the medieval York crucifixion play as part of a survey course. In that text, there is a comic scene of the crucifixion, as incompetent Roman soldiers can't figure out how to make a large wooden cross, and Jesus has to give them pointers. I was having a tough time teaching the text until a bold student said that she found the play shocking and offensive, and proclaimed what Jesus meant in her life. I was inwardly cringing, but the rest of the hour taught itself, as the students had a very mature and thoughtful—and personal—discussion about how to approach the historical contingency of religious literature.

I have been working, then, on trying to overcome my religious reticence, to craft a model of classroom discussion that allows space for questions about God but which is not overly confessional. This is tricky, because most of what students bring to the table for a conversation about God comes from their own faith traditions. These traditions are diverse (and I include atheism as a tradition), or for some students non-existent; therefore, there is a need for heightened sensitivity. And my own role as a conversational leader has not been clear: do I remain a neutral party, or do I identify my own religious orientation?

Until very recently, I had been trying the former approach; while I let the conversation run its course when students started talking about something they learned from their rabbi or catechism class, I maintained a firewall between the class and my own faith. On the course evaluations for a Milton seminar I led in this manner, there was an impassioned complaint—addressed to the department chair and college dean—that an atheist should not be permitted to teach the course. (It is in the context of teaching religion, more than any other subject, that I have found myself thinking, "Thank God for tenure!") I was not sure if the fact the student presumed I was an atheist was a pedagogical victory or a defeat. It meant that I had done a good job of maintaining the firewall, but what was the point? Especially in a seminar setting, where by the end of the semester most of the students had religiously self-identified, was it a form of pedagogic dishonesty to remain so personally opaque? Some students had hinted that they wanted to know where I stood, and I had refused the hints; to what end? If we were talking about gender, the students would see that I am a woman; if we were talking about race, they would see that I am white. That information would automatically inform the discussion. Therefore, the secrecy about my religious identity kept the conversation weirdly—and, I started to think, unnecessarily and even deceptively—mysterious in an unbalanced way.

The next time I taught the Milton seminar, I ended up with a classroom of classicists and political scientists; therefore, the conversation didn't naturally flow toward religion. However, the group after that was again very interested in Milton's religion, and wanted to talk about their own. (It was also a class that included a Muslim woman from Afghanistan—questions about religion were somehow on the table from the beginning.) This time, I changed tack, and at a point when many students had already self-identified, I confessed— awkwardly, stiltedly, and blushingly—that I am a Christian, sketching out the differences of Protestantism and Catholicism and locating Episcopalianism on the map. It felt hugely transgressive to me, but the students seemed unfazed. In fact, I felt that the seminar built up an unusually high level of mutual respect. For the rest of the semester, I felt liberated that I had shown my hand and could speak to the poem's religiosity from a transparent subject position, although I felt a heightened responsibility to ensure inclusivity. The student evaluation accusing me of atheism had made me acutely aware of how vulnerable faculty and students are when discussing religion. Perhaps, the teacher's role in this conversation isn't to be a personal cipher, but to vigilantly safeguard students' academic freedom.

My biggest challenges have been in office hours. I have, over time, had a steady stream of students wanting to meet with me to talk about their faith. I don't know if this is due to the subject matter of my courses, or that my firewall wasn't as impenetrable as I thought. These one-on-one conversations are tricky, and the rules—even the ethics—seem even less clear. When students start talking to me about their faith, I don't shut them down, and am willing to talk about my own beliefs much more than in the classroom, but I am not sure where the boundaries lie. I have had students who were raised in a Christian tradition come to ask me how I can really believe in the bodily resurrection and ascension. I can tell that they are wrestling with the religion of their childhood as they come into adulthood; is it my place to have this discussion (especially when, no, I don't believe in the bodily resurrection, another of my heresies)? I have had students who were clearly troubled wanting to use a poem by George Herbert as the vehicle for talking about their problems; for such occasions, I keep cards for the student counseling center on hand. I have had conservative Christian students, both an evangelical and a Roman Catholic, gently accuse me of not really being a Christian. I have had awkward conversations with self-defined "Christian" students (when used in a certain way, the term is a moniker for the religious Right) who assume that a common faith means common political opinions; but politically I am hard Left, in part because of my faith. I have had personal conversations with graduate students about the meaning of God. All of these conversations have been spread across many years; some have been long and some have been short or fragmented, some have been direct and some have been veiled. Some of them have emerged out of close reading a poem or helping a student with a paper. It is not as if I sit in my office all day having deep conversations about faith with my students. However, as long as my sensors aren't indicating that someone really needs to be talking to a therapist, I try to overcome the embarrassment that prevents us from talking to students about a hugely important topic in their lives.

The topic of faith was, and is, also a significant one for literary authors. If we are teaching literature, and that literature is questioning, exploring, seeking, or rejecting God, it strikes me that we are limiting our reading and reflection if we can't follow the texts in the directions they lead us. Embarrassment, in one of its definitions, means "to obstruct (a road, river, et cetera)" (OED 1b). Embarrassment about bringing faith into the classroom also obstructs the flow of conversation. To be sure, the primary goal of teaching the humanities is critical thinking. I am not suggesting that opening a space for the religious subject positions of students and teacher is an opportunity for a hand-holding love-in. On the contrary, allowing for diverse subject positions might facilitate critical thinking about religion. Given how powerful religion has become as a political force in our country, that's an important element of civic education as well.

NOTES

1. Borg, M. J. *The Heart of Christianity: Rediscovering a Life of Faith*, New York: HarperSanFrancisco, 2003. 63. Borg takes the term from its frequent usage in William James's *The Varieties of Religious Experience* (1902).
2. Interview with Gross, T. "Fresh Air." National Public Radio, July 15, 2011.
3. Tanner, K. *Christ the Key*, Cambridge: Cambridge University Press, 2010.

CHAPTER 18

RACE/ETHNICITY: RACE AND THE ACADEMY

Cathy J. Schlund-Vials

On June 7, 1998, in the small East Texas town of Jasper, James Byrd Jr. (African American, aged 49) accepted a ride home from three white men: Shawn Berry (aged 24), Lawrence Russell Brewer (aged 31), and John King (aged 23). Byrd was summarily taken to a far-out country road where Berry, Brewer, and King (all acquaintances) proceeded to severely beat him. Still conscious, Byrd was chained by his ankles to the truck's tailgate. Berry—with Brewer and King in the front seat—drove a distance of 1.5 miles (2.4 km), dragging Byrd to his death. Contrary to Berry's after-the-fact assertion that Byrd was deceased prior to being chained, the forensic evidence proved otherwise: Byrd, very much alive, had attempted to keep his head up during much of the horrific ordeal. Berry, Brewer, and King dumped Byrd's remains in front of an African-American church; they then drove to a neighbor's barbecue. Byrd's body—or rather, the 81 pieces that remained of it—was discovered the following morning. Brewer and King were known members of a prominent white supremacist organization; the murder was subsequently tried by the district attorney's office as a hate crime. All three were eventually convicted of Byrd's murder: Brewer and King received the death penalty; Berry (the driver) was sentenced to life imprisonment.

While many may vaguely recall Byrd's murder, I remain haunted by it. I grew up in Texas—Austin, to be more precise. Although most consider Texas part of the American West, it is quite "Southern" vis-à-vis its history, which includes slave-holding, membership in the Confederacy, and Jim Crow segregation. And whereas it is common-place to stress that Austin is a "blue haven" in an otherwise "red state," it remains a non-integrated municipality. Explicitly, Interstate Highway 35 (IH-35) divides the city not only in terms of east and west; the federal thoroughfare also segments the Texas capital along the lines of rich and poor, white and non-white. I attended the most impoverished school in the Austin Independent School District: Albert Sydney Johnston High (named after a prominent Confederate general), located on the east side of IH-35. Notwithstanding a stu-dent body that was 85 percent African American and Latino/a, our yearbook was titled *The Confederate*, our newspaper called *The Shiloh*, and our school colors (red and blue) were drawn from the Confederate flag.

My college alma mater, the University of Texas, was the primary setting for *Sweatt v. Painter* (1950), a by and large forgotten US Supreme Court case that was, quite significantly, the antecedent for *Brown v. Board of Education* (1954). To quickly summarize, the original suit involved Herman Marion Sweatt, an African American who fulfilled all requirements for admission to the University of Texas law school save for his racial identity; he was correspondingly denied admission due to Jim Crow's "separate but equal" segrega-tion. Eventually, Sweatt was admitted after the nation's highest court ruled that his fourteenth amendment rights—inclusive of equal pro-tection under the law and due process—had been violated. Traces of this history are evident in the university's architecture: as an under-graduate in the early to mid-1990s, I took classes in Painter Hall; in the university's older buildings, one could peel back the signs for "janitor" closets and see—stenciled quite clearly—signs for "colored" bathrooms. Returning briefly to the Byrd case, Texas's status as a Jim Crow state was dramatically confirmed by way of the segregated cemetery wherein the victim was interred.

That summer of 1998, I was working two full-time jobs and had, just three months earlier, been accepted into an MA/PhD program at the University of Massachusetts (Amherst), where I intended to pursue a focus in Victorian literature. Sadly, I don't remember the exact moment I heard the news about Byrd's murder. Instead, I immediately recall how hot it was that summer: fires raged just south of the US border in Mexico; the smoke extended far beyond the Rio Grande and settled oppressively over Austin, creating a distinctly dark haze. The average temperature was 105 degrees Farhenheit, although because of the smoke, the heat index hovered around 120 degrees. Many of my friends and most of my co-workers, upon receiving the news, expressed an understandable incredulousness. It was, after all, the turn of the twenty-first century; Bill Clinton was, as Toni Morrison (in)famously declared, the nation's "first black president." Two months prior to Byrd's murder, President Clinton—in his April 1998 tour of Africa—apologized twice for the slave trade (via speeches given in Uganda and Rwanda). The Clinton administration had also sponsored a high-profile commission, headed by John Hope Franklin, on race relations. In the aftermath of the civil rights movement, anti-discrimination legislation, and affirmative action, the nation seemed more liberal. How could this happen?

It is this question that resonated with me then (as I prepared for graduate school) and continues to preoccupy me now (as a tenured professor in Asian-American studies and comparative ethnic studies). While I initially went to graduate school intent on studying British literature, Byrd's death (along with my vexed reaction to it) prompted me to quickly switch to ethnic American literature and ethnic studies. Upon hearing the news, I, as a mixed-race Asian-American woman, consciously kept silent. On the one hand, Byrd's murder—an incontrovertible lynching—was disconcertingly linked to a systemic denigration of blackness fixed to the violent and all-too-recurrent degradation of African-American life. To draw an analogy between my own experience as a member of a so-termed "model minority" would troublingly elide very real differences and asymmetries between groups of color in the United States. On the other hand, my silence was fixed to a two-sided coping strategy: I did not want to make those around me feel uncomfortable, nor did I necessarily want to rehearse for public consumption my own experiences with racism. Indeed, by 1998, I had become accustomed to a certain type of race talk emblematized by flippancy; guided by the assumption that we had, in fact, achieved Martin Luther King's "dream" of being judged by the content of our character and not the color of our skin, the *de facto* response to contemplations of racial discrimination (along with other observations of identity-based prejudice) was the ironic retort of "political correctness." To admit that Byrd's death was an individual tragedy was in line with the status quo; to connect this to a larger imaginary of racial unrest (even in the shadow of the 1992 Los Angeles riots) was to occupy the role of an unwanted "troublemaker."

Even so, whereas many of those around me could not imagine such violence, I was not surprised by it. Although I had never been to Jasper, I had been to nearby Vidor, Texas—a known Ku Klux

Klan hub. I had been taught by my military father (whose family had initially ostracized him because he married a Japanese woman) to avoid small Texas towns and instead travel to major cities on road trips, which were allegedly "more progressive" in their racial thinking. Nonetheless, just 70 miles away from Jasper and five years earlier—in Beaumont, Texas—I was refused service at a restaurant on the grounds the establishment "didn't serve illegals." And just one month before, in May 1998, I was detained by border patrol at the US/Mexico border for a period of roughly one hour: when asked where I was born, I answered truthfully (Thailand) and was then questioned as to whether I "had swum over." These "big picture" indignities occurred alongside more quotidian dismissals, which in elementary school took the form of racist teasing (cue "slanty eye" gestures, comments about eating "stinky food," and allegations of unassailable foreignness). Upon adolescence, these dismissals were transformed into even more intimate critiques of appearance and minoritized non-conformity. While these various incidents in no way compare to James Byrd's murder, they do underscore the degree to which the question is not so much an individualized sense of "how could this happen" but rather a more systemic problem of "why it continues to happen."

The question of "why" in connection to racism, along with the refusal to relegate racialization to the annals of American history, circumscribes the experiences of faculty of color in the academy. Concomitantly, faculty of color—particularly those whose work deals specifically with racial formation and who have experienced (since childhood and over the course of their careers) a minoritized existence—are charged with the task of engaging what seems to be a *distant* racist past and situating it within the contours of a racialized present. To wit, we are responsible for reminding our students and colleagues that racism not only exists but that, politically, socially, and culturally, it thrives. We must tirelessly articulate the relevance of race-based exclusion to those who may not have the same histories or connections to racism. Within the dominant multicultural imagination, while incidents such as the James Byrd murder are cast as independent tragedies, the persistence of racism (along with sexism, classism, and homophobia) in contemporary life requires a Janus-faced acknowledgement of past and present. Such persistence, as I repeatedly remind my undergraduate students, is immediately evident in the different reactions afforded the 1995 Oklahoma City bombing and the 9/11 attacks. After all, the revelation that Timothy McVeigh and Terry Nichols were responsible for the deaths of 168 civilians did not lead to increased anti-white violence despite suggestions that one or both were influenced by white supremacist, far-Right organizations; in contrast, the 19 Muslim hijackers involved in the coordinated September 11 attacks promulgated a discernible rise in anti-Muslim, anti-Arab, and anti-South-Asian-American. In a more routine vein, one only has to log onto Facebook or YouTube, wherein racist posts are as common as "likes" and "dislikes," to ascertain that race still matters.

Admittedly and decidedly more hopefully, this task is by no means limited to those of us in identifiable ethnic studies fields (such as African-American studies, Latino/a studies, Native studies, and Asian-American studies); it is labor that is appreciably taken up by the majority of scholars in the humanities who take seriously the role that race (along with ethnicity, class, gender, and sexuality) has played in the making of particular histories and canons. Moreover, in my academic career, I have consistently benefitted from the mentorship of colleagues *outside* my field and racial group; they have constantly pushed me to make relevant and more wide-ranging my work as a scholar. Nonetheless, it is the particular expectations projected onto faculty of color—by undergraduates, graduate students, fellow faculty, and university/college administrators—in an ostensibly "color-blind" multicultural society that renders distinct their experiences in the academy. Put more simply, despite claims that we "no longer see race," faculty of color are (implicitly and explicitly) required (voluntarily and involuntarily) to constantly represent diversity and authenticate racial experience. Our bodies are read by the institution in terms of progress; our membership in a department is used as evidence of tolerance; and our courses—for better or for worse—are narrowly characterized as part and parcel of an often marginalized diversity curriculum.

These racially-driven expectations begin in graduate school and are amplified in an increasingly shrinking job market. There is a tacit (albeit mistaken) sense that students of color somehow have it "easier" on the job market because universities and colleges need them for diversity numbers; to access a sports metaphor, we are cast as "first-round draft picks" simply because we seemingly fulfill a set of largely unsubstantiated administrative metrics. This assumption fails to account for the paucity of available ethnic studies jobs (last year, in my field of Asian-American studies, a total of 16 tenure-track jobs were advertised in History, English, and Sociology, along with 12 non-tenure-track visiting appointments). It also ignores the threats facing "race-based" and "identity-focused" programs. Within an all-too-real administrative imaginary of budget cuts, metric-laden assessments, programmatic justifications, and shrinking faculty lines, ethnic studies (along with women's, gender, and sexuality studies) occupies a decidedly precarious position within the neoliberal university, which accesses free-market considerations to determine hiring priorities (e.g., the widespread dependence on contingent faculty), uses economics as a means of assessing curricular value (via job training and placement), and employs an individualized model of social responsibility that eschews collective culpability (particularly with regard to identity-based oppression). In sum, while academic critics and pundits alike have long decried the very real "crisis in the humanities" via defunding, the argument can easily be made that there is an analogous "crisis in ethnic studies." Consequently, it is not surprising that those on the ethnic studies job market often remark that they know everyone in the field. Anecdotally, when I applied for my current position at the University of Connecticut (in Asian-American literature), I not only knew everyone else who was being interviewed at the Modern Language Association conference, but also my best friend was among those selected.

The notion that scholars of color hold an academic job market advantage likewise disremembers the racial makeup of most university and college departments, which operates in contrast to national demographic trends. To illuminate, as per the 2010 US Census, people of color comprised 36.2 percent of the US population (13.1 percent identified as African American; 5 percent listed Asian; 16.7 percent were of Hispanic/Latino origin; 1.2 percent claimed American Indian status; and .2 percent identified as Native American and Other Pacific Islander Persons).[1] Between 2000 and 2010, more than half the growth of the total US population was attributable to an increase in the Hispanic/Latino population; in that same time frame, Asian immigrants and Asian Americans were deemed the fastest growing "major race" population; and, in California, the District of Columbia, Hawaii, and New Mexico, more than half the state population was "minority," leading to the characterization of these states as "majority–minority" sites. It is currently projected that people of color will constitute 49.9 percent of the US population by 2050.[2] Between 1998 and 2008, student enrollment in colleges and universities increased by 32 percent; approximately 33 percent of incoming students were from under-represented racial and ethnic groups.[3]

Despite such demographic shifts—in the country and within the college or university—faculty of color remain a very real minority in higher education. As a recent Association of Public and Land-Grant

Universities 2010 report makes clear, faculty of color represented (in 2009–2010) roughly 18 percent of all full-time instructional faculty members in degree-granting institutions: of this number, African Americans and Latinos represented 5 percent and 4 percent of the faculty ranks respectively; Asian/Pacific Islander/Americans constituted 8 percent; Native Americans represented the smallest percentage (less than 1 percent).[4] According to the National Center for Education Statistics, in 2011, women constituted 50 percent of the faculty workforce, although it should be noted that part-time faculty represent half of all professors in the United States and that only 17 percent of the faculty force was tenured; moreover, within the full professor ranks, 60 percent identify as white males.[5] Among faculty of color, Asian-American women are more likely to be denied tenure than any other minority group.[6]

Faculty of color are by no means immune to the exploitative nature of the neoliberal university, which consistently performs cost–benefit analyses to the detriment of field and profession; in fact, they must contend with the same pressures facing their junior colleagues (inclusive of scarce publication venues, increased teaching loads, and defunding). Yet, unlike others, we are hypervisible on our respective campuses, leading to differential service expectations. We are repeatedly called to represent the institution at dinners and academic functions; we are, likewise, asked to recruit and mentor students of color although racial similarity is by no means an adequate or proven basis for success. Our faces are featured on university brochures as a sign of progress; we are also the first ones asked—by upper administrators and the press—to respond to racist incidents on campus.

Although it may seem easiest to "just say no" to service, denial carries the potential for disastrous consequences: faculty of color may be characterized as "bad citizens" (at best) or irrelevant (at worst). Such categorizations of course vary due to the specific histories of an institution and departmental politics. For example, it may be that, due to a racist incident or university diversification directive, a department is forced to hire in an ethnic studies area when other subfields were deemed more pressing. Alternatively, an applicant for a non-ethnic studies field may "happen" to be a person of color (a so-termed "two-fer") who is then expected to teach a "diversity" class notwithstanding his or her specific training. While individually distinct, both scenarios, nonetheless, converge by way of increased and often disproportional service to the university. These enhanced service loads can dramatically impact research productivity and teaching effectiveness. Whereas service is certainly part of the job, its weight in the tenure process (as is the case for all junior faculty) is often minimized and at times quite meaningless. Like all faculty, faculty of color must completely comprehend what is required on the tenure track. This involves clarifying from the outset (at the point of hire) the department's expectations for tenure, talking with recently tenured faculty (who have been through the process), and meeting with editors at conferences (so that there are publications in the proverbial "pipeline").

However, faculty of color must also communicate, to a greater degree, their service loads and be ever mindful of their perceived role in a department. Indeed, if what guides our intellectual labor is a sense that "race work" represents an unfinished project, then we must at least be open to the possibility that our colleagues are unaware of such demands. Further, although we may have been hired to fill a so-termed niche field (e.g., Asian-American literature), we have to militate against assumptions of pedagogical narrowness which threaten to marginalize and render irrelevant the work we do. Teaching service courses, for instance, carries the potential to expand the canon and engage a more progressive academic agenda. Recently, I taught the introductory literary studies course in my department; in addition to more canonical work, I included texts by Asian-American authors. Consequently, I acquainted students with my primary research area while building a potential base for a future class (e.g., an advanced seminar in Asian-American/ethnic American literature) in a manner that was compatible with department needs. In so doing, I was able to move what had previously been considered marginal (Asian-American studies) into the mainstream (literary studies).

This pragmatic notion of moving the margin to the mainstream, and rendering relevant what faculty of color do to a larger imaginary, brings this contemplation of "race and the academy" full circle.[7] To concisely summarize, the inclusion of alternative voices and minority viewpoints is not limited to particular affiliations but is, instead, germane to a much larger imaginary. To think about civil rights acts which expand Fourteenth Amendment protections as exclusive to African Americans fails to see how all Americans benefit from them. Comparably, to view ethnic studies and the work of faculty of color as limited to one set of rubrics disallows the very possibility of expanding the vistas and contours of field and department. Despite the often problematic politics which undergird the recruiting, hiring, and retention of faculty of color, it is important to remember that we need not be relegated to the margins because the work we do is very much mainstream; instead, we can continue to foster coalitions, collaborations, and alliances that strengthen rather than diminish our work.

NOTES

1. "State and County Quickfacts, USA (2012)." U.S. Census Bureau, accessed July 1, 2014, http://quickfacts.census.gov/qfd/states/48000.html.
2. "2050 Projection: U.S. Census Bureau, Table 1A, 2000 – 2050." U.S. Census Bureau, accessed July 1, 2014, http://www.census.gov/population/projections/files/usinterimproj/natprojtab01a.pdf.
3. "A New Hope: Recruiting and Retaining the Next Generation of Faculty of Color." Association of Public and Land-Grant Universities, accessed July 1, 2014, http://www.aplu.org/document.doc?id=3055.
4. Ibid.
5. Newman, J. "Racial Gaps in Attainment Widen, as State Support for Higher Ed Falls," *The Chronicle of Higher Education*, May 30, 2014, accessed July 1, 2014, http://chronicle.com/blogs/data/2014/05/30/racial-gaps-in-attainment-widen-as-state-support-for-higher-ed-falls/.
6. Hune, S. "Asian American Pacific Islander Women from PhD to Campus President: Gains and Leaks in the Pipeline." In *Women of Color in Higher Education: Turbulent Past, Promising Future*, J-M. Gaëtane, and B. Lloyd-Jones, eds., Bingley, UK: Emerald Group, 2011. 163–190.
7. Okihiro, G. *Margins and Mainstreams: Asians in American History and Culture*, Seattle, WA: University of Washington Press, 1994. xix.

CHAPTER 19

GENDER: SPINSTER PANIC

Claudia Calhoun

The offices of my home department, American Studies, are located within the building that is the center of graduate school life, the Hall of Graduate Studies. It's a beautiful neo-Gothic building, built in the 1930s but evoking the architecture of its Anglo-Saxon predecessors—Oxford and Cambridge.[1] As you face the building, there are three entryways. The imposing iron gate directly in front requires you to lean into it with your full body weight, until you are rewarded with a view of the manicured courtyard. The door to the right takes you past the Graduate School's administrative offices and into the Common Room, where you try to run into friends between meetings. The entryway to the left is of particular importance to me, as it leads to a hallway of offices belonging to the professors of American Studies. At the end of that hallway is the American Studies seminar room, in which all of the major life stages occur. There, I was welcomed into the program by the director of graduate studies; there, I shook with anxiety throughout my qualifying exams; there, my dissertation proposal passed my full committee.

It's an ordinary hallway, except for its sole bathroom, which is a remnant of times past, and not yet passed. On the door, in gold letters, are the words "faculty" and "men." I'm not sure which was stenciled first, but they both, no doubt, date from a time when the latter was a redundancy. To the left is the modern sign, in dark blue with two white figures, one in a dress, one in pants, indicating that, in these days, men and women are permitted. There are two stalls, but there is a lock on the door, as if it were a single-occupancy room. At least one female professor confessed to locking the door whenever she went in, to prevent any awkward encounters. I often leave the door unlocked as a sign of courage, but I nonetheless move quickly, terrified of encountering one of my male committee members. I don't know what the male professors do.

Sitting outside of the seminar room, while, say, waiting for your dissertation committee to determine whether you've passed your oral examinations, provokes its own questions. You can't help but wonder, or worry, where you fit in the life you're fighting your way through. When you're a woman having those thoughts and staring at that conspicuously marked bathroom door, your mind leaps from the personal to the political—to discover, again, that they are indeed the same.

My generation of academics inherited a professional culture reflected in that doorway—a patriarchal system that has been amended but not yet displaced. Academic culture has changed dramatically since the Hall of Graduate Studies was built, when aspiring female scholars would have been advised that the inherent weaknesses of their minds and bodies made them ill-suited to the rigor of academic life. Generations of women cleared the path for me and women like me, so that we might pursue graduate study without being condescended to. Culture is much improved, but much of the structure of academic labor has retained the markings of an older gender system.

The legacy of patriarchy is most evident in our schedule of academic training. In our system, a five- to ten-year chunk of youth is reserved for apprenticeship (graduate school), which is then followed by a six- or seven-year probationary period (assistant professorship) in which there can be no significant interruptions. For the male faculty member who occupied the HGS hallway before any clarification of bathroom signs was necessary, this was no structural problem. It was assumed that his professional work was supported by the domestic duties attended to by an amenable wife.

In recent years, the transitional period between graduate school and semi-permanent employment has been extended, as it becomes more common for young scholars to spend several years on the job market, taking postdoctoral positions and short-term teaching jobs, bouncing around the country and even around the world while awaiting a tenure-track offer. This is difficult even for the modern man with an amenable wife. For a single woman who wants a family she hasn't yet created, it seems almost hopeless.

I sit on the professional border between graduate school and the tenure track—a razor's edge of uncertainty that exacerbates all of life's anxieties. An anecdote best illustrates my current state of mind: when

I was an undergraduate, my thesis advisor told me about how she had managed her young family while in graduate school, nursing a baby in one arm while typing her dissertation with the other. At the time, as a senior in college, I was astonished and impressed. Now, as a graduate student, finishing my dissertation with both hands, when I remember that conversation, I am bitter with jealousy. My mind screams, "How did you get a partner and a baby, Robin Blaetz? HOW?"

This is the voice of spinster panic.

The specter of spinsterdom, and its attendant panic, rose from the depths of my unconscious without warning, revealing to me the lingering cultural shame associated with being an unmarried woman of a certain age. I was born into a world transformed by feminism, and yet from the grave of memory rises the sad, lonely figure on the cover of the deck of "Old Maid"—one of my favorite card games as a child. You never forget the feeling of holding a single card in your hand, looking around and seeing everyone else's stacked pairs. Left alone, you lose. Cultural memory, past but not yet passed.

I study gender, as well as US cultural history and media studies, but more importantly for this essay, I am an unmarried, cisgender, heterosexual, African-American woman of 31 who wants a husband and children. My colleagues who are different, or who want different things, would write different essays about gender and the academy. However, I believe that all of our essays would agree that we want an academy that is a humane place for everyone. I make my personal struggles visible in order to make this conversation possible.

There are a number of books and articles about managing life on the tenure track and slightly fewer about managing life in graduate school.[2] No part of academic life is a walk in the park. But the period I have entered—what Mason, Wolfinger, and Goulden call "the pressure cooker years"—is made more difficult by the insecurity, not knowing where you'll end up, where you'll go next, how the money will work out.[3] And if you aren't already in a committed relationship, it's hard to imagine how you might meet someone. In these years, the professional and the personal are both inextricably entwined and diametrically opposed.

Until the comparative respite of the tenure track, the academic job market will make my decisions for me. From this position of relative powerlessness, I feel some trepidation about laying open my inner life. It's the fear that all vulnerable populations feel when raising a challenge, lodging a complaint, confessing an insecurity, or making an objection. I worry that the confession of my throbbing ovaries makes me a less serious scholar in your eyes. But I worry more about what will happen if I don't let you in. The late Maya Angelou liked to say, "When we know better, we do better." The doing depends on the knowing. So I'll tell all.

I grew up in the middle-class suburbs of Houston, Texas. My mom is a public school teacher and the sister of three brothers; my dad, a store manager, is one of a blended family of six children. My older brother, younger sister, and I spent Thanksgivings and Christmases surrounded by my dad's family in Houston; during vacations, we visited my mom's family in New Orleans and Atlanta. Surrounded by iterations of my immediate and extended family, I never considered that my life would look any different when I grew up.

I left home at 18 and returned only for brief stretches. I went to college and graduate school far enough north that many of my friends and relatives have felt no need to distinguish between the states in which I've lived, as they're all "up there." The distance from home has exposed me to radical alternatives to my family—warm and loving families of choice—but I, nonetheless, find that I most want what my parents have. I want to recreate in my own way what they gave to me: stability, warmth, and confidence. Even if I can never go home again, I have discovered that I can't leave it behind, either.

Time, however, is not on my side. I entered graduate school in my mid-20s, and I am now in my early 30s. The years matter. If all goes well, I'll receive my doctorate and begin my first temporary job at 31. At 32, I'll start my second job or postdoc. At 33 or 34, I might get a tenure-track job, or at least a long-term position. If I haven't settled down yet, then at that point, I will have to convince someone to marry me and have a baby within one to three years, so that I can do it before I'm 36—at which point I will have reached advanced maternal age—so that I can have a break and another baby before I hit 40, which is when Jean Twenge tells me that my chances start to get really dicey.[4] If I want more children—I'm one of three, so it's a number that makes sense to me—then I really need to have started five years ago. I need to have started grad school when I was 19.

It's a lot of pressure, to lay groundwork for both a personal life and a professional career while bouncing from job to job and place to place. And my worries about being alone forever are also complicated by race. Or at least, I think they are—my black self and female self are indivisible, so I can't control for the influence of either. It's certainly true that black women have felt for a long time that we are the least desirable partners for men of any color. I have a visceral but only partly substantiated fear that being single in a city that is majority white would be harder than being single in a city that has a significant black population.[5] Yet, my personal situation can't be predicted or ameliorated by statistical knowledge. My reality is binary to me, not relative to numbers: these things will happen, or they won't. And this reality is, at the moment, distressing.

For the eight months that I was on the job market this year, I stared down full days and an empty future. As best I could, I leaned on gratitude. I was grateful for the food in my refrigerator and the clothes on my back, for the heat in my apartment and the gas in my car. I selfishly soaked up the positive energy of friends and family. At night, I counted my blessings instead of sheep. And yet, on many days, I vacillated between ineffectual worry and unbanked rage. That is, until I got a job offer—one year's release through a visiting assistant professorship—and then everything made sense.

Some measure of affirmation and security made it easier to remember why I chose this life. There's so much about academia that supports full humanity. A life of the mind, yes; but also a life for the whole person: a living wage, benefits, job security, community, respect, flexibility, and autonomy. The best that an academic life can offer is the best than any life can offer. But these transitional years are wearing on the soul.

I have my problems, but I recognize that there are enough problems to go around. We are all concerned about how to maintain the best parts of academia while the academy goes through its own transitional years. Each of us is, in some way, floating within a tenuously connected network of decentralized university systems that are fighting troubling changes. A casualized labor force has stuck too many competent academics in dead-end positions as underpaid adjuncts. Colleges and universities have increased tuition to pay for the amenities that students seem to expect. Publics have faced even bigger financial challenges as state funding has declined, forcing schools to raise in-state tuition and rely on out-of-state residents, pricing out the students that these universities were founded to educate. Every college and university employee—faculty, graduate students, staff—has felt uncomfortably squeezed by the corporatization of the academy, in which departments compete for limited resources using metrics they don't believe reflect the value of their work. There is enough weariness to go around.

How can our collective disquiet be transformed into something like action? How can we make this period of transition in higher education—which has brought, most hopefully, a new awareness of pressing problems—into an opportunity to address the challenges?

These are not rhetorical questions; there is much I don't know. But, it seems important to move forward with more inclusive language to describe the ideals of professional life. My reflections on "gender" have turned, necessarily, to issues not strictly of gender but of human experience. I propose a shift in language, away from "work–life balance," which presumes a separation that doesn't truly exist, and toward "whole-life acceptance." In a recent gathering of graduate student teachers, a working-class colleague from Colombia spoke openly about coming to the United States and feeling that he had to "lock away" parts of himself in order to fit in. So many of us have kept so many parts locked away, he said—what do we lose, as a community, by keeping them there? My colleague was speaking from his experience as a recent immigrant, but everyone's different experiences are of untold value.

We can only grow by being open to all parts of a scholar's life. As humanists, we can see this if we reflect on the welcome changes within our disciplines over the past few decades, as students and scholars from diverse backgrounds have pushed scholarship in new directions, forcing into the mainstream studies of women, African Americans, Latin@s, and LGBTQ (lesbian, bisexual, gay, transgender, queer) communities, marking out interdisciplinary space and transforming established disciplines. Direct personal experiences and lived identities have expanded the boundaries of scholarship and raised questions about aspects of personhood that had formerly been locked away. In today's scholarship, we can see clearly the crucial contributions which have resulted from these new subjects of inquiry.

By taking into account academics' whole lives, colleges and universities would necessarily implement kinder, better policies and decisions that improve both individuals and campus culture at large. One change would make an immense difference for those of us in the pressure-cooker years: the minimization of one-year positions and a new commitment to longer term contracts for new PhDs. When departments are unable to offer new tenure lines, multi-year visiting assistant professor positions, postdoctoral fellowships, and teaching fellowships would allow for both flexibility and security for the scholar and for the institution. With more secure positions, young scholars can and will contribute more to their students, departments, and campuses. Humanists know better than anyone that it takes time to arrive at the thoughts worth thinking about. Our books' "acknowledgments" go on for pages because we owe a debt to others for the conversations, stretching back years, which make our ideas possible.

Time gives us all the ability to build and strengthen the relationships that make our work vibrant.

The availability of multi-year commitments would be of major benefit to those of us who are trying to compose lives as well as write books. With three-year or five-year contracts, we can get to know people, go on dates, explore a place—perhaps, even find happiness. But if the profession continues as is, without giving young scholars room to live and breathe, the academy creates a permanent, if revolving, underclass of professionals who are lonely, unhappy, and scared. Panicked, even.

Panic freezes the academy in place, when our circumstances compel us to *move*. I propose that we move with whole-life acceptance as a core principle. Starting now, we can rethink individual contributions to the academy, valuing each other not only in terms of what we write and teach, but in terms of who we are. The change that I have proposed responds directly to the need that I can see most clearly from the place in which I stand. Each of us, standing in different places across the academy, can see other needs. From wherever we stand, we will transform the academy if we push it in the directions in which we want it to go.

On some days, I swear I can feel an unfertilized egg making a hopeful journey from my ovaries and through my fallopian tubes before expelling itself in a wave of disappointment.

This is spinster panic.

In my less anxious moments, I know that my current emotional space results from the urgency and uncertainty of this transition in my academic life, and that it is not sustainable. Five or ten years from now, this anxiety will have faded into memory, either because I am no longer a spinster, or because I've built a life in which spinsterhood is not a state of panic. I've already begun to try to embrace ways in which a family of my choosing can differ from the family of my expectations. With my VAP salary, I will begin my Wedding-or-Adoption Fund, whichever of those two needs to happens first. I'm giving myself time to adjust to changing realities.

As I put my own future together, I watch carefully for hopeful signs of change around me. I know that the Hall of Graduate Studies is due to be renovated in the next few years. Future graduate students in American Studies will likely sit on a more comfortable bench outside of a less evocative bathroom door. The door itself will be easy enough to fix—the gold lettering can be sanded off and painted over. However, the problem it represents requires more sustained attention and effort. Each of us in the academy contemplates, at different crucial moments, where we fit in the life we're fighting our way through. But in the best version of the academy, these are assessments of readiness, effort, and desire, rather than of systemic barricades. As we determine our individual futures and the collective future of the humanities, our policies and decisions, as well as our signage, must take into account that it takes great lives to produce great work.

NOTES

1. Although today's visitors are more likely to point out excitedly that the whole thing looks like Harry Potter's Hogwarts School of Witchcraft and Wizardry.
2. In addition to many excellent pieces in *The Chronicle of Higher Education,* recent books include Mason, M. A., N. H. Wolfinger and M. Goulden. *Do Babies Matter?: Gender and Family in the Ivory Tower,* New Brunswick, NJ: Rutgers University Press, 2013; and Cooper, J. E. and D. D. Stevens, eds. *Tenure in the Sacred Grove: Issues and Strategies for Women and Minority Faculty,* Albany: State University of New York Press, 2002. During my time as a graduate student, this collection's predecessor accompanied me on that sometimes-rocky road: Semenza, G. M. C. *Graduate Study for the 21st Century: How to Build an Academic Career in the Humanities,* New York: Palgrave Macmillan, 2005.
3. Mason, Wolfinger, and Goulden, *Do Babies Matter,* 83.
4. "Advanced maternal age" is commonly used, clinically, and colloquially, to refer to women 35 and older who are pregnant or are trying to conceive, as research indicates that risks for the mother and child are higher. See Mayo Clinic Staff. "Pregnancy after 35: Healthy Moms, Healthy Babies," *Mayo Clinic,* accessed July 5, 2014, http://www.mayoclinic.org/healthy-living/getting-pregnant/in-depth/pregnancy/art-20045756. Twenge, J. "How Long Can You Wait to Have a Baby?" *The Atlantic,* August 2013, accessed July 5, http://www.theatlantic.com/magazine/archive/2013/07/how-long-can-you-wait-to-have-a-baby/309374/.
5. Black women may or may not marry for a variety of reasons, but a lot of anecdotal evidence points to a scarcity of suitable partners, especially if looking for a partner of similar race and/or educational background. Stanley, A. "Black and Female: The Marriage Question," *The New York Times,* December 10, 2011, accessed July 10, http://www.nytimes.com/2011/12/11/opinion/sunday/black-and-female-the-marriage-question.html.

CHAPTER 20

DISABILITY: REPRESENTATION, DISCLOSURE, ACCESS, AND INTERDEPENDENCE

Brenda Jo Brueggemann and Stephanie Kerschbaum

CLAIMING AND REPRESENTING

We must begin with representational (dis)claimers. We are deaf. Which is to say, in a way, that we are disabled. But it is also to say, in a contradictory way, that we are not (disabled)—that we occupy a space curiously related to disability. Although it is not necessarily common public knowledge, those who identify as "deaf" or "disabled" often understand that the two identities are not parallel or mutually inclusive of each other.

A good bit of claiming and clarifying is always taking place when you have a disability. Because we still don't see the "difference" of disability represented much for faculty members, it can be all too easy for a single disabled scholar to come to represent, in the minds of her academic colleagues, ALL disabled people. A graduate student that one of us (Brenda) once worked with was a first-generation Chinese American from the Detroit area who moved through the world in a wheelchair and had cerebral palsy; on countless occasions through his graduate career, I was approached by my faculty colleagues and his fellow graduate students about how to "deal with" him in several situations related to his access on campus and in their classrooms. He and I shared really nothing in common in terms of our life experiences, yet somehow, we were collapsed—as members of "the disabled" community—in many of their minds. Even in and of itself, deafness too often gets collapsed into a more familiar frame of reference—often that of someone's very hard-of-hearing grandfather.

Yet nothing could be further from the representational truth. The focus of disability studies as a field has been, in one important way, to demonstrate how disability is "social"—how it exists in relational and situational contexts and in the environment and not just in the medical diagnosis and "treatment" of it. So it is, then, that we have chosen to collaborate on this essay on "disability"—yet doing so from a (deaf) position that often sits in an uneasy, unsure, sometimes contested, and yet sometimes tightly stitched relationship with the identity or condition of "disability." Throughout, we will reference other academic narratives about disability; in this way, we hope to widen and deepen our own representations as authors of this piece. We begin with the start of our academic careers (separated by approximately 15 years) and move into some specific elements of (disabled) academic faculty life: satisfying (working for and with) supervisors; interacting with curious (but shy and sometimes uncomfortable) colleagues; and teaching a college class.

ON THE STARTING BLOCK

Brenda

When I went on the academic job market (in 1991), I did not use interpreters or captioners for my interviews. I would like to say that I didn't really need them (I did). Or that they weren't yet really available (they were, although not at all very common, especially for advanced degree students). It was really only because I knew better (or thought I did). The sheer stigma of asking in such a high-stakes situation (job interview) was just potentially too crushing. Better to bear my own exhaustion and literally blinding tension headaches at the end of the day. Several of my 14 different sets of interviewers in those Modern Language Association hotel suites and bedrooms guessed at the truth anyway. Yet no one asked, of course. And I'd like to imagine this was because they all were already knowledgeable about the Americans with Disabilities Act (ADA) and my rights around disclosure (they weren't). Mostly, it was because the stigma—even if imaginary—was likely too crushing for all of us.

I didn't start keeping records when I began my first faculty position in 1992 at The Ohio State University (where Stephanie was an undergrad during the late 1990s), but approximately ten years ago when Ohio State hired our first campus-wide ADA Coordinator, I started filing every email I received that was related to arguing for my access in the academy: every request for CART (real-time captioning), every request for CART + interpreting (for invited speakers or events I helped host), every query about whether or not a film or event I wanted to attend would have captioning, and every query sent to me from local or far-flung correspondents (sometimes, from outside the country) asking for advice about accommodating (another) deaf / hard-of-hearing faculty member or student. The records I've kept this last decade include just over 2,000 emails that were exchanged just in order to make it possible for me to do my job as a faculty member. I won't count the lines written—or try to imagine the total time spent in those additional emails—because doing so would only increase the time and effort I've already spent addressing my "needs."

Stephanie

As a student—both graduate and undergraduate—I was fortunate to receive strong interpreting and real-time captioning services in the classroom and for my teaching. I'd also been lucky enough to attend several academic conferences that provided interpreting services. This taste of access made me realize pretty quickly that if I was going to be satisfied or fulfilled in an academic job, I needed to work at an institution with a clear commitment to access as well as resources for making that access possible. When I went on the job market in 2005, I was fairly explicit about my disability. I mentioned in my job letter that I had "a personal and scholarly interest in disability studies" and, upon securing interviews, immediately requested sign-language interpreting. I didn't want to risk having trouble understanding someone in the middle of a high-stakes job interview. Plus, I figured that the sooner hiring committees got familiar and comfortable with the sorts of access moves I'd need them to make, the better.

I've worked as an assistant professor at two universities now. At both institutions, I made it explicit that, in addition to requesting interpreting for my classes and department meetings, I would also need to be able to plan for and schedule things on short notice, as many of my colleagues often do. Both institutions made a clear commitment to providing interpreting services and were open to my requests about interpreting needs and scheduling. In practice, however, making these accommodations happen has been a different story. At one institution, I had a direct line to an interpreting agency (who then billed the university), and I arranged all events through the owner of the company. At another, the Office of Disability Services coordinated interpreting, but due to a paucity of interpreters available for last-minute midday meetings, scheduling events almost always involved a slew of back and forth emails, negotiations about particular interpreters' availability and qualifications, and their ability to meet my interpreting needs for a given event. Thus, even with strong commitments from others and institutional resources at the ready, in order to show up and be present at myriad social and professional events, I do a lot of behind-the-scenes access work imperceptible to everyone else around me.

Satisfying Supervisors

Stephanie

Midway through my second year as a tenure-track faculty member, I walked into an in-service meeting and immediately felt anxious: there was no interpreter in the room. It wasn't unusual for an interpreter to be late on occasion—traffic and parking issues are endemic on my campus, and people often get lost trying to find the right room—but this time, I was particularly worried because I'd received no response to my interpreting request. Again, the lack of confirmation in and of itself wasn't all that unusual, but I was worried that this particular interpreting request, because it had been made during a semester break, had not even been processed.

When no interpreter materialized and the lights were turned off for the presenter's power point, I waited 15 minutes and then cut my losses and left, feeling embarrassed and anxious, but mostly angry. I didn't have time for this. I needed to finish my pre-semester prep, and my to-do list was a mile long. Thinking about my actions later, however, I felt anxious: would I be penalized for being unwilling to sit through yet another presentation I couldn't follow? Would it have been better to while away the time on my computer in the back of the room? Acutely aware of my tenure clock, the annual evaluations performed by my chair, and the myriad ways that things like interpreter availability and scheduling, which were largely outside of my control, were going to impact how I was perceived by others, I knew I would have to say something.

Advocating for access has always been part of my unofficial job description—part of the work I have to do in order to be able to do the work I need to do to be successful. However, I've also learned that I need to recruit others to help do this work with me. In this particular case, I contacted my department chair, who was then able to advocate on my behalf with the Disability Services office. Such institutional structures, including supervisors, administrators, colleagues, and staff members, have been vital to my success as a faculty member.

Brenda

As in Stephanie's case, advocacy is the one very large part of my job that doesn't often appear on my CV. In addition to working to ensure my own access and accommodations, I have also spent almost every day of my faculty life engaged in a larger project of advocacy and education around disability more generally. Here is just one (significant) example. I have always dealt with tinnitus—a phantom ringing, buzzing, booming that comes from inside your own ear and is, in fact, fairly common for people with my kind of sensorineural hearing loss. While there is still no clear consensus on what (physiologically) causes tinnitus, what is known is that lack of sleep, stress, and too much ibuprofen are all quite likely to increase it. And I was definitely checking all those boxes off in my third year on the tenure-track.

This had an impact on my teaching. I would be in front of a class and a roar of bell-ringing tinnitus would overtake me mid-sentence. I would either completely forget what I was saying (and become further distressed about that) or my voice would apparently fade to almost nothing. These struggles were abundantly reflected in my student course evaluations at the end of that difficult fall quarter of my third year. I began to think that although I had certainly learned well how to accommodate myself and strategize my way around the classroom as a student, it could be that I really had no business being on the other side of the desk or, additionally, on the academic tenure track. Who had I been fooling, I asked myself.

Four days before the start of winter quarter, in the new year, I went to see my department chair and—in a shaking and tearful conversation—I asked for an official leave of absence for that quarter and to be relieved of (or permitted to bank back) the one course I was assigned while I sorted out whether or not I would resign at the end of the year. He was shocked and refused to let me consider resignation without some further thought about what we could do to better meet my needs and situation. He said "we"—and he meant it. Keep in mind, this was only five years after the ADA went into effect, and none of us really had any idea how to better—let alone, best—make this work for me. But we worked on it. We strategized. Various new elements of my work life were put in place.

Significant among those was that I would try out a new pair of (very expensive) digital hearing aids (with an additional frequency modulation feature on them for optimizing conversations in different kinds of classroom settings). However, these hearing aids were not covered (not a single penny) on my university's health plan. As a new faculty member with a fair amount of student loan debt, I didn't have the cash on hand to buy what amounted to two good used cars to place in my ears. And that's when I got feisty.

I knew that without the hearing aids, I would really need to use a sign language interpreter in all of my classes and at all university meetings and events that I needed to attend. (I didn't really prefer this solution because my own American Sign Language [ASL] skills are only middling—much like my German skills. And too, while having access to an interpreter is a wonderful thing, they do, quite simply, shift authority dynamics.) I also knew that, by letter and law of the ADA, the university would have to give me that interpreter (and once again, I thanked whatever spirit had made me think to put a full audiological assessment in my personnel file the moment I began the job.) I pulled out my calculator and quickly added up the cost of having such an interpreter by my side. I kept the duties basic and the hours minimal. But whoa, the total cost for one year of an interpreter was anything but basic and minimal—comparable, in fact, to the cost of the two hearing aids I needed.

My Human Resources director got the point. Now, I hadn't wanted to use the "cost" and "burden" argument; I would have preferred for an appeal to "social justice" to matter more, but I knew where the bottom line was. What mattered most was getting the change to happen—getting the university to actually cover the cost of the hearing aids on our employee health plan—and then changing the attitudes and thinking of others more fully later. The very next year, the university rolled out a new health plan that included coverage for hearing aids (a basic sum, but still a sum), plus the option to cover further costs related to hearing aids through the use of a Flexible Spending Account. My own university clinic audiologist told me, a number of years ago, that literally thousands of university employees had since been able to make good use of that new coverage. Advocacy matters. And working with one's supervisors and colleagues—as a "we"—also really matters.

Curious Colleagues

Brenda

One of the first things people usually notice about my office is how many objects there are in it—physical objects to hold, examine, play with, question, and converse about. These objects have been deliberately selected and placed. For the most part, they are my Disability Artifact Archives. And they open up a comfortable space for talking about disability, a subject that tends to make academics shuffle their feet and cast their eyes downward. The best of all the conversation-starters there is The Barbie Corner. ASL Barbie (made in 2000) is paired with Share a Smile Becky (made in 1996), Barbie's wheelchair-using friend. The ironies and whimsy abound. Although "disabled," it turns out that Becky is really the only Barbie with jointed limbs that can move in "real" positions. She also has flat feet so, miracle of all miracles, this crippled girl is the only Barbie really able to stand on her own two feet. Her waist bends, her hips rotate whereas her Barbie friends all just stand stiff, on their tiptoes (and here a conversation about a possible autistic diagnosis can be had). Most people will not have seen either ASL Barbie or Share A Smile Becky (they are both vintage collector's items now), which also allows me to make an analogy with the strong presence—yet paradoxical invisibility—of disability in our lives and culture. Becky was recalled shortly after her original distribution in 1996 because, alas, her wheelchair would not fit into any of the Barbie Dream Houses. Go figure.

Nonetheless, ASL Barbie is not without issues, it turns out. Her right hand, for one thing, is frozen rendering the "I Love You" sign. (I have some reservations about how appropriate it is for a young attractive woman to go around signing that at all times and to all persons.) It is also the case that she probably isn't actually deaf herself—a particularly salient point for deaf people about *who* represents their own language or identity and *how* that representation takes place; she is apparently an ASL teacher (and so, more than likely, she is hearing). She originally came with a chalk board and little stickers to put on that board that demonstrated different signs (*house, cat, duck,* etc).

In the Classroom

Stephanie

- The hearing impairment of course inhibits the communication level between students and teacher, but that is a side point.

- The only weakness with this instructor is her speech and hearing impairment, but I did not have a problem in interacting with her because she did have an assistant present who did sign for her.
- Even though she was deaf, she was so amazing at teaching. She really connected with the class and made us laugh.

Every so often, comments about my disability appear in my teaching evaluations. Even when the comment is positive overall, the mention of my disability almost never is, and reminds me of the work I have to do to explicitly acknowledge my disability in my teaching. I've made a number of shifts in my teaching practice with regard to disability. I address it much more openly than I used to, for one thing. On the first day, I introduce my interpreters and mention my deafness, describe ways that I'll need students to interact with me (e.g., raising their hands, moving in a way that visibly indicates that they want to speak, understanding that if I look away at the interpreter, they don't need to stop speaking), and I often need to keep reminding students to make these moves as the semester proceeds.

However, at the end of the semester, when comments such as these appear in my teaching evaluations, I'm left wondering where and how teachers' disabilities enter the classroom and when—if ever—comments about disability can be positive.[1] Indeed, whenever disability shows up in my teaching evaluations, as in the comments earlier, it is either via a backhanded compliment ("Even though she was deaf, she was so amazing at teaching") or as an outright critique ("the only weakness with this instructor is her speech and hearing impairment"). Or it's not mentioned at all, which is more common, and yes, still problematic.

I experience an odd paradox here. I have to talk about my disability: I've learned the hard way that not talking about it results in difficult interactions, awkward situations, and misunderstandings. It's important to me that students feel comfortable interacting with me *and* with my interpreters; so, I work to build experience and knowledge by making explicit some interactional guidelines and inviting questions and conversation. And I try to do this in a way that makes my deafness a fact of life, not a problem to be overcome in the classroom. But then, I'm reminded over and over again that, despite my modeling work, despite the efforts I make to use language that others might productively adopt where disability is concerned, when deafness and disability are topics that others take up, it's in negative terms, as when colleagues say wistfully they wish I could have heard the passion in a poet's voice during a reading or express concern about classroom management techniques because I can't overhear students talking before class, or even when they use phrases like "fall on deaf ears" as an everyday colloquialism.

Brenda

Throughout my 23 years as a university faculty member—a period that aligns almost directly with the passage of the ADA—I have written, many times over and often in collaboration with others, about my deaf (and female) body in front of a classroom. In these essays, rather than aiming to be an inspiration or letting myself and my story be wrangled into the "narrative normalcy" of the disability-overcoming story, I have endeavored to explore how disability can enable insight. I enact "deaf gain" rather than "hearing loss."

To do this, I use myself, and my "hearing loss," as a "deaf gain" move that asks us all—in collaboration—to take shared ownership for discussion and listening in my classroom. For example, I rely heavily on small-group discussion (led usually by prepared prompts I give the students); then, I encourage the small-group discussions to unfold into whole-class discussions, with one of the groups always taking the lead (assuming a co-teaching position beside me). Not only does this technique distribute the ownership of class conversation, but it takes all the discussion-hearing pressure off of me! Likewise, I often ask a couple of students to come to the front of the classroom and record the major points of the discussion (i.e., take notes), which are displayed at the front of the classroom on a projector screen. I ask them to do this in pairs (so they can help each other hear and type) and so, once again, the burden of listening can be shared. (And too, I am relieved of being "The Big Ear"—that organ that traditional classrooms tend to place on teachers as the conduit through which all the classroom voices must come and go.) One thing that happens always—yes, always—in my classrooms is that, through the use of real-time captioning (which I usually project on a second screen or a wall so that I can roam throughout the classroom and see it from any vantage point—as can my students), my students soon notice how much they are learning through the "accommodation" seemingly afforded only to me. We are all then immersed in deaf gain and disability as insight.

CONCLUSION

As the vignettes here illustrate, many of our moves within the academy contribute to richer spheres of life, not only for ourselves, but for those around us. Indeed, life with a disability in higher education is as much about ourselves and our disabilities as it is about the others who are moving along with us and the ways that we can support and cultivate interdependence within different pockets of the humanities. What's more, even as we recognize our ways of moving in the academy, we also know we are still not quite disabled "enough" in that our experiences cannot fully represent the breadth of disability experiences and the many ways that disability manifests throughout the academy: as two white deaf women, we write from a stance of relative freedom to explore the ways that (a certain kind of) disability influences all of our experiences, even as we acknowledge (some of) the limits of our own vantage points for writing about the experience of disability in the academy.

NOTE

1. See, for example, Freedman, D. P. and M. S. Holmes. *The Teacher's Body: Embodiment, Authority, and Identity in the Academy*, Albany: SUNY Press, 2003.

CHAPTER 21

SEXUAL ORIENTATION: LOST AND FOUND—STORYTELLING, MENTORSHIP, AND ETHICAL RESPONSIBILITY

Margaret Sönser Breen

I have this memory from early childhood. I am about four or five and wearing only my underwear. I am running. My arms are spread out, and I am pretending to fly. Darting and whirling around the living room, I shout, "I am Peter Pan; I am Peter Pan!" My mother is standing nearby. It is time for us to go out, and she is holding up a pair of soft, light grey trousers. "Ja, you are Peter. Now, Peter, put on your pants!" Framing this memory for me are the voices of my mother, my aunt, and grandmother; their chorus in an Austrian dialect I heard throughout my youth and well into adulthood: "An Dir is weu a Bua verloren g'anga!" (In High German: "An Dir ist wohl ein Bub verloren gegangen"; in English, roughly: "With you, a boy was certainly lost.")

Several things strike me about this memory. First, there is its annunciative quality. While it would be decades before I realized that many lesbians shared this identification with Peter Pan,[1] I discern and treasure in this moment from nearly 50 years ago the makings of a lesbian life. I am aware as well of the stirrings of intellectual possibility. Given my early passion for stories, it is hardly surprising that I have become a literature professor, someone who recognizes the multifaceted and even contradictory workings of texts, at times both liberating and affirming and punitive and reductive. (J. M. Barrie's 1904 representation of perpetual boyhood is, among other things, steeped in British imperialist ideology.)[2] Finally, I am moved by the empowering role that my mother plays in this memory. The verb here is deliberate. As audience, she *plays* alongside me. She indulges me. She enters into my fantasy and sustains it, and she draws it into the world beyond the living room, beyond Never Land, the everyday *outside* world. She bears witness. When I think of how she might have reacted (with derision, fear, disgust) but didn't, I recognize how her support and encouragement have been vital to the development of my self-understanding, my intellectual commitments, and my ability to mentor others. I am the lost boy: the boy whose enthrallment with stories such as Peter's enabled me to find my lost [lust] self.

In many ways, this reading of a childhood memory helps me clarify my responsibilities to my students and to academia more generally. This essay focuses on three of those responsibilities, particularly as shaped by my mother's legacy: the importance of ensuring the regular availability of LGBT (lesbian, gay, bisexual, and transgender) literature courses; the importance of my role as a mentor; and the importance of laying out a broad vision of feminist and queer ethics.

I have taught courses in LGBT literature and gender and sexuality studies over the past 20 years. During that time, the range of reasons that students have given for why they want to take these courses has expanded, and the courses themselves have become part of the regular curriculum. For the most part, this integration has been a success.

The LGBT literature course that I taught in the spring of 1995 was the first undergraduate queer course offered at the University of Connecticut. I do not remember whether I proposed teaching the course or whether one of my senior colleagues suggested it. I do know that it had the immediate support of a number of the old guard, two of whom had lesbian daughters who were about my age. Over these past two decades, the English Department has consistently shown its support for LGBT studies. Some 15 students enrolled in that first course. One was an English PhD candidate. Most of the students identified as either lesbian, gay, or bisexual; many also defined as feminist. One was Latino; the others were white. What I remember most vividly is their passion, their intellectual hunger. They wanted access not only to texts that focused on their lives or lives like theirs, but also to queer and feminist analytical approaches that would allow them to read themselves and their questions into literature in general. They yearned to see themselves and see themselves intellectually affirmed. Our texts included sexological case histories, coming-out narratives, and *Bildungsromanen*. I assigned essays, as well as a presentation on a topic of their choice. At the end of the term, we held a symposium, to which we invited the general public. Throughout the course, but especially on the night of the symposium, there was a celebratory feeling. We were all aware of how we were breaking new ground for study at the university. For the final exam, I asked students to write about how LGBT literature, as well as queer materials in general, might be integrated into the curriculum. They argued for both the development of queer courses and the inclusion of queer material into course offerings. I am happy to say that, 20 years on, much of what they argued for in terms of the curriculum has taken place.

In the mid-to-late 1990s, the students who enrolled in LGBT courses were aware that they did so at some personal and professional risk. Toni McNaron, in her landmark study *Poisoned Ivy: Lesbian and Gay Academics Confronting Homophobia* (1997), characterizes this period as one of mixed conditions—a combination of new and unexpected possibility as much as continued prohibition. Employing the language of spiritual pilgrimage, she observes of gay and lesbian professors, "We are asked to inhabit a middle ground between exhilaration and watchfulness, between the beginning of ease and the necessity for alertness."[3] McNaron's description applies to the students of 15 to 20 years ago as well. They approached LGBT courses with both enthusiasm and wariness. They wanted the offerings, but they explicitly voiced their concern about the potential fallout. In the mid-1990s, the university offered queer students very few possibilities for community support. Although some students found welcome within the Women's Center, it was not until the late 1990s that the university established an LGBT center. Within the context of university micro-communities or social networks, students may have been out, but they were not necessarily out to either their parents or their academic advisors or professors in their major field of study. Queer mentorship during those early years was a tricky business. In some cases today it still is. In the mid-1990s I was a newly minted PhD with a commitment to, rather than an expertise in, lesbian and gay studies. I was trying to become competent as quickly as possible, and my awareness of students' intellectual and emotional investments in the field added meaning and focus to my work. I could not think of my scholarship apart from my mentoring responsibilities. I realized the importance of being present for my students: listening to them, whether in the classroom or the office; helping them clarify their ideas and questions without attempting to answer them myself; keeping confidences—in effect, bearing witness to their journeys of self-discovery ("Ja, you are Peter").

I have not always mentored well. I recall one student who was part of that initial LGBT literature course: he came out to his parents that semester, and they disowned him. A third of the way through the term, he disappeared. One of my great regrets is that when, at the end of term, he came to me, explained why he had missed the last nine weeks of the semester, and asked if he could make up the work, I said no. Wanting to prove to the department and most especially myself the merits of the course, I responded to him by saying that the course's requirements were as rigorous as those of any other literature offering. He had missed most of the semester, had handed in none of the assignments. His situation was regrettable, but there was nothing to be done; he should withdraw. At least now, the painful irony of my response is not lost on me. My definition of course rigor left me no room to advocate for the student. Arguing in the abstract, I neglected to respond to the situation in front of me: the obstacles thwarting the student's own academic achievement. I did not consider how the young man's absenteeism reflected not his own volition but his parents'. They had put him in an impossible situation, and I proved unable to respond in a way that, at least for our course, could effectively absorb the blow of their emotional and financial withdrawal. Bearing witness is not a passive posture. In Adrienne Rich's terms, it requires an act of re-vision: "the act of looking back, of seeing with fresh eyes, of entering an old text [insert 'a traditional academic structure'] from a new critical direction…an act of survival."[4] My unwillingness to advocate for him reflected my own investment in academic structures inadequate to deal with homophobia—reflected, in effect, my own acquiescence to homophobia. I should have given him an incomplete and, with it, the opportunity to find both the time and money to complete the course. This experience has offered me a bitter lesson in the importance of good mentorship, and my hope is that that lesson learned has informed subsequent relationships with students.

I tried to do better when subsequent challenges arose. There was a student who wanted to take the course the next time I taught it, a few years later. She was working on her teaching certification, and she was concerned, rightly, that the appearance of any LGBT course on her transcript might prove a hiring liability. Thereafter, another student came to me. She was from a family whose religious beliefs could not sanction an intellectually independent, much less a lesbian, woman. Like the student who had been disowned, she, too, risked losing her family. In both of these later cases, I had the students register for an independent study. They attended the LGBT course, participated in the discussions, and completed all of the required work. Their transcripts, however, only listed a generic independent study. Sometimes, it's necessary to go stealth.

These days, thankfully, I encounter fewer situations of institutionally and socially sanctioned homophobia. In sync with the increased acceptance of LGBT people and the expansion of rights and protections for gender and sexual minorities nationally, LGBT course offerings and research have become part of my university's academic mainstream. There are more LGBT faculty and more faculty engaged in research in gender and sexuality studies. There is an LGBT center, which offers a speaker series and sponsors a variety of student groups. In terms of curriculum, LGBT courses have been integrated into major course offerings, and many fulfill university-wide as well as school- and major-specific diversity requirements. Such courses are in high demand. They are offered every year; in some cases, every semester. They regularly fill to capacity.

Over the past 20 years, the composition of LGBT classes has changed, and the range of reasons that students give for enrolling has broadened. There are still queer students in the classroom, but most students identify as heterosexual. There are more students of color. Intellectual and emotional urgency still characterizes many of the students, but the motivation behind students' urgency is more varied, as are the resources available to them. Some students, like so many from 20 years ago, come to learn about their own queer selves. There are also many students now who say that they have signed up because they have friends and/or family members who are gay. And even as there are undoubtedly some students who have only signed up for the course because they are obliged to meet a distribution requirement, others have enrolled because they care about social justice issues. Students now also have access to technological resources that can enrich and extend classroom discussions. In terms of professional training, there have been significant developments as well. For a fair number of undergraduates, LGBT courses are now part of their preparation for careers in counseling and social work, and, in contrast to some 15 years ago, LGBT literature courses are now a desirable component of elementary, middle-, and high-school teacher training. LGBT studies has become part of the university's academic landscape.

For more than a decade, academics have debated the significance of such curricular mainstreaming. We have underscored the powerful possibilities for knowledge production outside and alongside institutional frameworks. In my scholarship and teaching, I draw attention to the limits (including limitations) of traditional structures—whether within literature, the university, or society as a whole—for encountering and understanding queer lives. What does it mean to pursue the discipline (as well as disciplining) of LGBT studies; by privileging one frame or set of frames of knowing, what other ways are overlooked or disregarded, and *what* is rendered unintelligible in the process? *Who* is lost? Judith Butler has written of the interdependence of our lives—even at those moments when we assert our needs (because doing so occurs at the expense of others'); "Let's face it," she says. "We're undone by each other. And if we're not, we're missing something."[5] How do we come to recognize that "something" or *somethings*? For me, awareness comes so often through the empathic engagement with LGBT stories—an engagement that I share with many of my students.

Of course, the selection of texts, whether I am writing about them or teaching them, is itself part of the disciplinary regulation of LGBT studies. Still, I would hope that my choices, together with the exchanges that they engender, invite an undoing of that regulation. In class, we often focus on texts that promote a vision of political solidarity across various political movements (e.g., workers' rights, immigrant rights, women's rights, civil rights, and LGBT rights): texts such as Audre Lorde's *Zami*, Amber Hollibaugh's *My Dangerous Desires*, and Sarah Waters's *Tipping the Velvet*. We read these works as much for the connections that they forge as for the disconnections that they acknowledge. Encounters with stories engage us in a process of loss and discovery and remaking. I think of the student for whom Susan Sontag's *AIDS and Its Metaphors* offered an opportunity to mourn the uncle whom she had lost when she was six: the uncle whose death from the disease and whose life as a gay man her family wanted to keep quiet. I think of how *Stone Butch Blues* has offered my students so many points of contact. One woman stopped to see me after class: she wept as she told me that she recognized in the narrator-protagonist Jess an image of her own stone lover. Another student found in Jess's story a version of her trans partner's experience. Then there are the novel's scenes of sexual violence. Jess's brutal coming of age may take place in the 1950s and 1960s, but students discern in it something of their own reality or the realities of others whom they care about. By the time they leave the privileged space of university, one in four or five women in the United States will have been sexually assaulted.[6] The figures for women of color and for transgender individuals are higher.[7]

At times listening to students and acknowledging the value of their engagement with queer texts entails bearing witness to unbearable sadness. At times, but not always. LGBT stories can also occasion fun. Sometimes, poignancy and foolishness even coincide. My mother has recently reminded me of as much.

These days, I recognize my mother's increasing failing, in mind and body, and I struggle against the standard narratives of othering that threaten to accompany it. In a society defined by the centrality of what Lee Edelman has termed reproductive futurism,[8] little respect is accorded people who do not readily conform to those norms of gender, sex, sexuality, race and ethnicity, ablebodiedness, and age (to name just a few constructs), which commonly serve as measures of our personhood. From this perspective, my mother has become something of a gender and sexual outlaw. In a culture that regularly dismisses as ludicrous the attractiveness and attractions of the elderly, she is, with all her dishiness and desires, in danger of being dismissed. Still, she continues in her happy affronts to acceptable behavior. Slow moving, she enjoys an unhurried pace. Mishearing words and whole sentences does not really phase her; she rather delights in the resulting wordplay. She may be at renewed risk for not being taken seriously (as a woman and a foreigner, she has always faced this risk), but her ingenious capacity for pleasure reframes the issue for me: perhaps, it is that her age (or agedness) is taken too seriously, as if it were a barrier somehow to acknowledging her acceptability, her vitality, and her humanness. Paying attention to my mother, I recognize on a daily basis that growing old is a feminist issue and a queer issue. Judith Halberstam has written that "failure allows us to escape the punishing norms that discipline behavior...Failure preserves some of the wondrous anarchy of childhood and disturbs the clean boundaries between adults and children."[9] My mother teaches me anew of the pleasures of such failure. Neither economically productive nor sexually reproductive, she is far more interested in inhabiting the present and enjoying the silliness of the moment than in curbing her thoughts and problem solving for a future. In her forgetfulness, she reminds me of absurdity's rewards.

It is both heartbreaking and heartwarming to bear witness to my mother's capacity to revel in her own inevitable undoing. This is another lesson for LGBT studies—a lesson with ethical, aesthetic, and political dimensions. My mother reminds me...if they're to find themselves, lost boys need to play...even when they're lesbian professors. The hot octogenarian out-queers me.

NOTES

1. See Wolf, S. E. "'Never Gonna Be a Man/Catch Me If You Can/I Won't Grow Up': A Lesbian Account of Mary Martin as Peter Pan," *Theatre Journal* 49 (1997): 493–509.

2. See Deane, B. "Imperial Boyhood: Piracy and the Play Ethic," *Victorian Studies: An Interdisciplinary Journal of Social, Political, and Cultural Studies* 53 (2011): 689–712; and Rose, J. *The Case of Peter Pan, or The Impossibility of Children's Fiction*, London: Macmillan, 1984.

3. McNaron, T. *Poisoned Ivy: Lesbian and Gay Academics Confronting Homophobia*, Philadelphia: Temple University Press, 1997. 213.

4. Rich, A. "'When We Dead Awaken': Writing as Re-vision," *College English* 34 (1972): 18–30, 18.

5. Butler, J. *Precarious Life: The Powers of Mourning and Violence*, London and New York: Verso, 2004. 23.

6. See Chemaly, S. "50 Actual Facts about Rape," *Huffingtonpost.com*, October 26, 2012, accessed July 5, 2014, http://www.huffingtonpost.com/soraya-chemaly/50-facts-rape_b_2019338.html.

7. Bolles, A. "Violence Against Transgender People and People of Color is Disproportionately High, LGBTQH Murder Rate Peaks," *glaad.org*, June 4, 2012, accessed July 5, 2014, http://www.glaad.org/blog/violence-against-transgender-people-and-people-color-disproportionately-high-lgbtqh-murder-rate.

8. Edelman, L. *No Future: Queer Theory and the Death Drive*, Durham and London: Duke University Press, 2004. 3.

9. Halberstam, J. *The Queer Art of Failure*, Durham and London: Duke University Press, 2011. 3.

PART IV

LIFE OFF THE TENURE TRACK

Chapter 22

Life as an Adjunct: What Should Parents Know (and What Can They Do)?[1]

Joseph Fruscione

I remember a nice spring day in 1999—my second semester of teaching. I was walking past a campus tour group and saw one of my students leading it. The timing couldn't have been more perfect: as I was passing the group, a parent asked if all university faculty were full time. "Yes," my student said. I was taken aback, because I'd told my classes about being adjunct, as well as a bit about what "adjunct" meant and how many of us there were in the English department alone. The next day, I pulled him aside after class and asked him about it. "I'm not mad at you; I'm just curious: your class knows I'm a graduate student, not a full-time professor with tenure. I don't even have my PhD yet. Why did you tell that parent all university faculty were full time?" "That's what the university wants us to say to parents," he replied.

Here's a thought experiment:

Imagine you're asked to address an auditorium full of parents at your university's orientation for new students. Maybe you're a PhD student just getting your feet wet in higher education; maybe you're a long-time adjunct or other contingent university worker who simply has had enough. Either way, you want these parents to know much more about the student learning conditions and faculty working conditions than the school is willing to tell them. You have the knowledge and experience to set them straight; you know most professors don't have the easy, stress-free lives some stereotypes still describe. You know how much work being an academic entails—and how much harder university administrations are making such work. With all this in mind, you're most interested in sharing some of your more galling or frustrating memories of academia, because you want to determine the narrative of higher education. The true one. Perhaps you'll recall:

> That time your department chair forwarded an announcement from the dean (one of them, anyway) announcing budget cuts and hiring freezes...around the same time yet another new provost was hired at a six-figure salary. Many adjuncts—including several in the department where you earned your doctorate—would be out of work at the end of the semester because of the cuts.

> When a smart, engaged student asked you to mentor her senior thesis—which would be a great opportunity for both of you—she was basing on a paper she wrote in your class...only to be told by a "real" full-time professor that adjuncts aren't allowed to mentor such projects because they might leave at any time. (So much for sustained relationships with students.)

> When you're teaching three, four, or more classes in a semester yet overhear a senior faculty member quasi-complain about a sabbatical not being long enough...then fumble to correct himself when he realizes you teach twice as many courses and students for a quarter (or less) of his pay.

> Those times you couldn't meet with students needing help with their writing, because you had to trek to your *other* campus and teach your *other* students so you could make a little extra money to pay down some of that student loan and credit card debt...while wondering how many lost hours there've been in your semester so far commuting.

I'm going to conduct my own thought experiment here by interspersing some argument and background with a few short sections imagining what I'd say to an audience of parents. I recognize that I'm using an approach that might seem peculiar; however, I want this rhetorical tactic to help current, former, and future faculty (at all levels) understand how important it is for parents and students to know the truth about higher education. The 70 percent to 75 percent of university faculty teaching off—*way off* in some cases—the tenure track are neither invisible, nor are they simply course coverage hired in the name of economic austerity. Many adjuncts continue to be vocal on their campuses and online; many more continue to fear doing so. (In light of the Steven Salaita situation at the University of Illinois at Urbana-Champaign in 2014, many tenure-line faculty may have similar fears.) Given the chance, the majority of concerned faculty would surely jump at the opportunity to speak frankly to their students' parents.

There are many moments in my career I'd like to revisit with the knowledge and dedication to activism I have now. Graduate students (in the humanities especially) can expect to teach part time under various sobriquets: lecturer, teaching assistant, visiting assistant professor, postdoctoral fellow, professorial lecturer, and so on. At some level, each of these positions grows increasingly contingent in a profession that is more broken by the day. Part of me thinks it would be worth the effort to hit the road and visit as many colleges as possible during spring tours and back-to-school move-in time. My 15 years of adjuncting—six as a PhD student, nine as a hopeful jobseeker—have given me a lot of rich, sometimes troubling, experiences that I'd love to share with parents and students. Whether we make such trips, or simply write and speak publicly, it's up to us as insiders to tell parents, students, and anyone else who cares about higher education in America what schools won't tell them.

I wish, for example, that a parent was with me that time I was in the elevator with my department chair—who mildly complained about having to teach one class in a semester when I had four first-year writing courses and 74 students across two schools. (To be clear: I'm not questioning how much work and how many demands chairs have. I'm questioning the myopia of this person's comment.) "I guess I shouldn't complain about this to you," she said. I could only reply, "Yes, but it's fine. I manage."

Had some parents been with me, I could've added this: "Maybe you can explain to them why the university thinks it's good to give students—especially freshmen—a string of part-time professors who may also be teaching at other schools to make ends meet. Can you or one of the provosts meet with my students while I'm teaching somewhere else to approach a livable wage? Is this a good way to introduce students to college life?" At the time, I was playing nice because I'd hoped (naively) that I could move up the ranks in the department to a full-time position. Perhaps I should've damned the torpedoes and just spoken my mind. Playing nice rarely helps adjuncts move up at any school.

I always wondered why my fellow adjuncts and I were never rewarded for our 10–15+ years of teaching experience—and instead were made to just hit RESET every year with no promotion or rise in status. Why were we good enough to be renewed for the same thing, yet not good enough to be promoted? Why should schools supposedly save money at the expense of student learning? If part-time professors are always on the hunt for full-time jobs at other schools, how can we focus on the job—or jobs—we currently have? In hindsight, I regret the occasional short-changing I had to do with some students for meetings, grading, and preparing class discussions. At the time, it was the most pragmatic and time-efficient thing to do given my schedule and limited resources. I had no TA and no paid leave; I had me.

Students, parents, professors, alumni, and anyone else connected to a university should be troubled by how much higher education has devolved in the last 30 or so years. Insiders—whether current or former professors, graduate students, or other university employees—need to share their knowledge far and wide. When more and more universities spend time and resources hiring senior administrators (and keep raising tuition in the process), they devalue teaching and teachers. Often, more highly paid senior administrators mean fewer full-time faculty hires; with fewer full-time faculty, of course, come more part-timers. (If you give a school a provost, it's going to want a few assistant vice provosts to go along with him or her.) These deliberate budgetary choices consequently create strained learning conditions for the most important demographic of any school: students. Such massive financial disparities as well as the casualization of educational labor does a lot of things, but helping students be the writers, thinkers, and researchers we need them to be in the twenty-first century isn't one of them. *We* know it, so let's make sure parents and students know it, too.

I kept trying to understand why a school would knowingly create a contingent, largely part-time labor force to teach the majority of its students—especially freshmen. Why not give experienced, accomplished faculty more stability and promotion potential to make them better, more accessible teachers? Then, I realized that education is an increasingly lower priority at many colleges and universities, and (in the words of a fellow activist) that professors are increasingly seen as lines on a ledger, not educated professionals.

I'm far from the only person eager to talk with parents. I asked my professional network what they'd most like to say to parents. I got some smart, wonderful responses from some folks who would make great guest speakers:

> *Natalie Dorfeld*: I'd ask them how they would feel if they knew some of their children's professors were on food stamps.
>
> *Brianne Bolin*: I'd tell them that at my school, 78% of classes are taught by adjuncts who get 8% of the extortionist tuition that

they're shelling over. I'd also ask them if they were more concerned with an education or a piece of paper.

Desirée Sunshine: Don't go into debt. If you can't pay as you go, it's not worth it.

Miranda Merklein: Do not send your kids to schools with a pattern of low-wage contract labor, budget cuts to faculty (reduction in costs to instruction), and tuition increases. That pattern demonstrates a lack of concern for education.

Seth Kahn: Make the effort to understand contingency. Know the differences among different kinds of academic jobs. Senior administrators (president, provosts, chancellors, and deans) and faculty are very different; there are ranks of faculty even within tenure track, and those titles mean some concrete things.

Melissa Bruninga-Matteau: Absolutely know the ratio of tenure-track faculty to adjuncts, and ask what percentage of classes are taught by non–tenure track faculty, including if there are any grad students teaching classes.

Gordon Haber: Parents must insist their kids graduate without debt, even if that means a less fancy degree. Parents should lock their kids in the basement rather than let them attend for-profit colleges.

Amy Lynch-Biniek: Ask about labor conditions; insist that working conditions equal learning conditions.

Jeana Jorgensen: Parents should know how many classes are taught by adjuncts and other impermanent staff—as well as how this affects student learning.

Emily Schmidt: Ask about how many adjuncts teach at their kids' colleges/universities, adjunct compensation, and adjunct access to library and office space.

Professor Never (a self-described "ex-academic alive in the real world") had even more to say:

As a parent of a rising high school senior, I have found touring colleges with my son a sort of revolting experience. I wasn't the rebel I'd planned to be on the tours as I found the all-smiles-come-to-our-college/resort atmosphere sickening and oddly oppressive. While I was disappointed in myself for not doing a better job of educating the other parents on the tours with me, I take every opportunity I can to educate all the other parents I know who have kids of similar age about how universities are spending their money. Parents need to know they are getting state-of-the-art stair machines instead of well-compensated professors. They need to know they're getting luxury dorms instead of professors who have office space and health care. They need to know most universities care more for attracting students than they do about educating them.

Touring colleges should be a lot of things, but "a revolting experience" should never be one of them. (Ever.) These pieces of advice are the proverbial tip of the iceberg. Remember, this comes only from people in one writer-activist's social network. Surely, the tens of thousands of non–tenure track faculty across the country would have more to say. The more we can get parents to encourage their children and others to follow their lead in asking tough questions, the more American higher education can change.

I was once at a dinner at the home of one of the provosts. I forget what this one's long-winded title was; I learned later that he makes over $700K per year. (Remember that the next time tuition is raised or extra fees are added.) He was sharing the new strategic plan and anticipated a growth of full-time positions. I remember tempering my expectations about this hiring plan given the school's track record, aggressive anti-union efforts, and practice of hiring more non-teaching administrators. Sure enough, a little over a year later, several part-time lines were eliminated in the name of "spending cuts" and "enrollment declines." How, I wonder now, has the strategic plan been revised? Where did those tuition dollars go?

We are all a part of higher education's culture of contingency, regardless of whether we're students, parents, staff members, TAs, or professors—or activists trying to shine a light on higher ed. The volatile and strained working conditions for the majority of university faculty mean that adjunct and other non-tenure-track faculty must often choose between their desire to teach and their desire to deal with the financial realities of what is, essentially, full-time part-timing. In such cases, students suffer when professors have to curtail office hours, grade and comment on their writing when they have 70–80 (or more) additional students across several campuses, and otherwise splinter their time and attention. Ultimately, this is about making all professors better, more accessible teachers for their students, which requires helping them feel more professionally and financially stable at the university.

When I was spending semesters—seven years' worth of them—as a "road scholar" commuting between two schools, I kept realizing how much time I was wasting while traveling. I couldn't grade on the subway, bus, or in my car, so the 70–80 students I had those semesters each got a little less of my time and mental energy. Yet, there was always a reason that qualified, experienced adjuncts couldn't be promoted to full-time positions, which would've allowed us to work exclusively at one school. We heard a few times about some "upcoming retirements" and "expected full-time lines ideal for someone of your experience," yet things never quite went to plan. Whatever the reasons—legitimate or self-

justifying—were for these hiring decisions, having more engaged and accessible faculty to help students certainly wasn't one of them.

Parents and their college-bound children have every right to know exactly where their tuition dollars are going, how university administrations and policies are harming children's learning conditions, and how children's teachers are not always treated professionally and equitably. If I were talking with parents, I'd offer them a few steps to becoming more active and engaged in helping improve their children's college experiences and making their voices heard. Here are some simple yet effective ways we can help them get started. Think of these as starters for PowerPoint slides:

- Understand that the fracturing (or "adjunctification") of college teachers keeps hurting students because professors have limited time to hold office hours, often have to work multiple jobs to make ends meet, and must further subdivide their attention among additional students, campuses, and income streams.
- Encourage your children to know more about the contingency of their adjunct professors, as well as how it affects their learning environment. Being an adjunct does not simply mean the professor is paid less or lacks tenure. Remind your children that financial necessity leads many of their professors to teach at other schools, and perhaps do extra tutoring and editing on the side to make ends meet. When their professors are full-time part-timers cobbling together a living, students suffer.
- Ask your children to contact the university newspaper about writing stories or op-eds about their adjunct professors. They have a right to make their voices and concerns heard for the entire university community. The vast majority of first-year students alone will have at least one adjunct professor this year (and next year).
- When your school is trumpeting the new facilities (but perhaps not those for their leaders), the newly hired star professors (who probably won't teach undergrads), and its view of the campus as a "business" valuing its "customers," ask instead about the working conditions and job stability of their non-tenure-track faculty—that is, the likely majority of professors your children will have.
- Follow the advice from other professors (see above) about what you need to know, what you can do, and how you can do it. Learn more about these and other writer-activists dedicated to improving American higher education. Share their work with other concerned, tuition-paying parents whose children might be facing record levels of student debt after they graduate.

The school had been heaping praise on the new dean of Arts and Sciences it hired away from an elite institution. I was pretty hopeful, because I'd initiated talks with my chair about what our department could do to enhance job security and promotion potential for its adjuncts. The next step was proposing a meeting with the new dean—my chair, at least, didn't oppose such an overture. I was happy to be the point person to help my colleagues in my department and the others in Arts and Sciences. Yet—and not surprisingly—things fell through. I gave up my plan when the school announced pending cuts to adjunct and full-time faculty lines, as well as other educational services, in the dean's first year on the job. Yet again, the part-timers stayed part-timers.

Regardless of how experienced and/or engaged we are as writers and activists, we can also encourage parents to ask someone in charge—a dean, provost, admissions director, and so on—questions like these the next time they're on campus:

- What percentage of your faculty are adjuncts? Approximately how many of your faculty have to teach at other schools?
- How much do you pay adjuncts per course? How do adjuncts' salaries compare to those of full-time tenured or tenure-track faculty?
- What percentage of your general education faculty are adjuncts? How many, if any, tenured professors teach first-year students?
- What are the salaries of the school's upper-level administrators, and how many (if any) courses will they teach this year?
- How is there funding to install posh new facilities or pay star professors who probably won't teach my freshman, yet not enough to pay the majority of our children's professors a living wage or give them meaningful full-time positions?

Even if parents are not visiting campus, they can call or email the school. They might get the truth. They might not. They might get some spin or adminspeak about "valuing all faculty equally," "financial realities," and "some faculty choosing to teach at multiple schools." If they contact their schools, I'd strongly suggest they take notes about whom they're speaking with, what he or she says, and so on. When more parents start asking these kinds of questions, university administrations will realize that their actions to undermine higher education are not going unnoticed.

Parents: college students and faculty need you on their side if higher education is going to change. Follow the advice I've given. Know where your tuition dollars are going. Know more about how the "budget shortfalls" at your children's schools affect their learning but not senior administrators' bloated salaries or efforts to further erode professors' job stability and academic freedom. Ask the questions your children's schools may not want to hear. Talk with other parents about next steps and effective strategies. Encourage your children to ask the same kinds of questions and be as proactive and engaged as you are.

As long as colleges pay enormous salaries to their upper-level administrators, erode faculty stability by dismantling tenure and moving faculty to piecemeal adjunct positions, or treat their students like customers and their faculty like cheap and renewable labor, we need to keep encouraging parents and students to speak out.

Hopefully, the next time parents touring a college campus ask about the numbers of full-time faculty, they'll hear something more promising than what I did 15 years ago. If they hear something like, "We have recently restructured the budget to give faculty pay raises and improved office and classroom spaces" or "Only 15% of our faculty are now part time"—and if and only if this is the truth—it'll be because experienced insiders and activists had parents lend them their ears. We know what we want them to do. It's now up to us to tell them.

NOTE

1. Parts of this piece were originally published as "What Parents Need to Know about College Faculty," *pbs.org*, August 14, 2014, accessed September 10, 2014, http://www.pbs.org/newshour/making-sense/what-parents-need-to-know-about-college-faculty/.

CHAPTER 23

LIFE AS A GRADUATE STUDENT: INFORMED CHOICES, POSITIVE ATTITUDES

Alex Galarza

Graduate school contains plenty of grimness, despair, and soul-crushing disappointment. Decreasing public funding for the humanities, casualization of academic labor, and the widespread failure to reform graduate study for the twenty-first century paint a disheartening picture for anyone contemplating life in academia. Yet, you can also consider this somewhat bleak landscape as an opportunity to join a generation of graduate students who are motivated to effect changes in the humanities and higher education. This chapter is about my own choice to attend graduate school at such a historical moment and the importance under such circumstances of developing an informed and positive attitude for anyone who makes the same choice.

The challenges you will face in graduate school are unique to you and I am in no way qualified to provide a comprehensive guide to the future of graduate education in the humanities. Indeed, I entered my PhD program in history with a blithe naiveté that was rocked by the intensity of my workload and the suspicion that I was out of my depth. However, I can reflect now on what I've learned in the hope that you will be able to relate to what I say and glean your own lessons from it. I've made it through five years so far, and I have been privileged enough over the last three to read and write about the issues facing grad students while serving as an editor of the collaborative blog *GradHacker*. Throughout these experiences, I've heard consistently helpful advice, which I've grouped into three categories: make informed choices, prioritize your wellness, and be conscious of your work habits.

CHALLENGES AND CHOICES

The warning label on graduate school is more prominent than ever before. For decades, you had to look somewhat hard for data on the poor tenure-stream job prospects of PhDs, for critiques of the overly narrow training they receive, or any information at all on the negative effects of stress and isolation they commonly experience. Nowadays, the advice on social media, blogs, and news sites has made these warnings roughly equivalent to the grotesque images on cigarette packs. Writers including William Pannapacker, Karen Kelsky, Sarah Kendzior, and Rebecca Schuman (among many others) have posted sustained critiques of the training and culture of graduate school; their messages have resonated and riled in equal measures. Do the research on your field and program, take this warning label seriously, and then make an informed decision about attending graduate school. If you are like me and became aware of such challenges only after you enrolled, you should still take the opportunity to reassess your decision. My own reevaluation of whether or not I should become a historian in higher education involved paying closer attention to the publications and annual programs of my professional association, the American Historical Association (AHA), reading higher education news sites including *InsideHigherEd.com* and *Chronicle.com*, and seeking out critical voices in social media and the blogosphere.

These extracurricular resources touched a nerve so deep that I briefly considered leaving my program. A few facts that made me question my choice: the numbers vary by discipline and program prestige, but at the *very least* it's fair to say you probably won't land a tenure-track position. Near 75 percent of American university faculty are now adjuncts, and approximately 40 percent of academic positions have been eliminated since the 2008 global financial crisis.[1] Compounding the contingent faculty problem is the fact that enrollment in graduate programs has either remained steady or slightly increased, depending on the discipline, thus producing a glut of highly competitive prospects for an ever-diminishing number of positions.[2] In the humanities, only 47 percent of doctorate recipients in 2011 reported definite employment at the time of graduation, down from 60 percent in 2006.[3] Increasingly, graduate students who manage to find permanent positions only do so after an additional year (or years) of a postdoctoral fellowship, visiting position, or adjunct position, tacking on yet more debt during a possibly fruitless and prolonged job search period. You'd be wise to look into how these trends have impacted your own field.

The personal anguish and the precarious living situations that I both read about and saw others experiencing also gave me pause. Because I am unmarried, healthy, without dependents, and my family lives less than two hours away, graduate school wasn't as risky a proposition for me as it might be for others. If you have a family, a committed relationship, or plan to build either of those during grad school, then consider that changes in your funding status, program timeline, or research commitments can be enormously disruptive and stressful. If you have a chronic illness or develop one during your program, graduate school can be downright dangerous. If you are not lucky enough to receive a complete funding package, adequate for living in your university town, you shouldn't attend that university. Realistically, you should expect at least seven years of foregone wages if you can finish and find employment earlier than the average PhD. Graduate school is also rife with reminders that academia is not a meritocracy, nor is it a progressive refuge free of discrimination. The culture of many programs convinces students that their self-worth is tied to outcomes they only have so much personal control over, such as funding decisions based on departmental politics. Graduate students often struggle with depression and low self-esteem, especially when they fail to obtain external funding or employment after excelling within their programs. Even if you are lucky enough to avoid these injustices and problems, many of your friends and peers will face them.

If you want to assess risk accurately, make informed choices, and develop a sense of purpose in your work, then you've got to pay attention to certain warnings and understand the ins and outs of your program and wider discipline. Know your field, your prospects within it, and the challenges ahead so that you can develop an informed and realistic outlook. Don't let your decisions be shaped *only* by your adviser or graduate director. These individuals will undoubtedly play an important role in shaping your career and should be vital resources for you, but they likely traversed a very different career path than the one you're on, and they will, in many cases, put the interests of the department ahead of yours. Temper all advice from your program or institution with that of friends, mentors, peers, books, and blogs. My first step in answering specific questions is, of course, to search the Web for relevant articles and posts, but I also post questions on forums,[4] consult the indexes and appendices of relevant books,[5] tweet at the #phdchat hashtag, and email or call friends. You should always be willing to look up a relevant contact online and send them an email as the worst they can do is ignore it; very often, you will receive a helpful response. Once you have made an informed decision to complete your degree and found answers to the fundamental questions, your next goal should be to develop a positive outlook about the process you're about to undergo; doing so will help you weather the various setbacks you're bound to experience along the way.

WELLNESS

Now that you are feeling positively cheery about graduate school and your future as an academic, let's talk about happiness. Prioritize your wellness, mental health, and happiness from the outset of your program. After all, an advanced degree isn't something you *have to get through first* in order to be happy, nor are years of misery a foundation on which you should build a career. This is not a call for Netflix binges or video game marathons (although these can be restorative). I mean taking your plan for long-term happiness seriously and figuring out how graduate school fits into it. You might begin by thinking about whether you *can* be happy with a career outcome that doesn't include a tenure-track position; if you can't, then re-read the previous section and consider adjusting your plans accordingly. Once you have a sense of what will bring you long-term happiness and how graduate school fits in, you can then start building that life. Taking your goals and overall wellness seriously will make you more resilient against the many challenges you will face in an academic career (or any career for that matter).

In my case, I'm determined not to let my success or failure in securing a tenure-track position impact my long-term happiness. Instead, I've shaped my goals around my dissertation topic and the professional development that comes with earning a PhD in Latin American history. My undergrad mentor told me to pick a dissertation topic I could be happy studying for seven years, so I took one of my biggest passions and developed a research project on soccer and society in Latin America. I've since refined that idea into a dissertation that examines the social, economic, and political impact of soccer clubs in Buenos Aires. The *most important* calculation I think I made was to avoid shackling my dissertation to my hopes for a tenure-track position; this has freed me to prioritize those intellectual and personal goals that I see as especially relevant to my long-term happiness. For example, I've taken what others may consider a professional risk in being very open with my sources during my fieldwork and in deciding to publish a digital dissertation. This, indeed, exposes me to being "scooped" and may alienate some publishers of a potential monograph (the golden ticket to tenure) but, in my mind, producing relevant and publicly accessible research makes the risks worthwhile.[6] Staying focused on the original idea that excited me has allowed me to carry over my passion into meaningful side-projects such as my creation of a web platform for soccer scholarship,[7] and my editing work with *GradHacker*.

Continuing to find satisfaction and meaning in my work even as I've gone deeper into it has kept me sane. Far too often, graduate students forget the happiness that their original motivation for graduate study brought them and invest all of their time and energy in the major milestones of comprehensive exams, dissertation proposals, and dissertation defenses. Certainly, one should take joy in such accomplishments, but too often reaching a big goal is accompanied by a sense of dread at the seeming impossibility of the next step—and there's always a next step. Such thinking also tethers your happiness to someone else's evaluation of a specific moment in your scholarly development. This is symptomatic of not knowing how these milestones fit into your long-term happiness. You won't be repeatedly subjected to comprehensive exams or having to defend a research proposal as a professor, but the underlying essence of these tasks (immersing yourself in a specific research topic, say, or synthesizing scholarship) is exactly what you'll be tapping into for the rest of your career in the academy. Beware the lottery-winning mindset, which delays gratification until tenure: "If only I could land a tenure-track job at a research university, then I would be truly happy!" Instead, build happiness around the work itself. Grading papers or getting through comprehensive exam lists isn't always fun, but this is the kind of work you signed up for and will continue to do as a professor, so why not adopt an attitude that looks for the joy in these tasks? I've labored to remind myself of the love I have for most of the work I do, and to find the positive in those other tasks with which I struggle or find tedious. (Of course, we all should also be aware that the "love of work" rhetoric can be abused as a justification for exploiting workers, including ourselves.)[8]

I've also found it particularly useful to think about the ways grad school has impacted my interests and hobbies, as well as how I prioritize them. Don't underestimate the effects of the frequent isolation and the sedentary work life that come with being a graduate student. As an active extrovert, I was surprised by the drastic effects that too little time with friends and family, and even for playing team sports, had on my work. During my first comprehensive exam, I isolated myself for a week and eliminated exercise because I thought I needed to study the whole time. This particular exam ended up being the worst I ever turned in, and I was miserable the whole week. You may hear from others that consistently pulling all-nighters or spending all waking hours working is normal or laudable; however, in my experience, it's an unhealthy way of solving problems. Again, take time to identify the most important aspects of your wellness, weigh them against your professional responsibilities, and then prioritize accordingly.

I've learned a lot about the importance of developing a positive attitude from Buddhist teachings about suffering and happiness. Before you roll your eyes, just consider that my point all along has been to encourage you to become more conscious of your negative and positive mental states. The Dalai Lama's book, *The Art of Happiness*, co-authored with an American psychiatrist, contains a number of lessons apt for graduate school.[9] It reminded me that suffering was an inevitable part of existence and that our attitudes play a crucial role in how we perceive this suffering. It also helped me to become more conscious of my negative and positive mental states, which in turn helped me to improve my baseline happiness and resilience in the face of mistakes and setbacks. The book also has a great deal to say about building your happiness and attitude around compassion, something that we could do more of in the sometimes toxic—meaning competitive, even cutthroat, and always critical—environment of academia. Learning to tolerate some suffering as part of any job can be healthy; just don't lose sight of the fact that it's also important to develop an informed and positive perspective that doesn't tolerate injustice. Be willing to fight for change where it's needed.

WORK SMART

It's a given that you're going to be working hard; so, spend some time thinking about *why* and *how* you're working. This means developing systematic plans that take into account both your short-term and long-term goals. Are you working toward your long-term happiness on a daily basis? For example, whenever I want to throw up my hands and ask "Why am I doing this again?" I remind myself that one of my long-term goals is to grow from the experiences and lessons afforded to me as a historian. Doing so allows me to contend with the daily stress and anxiety that can cause procrastination or worse problems for scholars. Having a sense of purpose doesn't eliminate my daily battles to remain self-disciplined or resist the temptation to procrastinate, but it has made them easier to win and profoundly affected my mood and levels of motivation. Working with a larger sense of purpose has given me peace of mind that I am doing the best I can and helped me to be easier on myself (many of you likely will relate to the experience of being your own worst critic). Being more positive and compassionate, even toward myself, has in turn reinforced my sense of purpose and contentment in performing daily tasks. Working on these issues is a constant struggle, and I've experienced my fair share of setbacks on all fronts. But I keep on struggling, and I keep on improving.

How you get your work done can be a touchy topic since individual work habits vary wildly. I am the type that needs to police himself. One of the most important techniques I used to develop a routine and maintain self-discipline involved tracking the time I spent working. Measuring my work with the Pomodoro method (which promotes working in relatively short increments with frequent breaks) has been vital to keeping me focused and giving me an accurate sense of how I function best. Technology has also helped me to manage my tasks better, to avoid wasting time on the Internet, and to develop a workflow that differentiates my main tasks of writing, reading, teaching, and focusing on professional development. Websites like *ProfHacker, GradHacker*, and the aforementioned blogs constitute great resources for learning about how others manage their routines and workflow. There are plenty of productivity books filled with rehashed common sense, but I found Neil Fiore's *The Now Habit* to offer a solid reminder of best practices.[10] What I can loosely call my own work "system" changes occasionally, but it is always geared toward counteracting my weaknesses by helping me to juggle (over-) commitments, stay organized, and cut down on distractions.

Be careful to not overemphasize productivity and get lost fine-tuning a system instead of *actually getting work done*. It's also worth questioning a relentless drive toward productivity, especially in cases where it makes you miserable or complicit in your own exploitation. Pay attention to the wider social and political issues involving graduate student and adjunct labor so that you can better negotiate the line between what's reasonable and what's exploitative.

Finally, I should note that I've benefitted enormously from a document my adviser insisted I create in my first year of graduate study, and which I have updated on a regular basis. You might call it a five-year plan, a long-term planning document, or it can even be viewed as a modified and expanded CV. The idea here is to create some sort of plan, tailored to your own personality and needs, which will allow you to check in on how you're doing, on a quarterly basis at a minimum. This plan should also be integrated into whatever calendar or system you use to generate automatic reminders about calls for papers, conferences, grant deadlines, and professional development opportunities. You can find an excellent template at Karen Kelsky's website, *TheProfessorIsIn.com*.[11]

CONCLUSION

The graduate students I've most admired and from whom I've learned the most tend to have two qualities in common that have made them successful both in and outside of academia: positive attitudes and resiliency. In addition, they all were individuals who were willing to rely on their own peculiar support networks—whether family, friends, or significant others. You can equip yourself with the right information, attitude, and work ethic, but you will also find yourself counting on and benefitting from the help of friends and mentors. You will benefit equally from performing the role of friend and mentor for others. By recognizing and even cultivating our dependence on one another, we foster solidarity in the academy, bringing more compassion into graduate school and the wider academic world—transforming the inevitable despair and grimness into something positive and productive.

NOTES

1. Kendzior, S. "Academia's Indentured Servants," *Aljazeera.com*, April 2013, accessed July 5, 2014, http://www.aljazeera.com/indepth/opinion/2013/04/20134119156459616.html.
2. Council of Graduate Schools. "U.S. Graduate Schools Report Slight Growth in New Students for Fall 2012," *cgsnet.org*, September 12, 2013, accessed July 10, 2014, http://www.cgsnet.org/us-graduate-schools-report-slight-growth-new-students-fall-2012.
3. American Academy of Arts and Sciences, Humanities Indicators. "Job Status of Humanities Ph.D.'s at Time of Graduation," *humanitiesindicators.org*, June 6, 2013, accessed June 10, 2014, http://archive201406.humanitiesindicators.org/content/hrcoII16.aspxHumanities.
4. I frequently bookmark useful threads at the grad school subreddit. Go to http://www.reddit.com/r/gradschool.

5. Semenza, G. M. C. *Graduate Study for the 21st Century: How to Build an Academic Career in the Humanities*, 2nd ed., New York: Palgrave Macmillan, 2010, and the dated but still useful: Peters, R. L. *Getting What You Came For: The Smart Student's Guide to Earning a Master's or a Ph. D*, New York: Noonday Press, 1997.

6. For more on my thoughts regarding open-access scholarship, see my blog post "Don't Keep Your Head Down: Digital Dissertations and Graduate Training," *gradhacker.org*, November 18, 2011, http://www.gradhacker.org/2011/11/18/don%E2%80%99t-keep-your-head-down-digital-dissertations-and-graduate-training/.

7. See *footballscholars.org*.

8. Shine, J. "Love and Other Secondhand Emotions," *chroniclevitae.com*, February 3, 2014, accessed July 10, 2014, https://chroniclevitae.com/news/309-love-and-other-secondhand-emotions.

9. Dalai Lama and H. Cutler. *The Art of Happiness, 10th Anniversary Edition: A Handbook for Living*, New York: Riverhead Books, 2009.

10. Fiore, N. *The Now Habit: A Strategic Program for Overcoming Procrastination and Enjoying Guilt-Free Play*, New York: Tarcher, 2007.

11. Kelsky, K. "In Response to Popular Demand, More on the 5-year Plan," *TheProfessorIsIn.com*, May 9, 2014, accessed July 5, 2014, http://theprofessorisin.com/2014/05/09/in-response-to-popular-demand-more-on-the-5-year-plan/.

CHAPTER 24

LIFE AFTER RETIREMENT: TWO
ALTERNATIVES IN DIALOGUE

Valerie Wayne and Linda Woodbridge

LINDA WOODBRIDGE

Hi, Val. Hope you're safely home in Honolulu. It was so great to see you at the Shakespeare Association of America conference (SAA). Good choice of restaurant! It was fun to have dinner with just the three of us—you, me, and Rachel. So we could celebrate Rachel's getting her PhD (in Shakespeare, what else?) and I could brag about how fine her dissertation was. And brag about Dana's new faculty position in speech pathology at the University of Montana, and about her winning four national short-story contests within twelve months. Didn't our daughters turn out great?

They were all pretty young, our three daughters, when you and I met: Rachel was only ten. Do you realize that was 30 years ago this year? The SAA met in Boston that year, 1984, and the reception was at Brandeis—remember that we met on the shuttle bus back? Just happened to sit next to each other, and now we've been good friends all these years. At how many Shakespeare conferences have we shared a hotel room? Remember the major blizzard at the Montreal conference, when we got snowed in, and instead of boarding our planes home to our paper grading and committee meetings, we were forced to stay in Montreal, eating in French restaurants, and shopping in fine boutiques? "Jesus, the days that we have seen!" And now we're retired and have six grandkids between us.

But you're still truckin'! I'm thrilled for you that you got the prestigious Bogliasco Foundation Fellowship, although I still can't suppress the niggling voice telling me it's unfair for someone who lives in Hawaii to be sent off to the Italian Riviera! Remind me—what part of your *Cymbeline* editing project will you be working on in Italy? (I know we talked about it over dinner, but that might have been at a point too deep in the wine for me to recall clearly.)

VALERIE WAYNE

Hi Linda. Yes, it was wonderful seeing you and Rachel at SAA. Your daughter's dissertation sounds important, and it's reassuring that she can continue to work right in Edmonton rather than go on the job market. I gather it's not easy to get there from Montana during the winter months, but your being within ten hours driving distance of one daughter with her two children, and just down the road from the other with hers, is enviable. Although I live in Honolulu with wondrous weather, I'm far from my two grandchildren on Vancouver Island. We get together as a family two or three times a year, which is not enough, but because we're over 2,500 miles from one another, that's pretty good. Skyping helps and so do phone calls. Both fill my heart with family news and fun.

I also just returned from visiting my daughter Sarah in Mumbai, where she had the lead in a film being shot there. Her children were too young to travel to India so they stayed home with their father, and I got Sarah's companion ticket. It's a fascinating, complex city, and I loved it there. Sarah worked 12-hour days, six days a week, but we enjoyed our times together. One of the good things about retirement is the ability to drop everything and shout "Yes!" when your daughter says, "Do you want to come to Mumbai for a week?"

Most of the time, I'm here in Honolulu working on my edition of *Cymbeline* for the Arden Shakespeare. I retired in 2010 to finish it and am in the home stretch. I applied for the fellowship to revise the introduction, so that's what I'll be doing when my husband and I are enduring the astonishing views of a coastal town south of Genoa next September. I know, I know, why should I have even more water views than on my walks here at home? But one can accomplish so much on a work retreat when ordinary obligations recede and the focus becomes intense. So I'll travel from one ocean to another in hopes that the depths of those seas will somehow affect the depth of my work. You, however, are in the mountains, scaling them almost every day, which must be beautiful in very different ways. What are you thinking about as you hike up those hills, and what are you working on?

LINDA WOODBRIDGE

What am I thinking about as I hike? Thinking about the beauty of Montana, worrying about my husband who isn't very well these days, smiling when I think of having good friends like you. What am I working on?

Well, nothing.

I know: nothing will come of nothing, speak again. I say again, "nothing." By that I mean I'm doing no research, writing no papers, drafting no new book, applying for no grants. Nothing. And feeling pretty happy about it.

This came as a complete surprise to me. I have always loved researching, thinking about literature in new ways, writing, rewriting, thinking, and rethinking. My book on revenge came out from Cambridge the year before I retired, and while I drew breath for a year or so after retiring from Penn State, selling a house and buying/renovating a new one, moving, and making new friends, I always assumed that once we were resettled, life would reassume its usual contours for me: I would embark on a new book project, enabled and invigorated by the sudden absence from my life of faculty meetings, committee meetings, office hours, annual reports, teaching evaluations, travel claims, and dissertation defenses. And (it must be said) the sudden absence of full-time teaching, which I had always loved, but which, in recent years, after 42 years in the classroom, I had come to feel just a little tired of. Nothing to do but work on a new book! Heavenly thought!

Now three years have passed, and I have not worked on a new book at all, and haven't even missed that part of my life. Nearly all my retired friends, when I meet them at conferences, are still "working on" something of that sort. Why not me?

Schooled by many years' familiarity with *King Lear*, I had expected that, when I retired, I'd be surprised to find how much of my identity was bound up in my profession. Instead, I'm surprised to find how little of my identity was bound up in my profession. I could and did just walk away.

That doesn't mean I've let my brain rot. At the foot of the mountainside to which I've retired sits the University of Montana, and I've made many friends here who like to talk about books and ideas and attend concerts and galleries. I'm reading more than I've ever read in my life, and it's the sort of reading I've always wanted to do—the disinterested pursuit of knowledge for the pure pleasure of the life of the mind. If the true intellectual life comprises broad reading, in many historical periods and across many disciplines from the humanities to the pure sciences, then I've never before had time to lead the intellectual life. All the years I was a professor, my reading resembled not "basic research," guided only by intellectual curiosity, but "applied research," channeled toward a single topic on which I intended to publish an article or monograph. Academic life leaves no time to be truly intellectual. Retirement has given me the time and the freedom to make full use of my mind.

And happily, although I'm taking a break from reading academic prose, I still love literature itself as passionately as ever, and have more time than ever in which to devour it. (Then too—I have taken an Alaskan cruise, sailed on the Queen Mary, and recently gone on an African safari).

VALERIE WAYNE

How wonderful that retirement has allowed you to lead what you call the "true intellectual life!" I can sympathize with your not having found time for that before. You sound happy and satisfied not only with the retirement you've chosen but with the person you are at this stage of your life, and that seems to me key. We don't know, do we, who we will be when we are free of those urgent, day-to-day obligations? It's hard to be sure in advance, and the first year of retirement can be so unsettling it's often unclear at that stage as well. Since we have so much in common in other ways, let me explain what has made my response different from yours, because I'm happily working away at a publication deadline.

For starters, I taught 32 years as a professor rather than 42. I worked for four years between my BA and MA, lived in England for a year, traveled pretty widely, settled two homes, and left Chicago for Honolulu right after getting my doctorate. I was hired at the University of Hawaii as a generalist, and the tenured faculty claimed all the Shakespeare courses so I couldn't teach in my specialty for several years. That would be unconscionable today, but it was standard practice then, and our course load was 3–3 for my first 12 years or more. Teaching composition used to be required every third semester of all faculty in my department, and we teach a lot of literature at the introductory levels. So while I can't say I was making full use of my mind during that time, I was able to stretch what I knew by devising lower-level courses in areas where I had some interest but not much expertise. What I was hungry for, however, was more time to devote to my research and writing.

That's now happening for me in retirement, which sometimes feels like a long-term sabbatical. One of the things I love about editing is taking a deep dive into a text and discovering how its subtexts radiate out to the culture at large. Both of my previous editions have been satisfying in that way. My work on *Thomas Middleton: The Collected Works* for Oxford required collaborating with lots of people around the globe, and editing *Cymbeline* has occasioned a broad reach, too. To know one subject well, really well, and to track its growth from localized beginnings to its current presence can be so satisfying! That kind of knowledge is also part of the life of the mind that an academic career promises but often doesn't deliver on. Your monographs testify to your having found the satisfactions of focused work again and again: they're wonderfully diverse and engaging books on great topics. I continue to find pleasure in a related kind of inquiry, and there is still good work in me, maybe my best yet. I also need to accomplish something I haven't yet managed to do. I'm lucky to have the resources in time, health, and financial security to work in an area I know well with the kind of uninterrupted focus that wasn't available when I was on the academic treadmill.

LINDA WOODBRIDGE

Oh, Val—how happy it makes me to hear of your great satisfactions in post-retirement scholarship. You did so much to make that award-winning *Collected Middleton* the magnificent edition that it is; and it's very fine to see you continuing to hone your already razor-sharp editing skills in retirement. And talking about satisfactions—I earlier said I was getting a little bit tired of teaching, toward the end of my career. And no wonder, since I taught three courses per semester for at least the first two decades of my career. But (another surprise) what do you think I've found I really missed? Yes, teaching. As soon as I reached Montana, I filled in for a prof on sabbatical, teaching a senior Shakespeare course at the university here. I was delighted with the students—very bright, and a very different demographic from Penn State, mostly older, nearly all of them parents themselves, which made teaching *King Lear* a lot easier. But I have to say, grading papers and setting exams and chasing down students who hadn't appeared in class for a while didn't grow any dearer. Or fighting for a better classroom—I was spared a third-floor walk-up classroom over a noisy basketball court only by a student who swore to the administration that walking up three flights after his recent knee operation would lead to his demise, and lawsuits. That was my last brush with the university teaching we have all known and loved. Since then, I have discovered a marvelous kind of teaching: the Osher Lifelong Learning Institute. Talk about a different demographic! These students are all over 50, many of them retired university professors—they are well-read, extensively traveled, smart, intensely interested in their courses, and willing to leap into discussions with verve. It would perhaps be ill-bred of me to mention that there are no exams, no essays to mark, no grades to assign, and no appeals for better grades from those who really need to get into med school. Just pure pleasure! I have taught several of these wondrous courses. And I've taken several—all excellent.

And another surprise. Last week, I was interviewed by a student who is doing a cultural history of the English department at the University of Alberta, where I taught for 24 years before my 17 years at Penn State. It seems that I am remembered at Alberta primarily for my term as chair of the English department. I have always recalled that era mainly as a time of stress and misery. And it is definitely unfashionable to take pride in administrative achievement. It has always been a beef of mine that university administrators are regarded with contempt, as if no one with respectable scholarly credentials would accept such a job, or accede to such an interruption of her intellectual career. But looking back on that era, a time of economic recession when the University's budgets had crashed and enrollments had soared, I find to my surprise that I feel good about what I was able to do. The English department had suffered losses in its tenure lines and was employing an army of fixed-term ("sessional" in Canada) lecturers at poor wages, everyone was teaching three courses per semester or more, and the average class size for first-year students, even in classes heavily devoted to composition, had shot up to 43 students! I very nearly had a breakdown trying to fix all this. But by the end of my term, average class size had been reduced to 32, teaching loads had been reduced to five half-year courses per year, and I had harangued/cajoled university authorities into granting the English department 11 new tenure-track positions and increasing benefits and job security for the sessional lecturers who remained. I now find that it doesn't matter at all to me that nobody at the University of Alberta remembers that I wrote a book called *Women and the English Renaissance*, or any other of my books. What I did during my term as department chair, although it nearly killed me and nearly annihilated my family life, made a real difference to people's lives—both instructors and students. Sitting on my Montana mountainside now, I find that I look back on that with real satisfaction.

VALERIE WAYNE

I like that picture of retirement: sitting on a mountainside, contemplating a past that nearly killed you, but with the satisfaction that it also improved the lives of others. Maybe that confirms we're all masochists. But that's got to be one of the best parts of this stage of life, knowing that you gave a lot at considerable cost while believing you made a difference. Teaching affords those pleasures as well as administrative work, and I deeply respect colleagues who serve their institutions in leadership roles as you have done. I deflected invitations to stand for department chair because research was my primary passion, but I did direct the graduate program. That was when the creative writers were fighting the literary critics, who were fighting the cultural studies faculty, who were fighting the marginalized composition specialists. Working with a great committee, I was able to revise the graduate program to allow for "concentrations" in each of those areas. The plan is still in place 17 years later because it provides everyone with a home in the department and diversifies the curriculum.

I surprised myself the other day by telling a colleague I might be willing to teach Shakespeare again once I finish my edition. I didn't see that coming, but if they need me, I may help out with one course a year because I've always loved teaching. We have an Osher Institute here too, so that's another option. During my retirement, I've always been working with one or two doctoral students, so I go into the office every week or so. And I have my office still, which is a rare boon. I attend some departmental colloquia and tune into the occasional crisis. Many of my close friends will be teaching for another ten years or more and I want to maintain those connections, so I've tried to inhabit an alternative form of retirement in my department. Apparently studies show that community is the most important factor in a happy retirement, and I believe it. To be surrounded with people you love and care about, those with whom you've endured institutional traumas but still count as good friends, matters a lot. I've returned to music recently, too, so in addition to research, I'm mentoring and singing and living a more balanced life at a pretty sane pace.

But Linda, this exchange could be depressing for some of those coming after us, who may not have a future with adequate resources from tenured jobs, pensions, social security, and investments to experience the kind of retirement we're enjoying.

LINDA WOODBRIDGE

Yes, that's too true. I worry about what is happening and will happen to the world we knew. Well, more than half of all humanities teaching is done by instructors ineligible for tenure, and those percentages are increasing year by year. What will those instructors' retirements be like? People are living longer, and those who think seriously about what an academic career can be need to devote attention and institutional energy to ensuring that the now-lengthening years after retirement can be as fulfilling as possible. That rests ultimately on economic security for retirees. Each retiree should be free to lead a life of her choosing, whether it be a life of continued scholarship and productivity, like yours, or—like mine—a life that freely acknowledges that "there is a world elsewhere."

VALERIE WAYNE

So professional knowledge remains central in my retirement, while in yours it's peripheral, but we're both using our minds to connect with a larger world and enjoying doing so. Because we've both been committed to feminism for all of our professional lives, those commitments have taken us beyond the academy too, and continue to do so. For each of us, this is a time to round out our lives, try things that have been untried, and complete things that have been unfinished. Retirement can be an exceptionally good time of life, one that is well worth sharing with the generations coming after us.

CHAPTER 25

LIFE AFTER ACADEME: GIVING UP
TENURE? WHO DOES THAT?[1]

Anne Trubek

My academic career has been absurdly idiosyncratic. Fifteen years ago, I accepted a half-time tenure-track position. (Idiosyncrasy No. 1: some small liberal-arts colleges like mine offer split appointments on the tenure track.) Twelve years ago, I was awarded tenure, and on the exact same day, divorced. (That's Idiosyncrasy No. 2, one I wrote about for *The Chronicle* back in 2004).[2]

Tenured, but unable to support myself financially, I began to do freelance writing to supplement my income. I enjoyed it—so much that it became increasingly hard to juggle my professorial and free-lance duties. The language of traditional scholarship was sounding increasingly foreign to me, and it became a tongue I no longer wanted to speak. I revised my writing courses to reflect the work I was doing in narrative nonfiction, cultural criticism, and book history. But then, when departmental and service duties ramped up, and espe-cially when it was my turn to become chair, I found myself pulled in too many directions. As a divorced mother with joint custody, I am geographically restricted (Idiosyncrasy No. 3), so the job market was not for me.

To stop the juggling, I chose to expand my freelance career and took an extended leave of absence from Oberlin College. I have been supporting myself with my writing since 2011. But in the fall of 2012, it was time for me to make a decision: should I give up my faculty line at Oberlin?

In my mind, my curvy odd career made me an outlier; so, giving up tenure would be as idiosyncratic as the rest of my story. I mean, who does that? Who gives up tenure? I kept tripping myself up on the oddity of the move, the seeming illogic. So many want what I have, and so few will attain it. Who am I to give up the golden prize? Nobody does that, I told myself, over and over.

But I was wrong. As soon as I started looking around, I could not stop finding examples of tenured professors who had resigned their posts.

Statistics are hard to come by, and I can make no claim about a trend or percentage. But *Nature* recently profiled four scientists who gave up tenure.[3] John Jackson wrote a blog post for *The Chronicle* about three faculty members in the humanities and social sciences who did the same.[4] Ann Daly gave several interviews about her recent decision to quit.[5]

Blog posts announcing one's departure are becoming a microgenre. Robert Kosara posted about quitting to join Tableau Software.[6] Terran Lane wrote a post elucidating his reasons for leaving academic science, which *The Chronicle* subsequently published.[7] Lane then wrote a follow-up for *Times Higher Education* on the enormous number of people who responded to his story: "The majority response came down to 'me too.' Many people said that they had left or were going to leave academia, or that they knew someone who had or was, for many of the same reasons."[8] Lane concluded that "erosions of resources, autonomy, flexibility, vision, and respect for learning" were "beginning to force a generation of scholars out of the field."

To continue the woes of academe, a *Chronicle* article titled "Why Are Associate Professors So Unhappy?" discussed the struggles of the post-tenure years.[9]

I took to Twitter to see if I could flush out more examples. "Anyone know of profs who gave up tenure?" Those few words elicited a torrent of responses. Within two hours, I had been given the names of, or been contacted by, two dozen people who had given up tenure. Dozens more wrote to let me know they were very interested in the topic, and could I keep them updated on what I found?

My tweet persuaded one lurker to make her own announcement (which she followed up with a blog post). Kathleen Fitzpatrick announced that she had resigned (effective in June) from Pomona College to work for the Modern Language Association (MLA). Her news set off a new wave of tweets. Everyone cheered her on, congratulated her for her decision.

The chorus in my head—those abrogating, "Nobody does that" voices—were silenced. Not only do people do that, but when they do, others cheer them on.

Fitzpatrick's move was motivated, not by a distaste for changes in higher education, but by her passion to pursue an academic issue outside the confines of her faculty position. She is now director of scholarly communication at the MLA. When she made the decision, she had just been promoted to full professor. "It was clear to me, with a few possible forks, what the path ahead was," she said. "I could keep teaching the same classes but update them, keep doing research and service with some changes. Or I could decide I wanted to move into administration. These were predictable, carved-out paths." When the MLA opportunity arose, it "allowed me to do work at a much larger scale and a national level where it might have some impact beyond my specialized field. I could actually do the things I had been writing should be done. That seemed way more important than lifetime job security."

She did not make the decision lightly. "At first it was really terrifying to contemplate it, to think about taking that chance. What if I decided it was a mistake? After this job, what next?" She added: "I realized that the fear was a productive fear. 'I don't know what I would do next' means I could do anything. That was the moment I realized, somewhere in the back of my head without realizing, I'd made the decision."

And if she had internalized peer pressure—the "Nobody does that" in my head—it was dispelled as soon as she tweeted. "I have been extremely surprised at those who wrote me via Twitter or left comments on my Web site to say congratulations. It's not that I don't think it's a great decision. I'm just surprised that it seems like such a positive move to so many others. I worried some would think of it as the squandering of a benefit they're still working to get close to. It feels like an extraordinary luxury."

Most of the dozen people I subsequently interviewed about leaving tenured jobs echoed the same sentiment: their news was received with congratulations and, often, envy. Kosara admitted he was "scared" when he met with his department chair and dean, but both surprised him: "They were calm, supportive, and very interested. They wanted to know more." So did other colleagues: "I expected more people to say, 'Are you sure?' But I think a lot of people are thinking about giving up tenure, even if not consciously. And they are a bit envious."

When Carin Ruff was considering whether to leave her tenured position in medieval studies at Cornell University, friends and colleagues advised her to go for it: "They said I should do this now and not wait until I'm 50." When Peter Suber left his faculty job in philosophy at Earlham College, "some said, 'Gosh, I wish I could do that, too.' Nobody said, 'You're making a big mistake.' Nobody said, 'What a terrible thing to do.'" His wife, Liffey Thorpe, quit her tenured post in classics at Earlham, too.

"All of us know senior faculty who are ready [to leave] but feel immobile," Suber said. "We were ready and didn't feel immobile. It was a scary leap, and that's the equivalent to being immobile for many people. I won't pretend that we weren't scared. We were."

Kosara acknowledged those fears as well, but said he was "not risk averse"—unlike many academics, for whom tenure is an important form of security.

For everyone I interviewed, the risk of giving up tenure allowed them to pursue something more meaningful. For Suber, it was to pursue his passion for open access. When he made the decision with his wife, they "gave up salaries, tenure, and tuition remission. We had nothing to take the place of it. Neither of us had new jobs. I had a cause, not a job. I had to apply for grants to fund me for that cause. Ever since, I have lived on grants and fellowships." (He is now direc- tor of Harvard University's Open Access Project and a faculty fellow at the Berkman Center for Internet & Society. Thorpe, his wife, is director of communications at George Stevens Academy.)

Of his decision to leave academe for a software company, Kosara wrote on his website: "I like doing stuff, but at the university I spent most of my time telling other people what to do instead of doing things myself." He wrote that he had "struggled to see my work have an actual impact." At Tableau Software, he has "more interesting and better" opportunities for his work.

Ruff, who left Cornell and now works in historic preservation, "feels so much better about life, and that trumps not writing that book. Out in the world it's normal to change jobs several times. Now the sense of who I am comes from myself, and not my work, and that's such a relief." She is also relieved of the persistent survivor's guilt she had felt since receiving her first tenure-track job. "My sense of lack of accomplishment by the time I got to tenure was influenced by having come up in this world where getting a job is a crapshoot," she said. "I got a job, but I knew 20 others who didn't. There is a high infant-mortality rate among medievalists. I felt complicit in an unattractive system, and so tenure did not feel like a relief."

The risks of leaving tenure are not just professional. They are finan- cial, too. Although the vast majority of Americans think nothing of working under contract or at will, professors find the prospect fright-ening. What if they were to get fired? Many who have made the move prepared beforehand. Eileen Joy, who left her tenured job at Southern Illinois University, "laid the groundwork." She paid off her debt and sold her house at a loss. Now she stays with friends as she travels to give talks or stays at her partner's home, in Cincinnati. Fitzpatrick noted that she had little personal debt, paid off her educational debt, and did not have children. (The majority of people I interviewed do not have children.)

Few of the people I interviewed expressed any regrets about giv-ing up tenure. Yet they didn't link their decision to frustration with academe, beyond the frequent refrain of being "kind of bored." None saw themselves as opting out of academe. They saw themselves as opting in to something else, which seemed more exciting, fruitful, and productive. Few had qualms about how others might perceive their decision, and none thought of it as any kind of failure or shift downward.

It would not be going out on a limb to say that academics can be self-important. To frame the question as "Why leave? Who does that?" as I did—and as the articles I mentioned do—reveals a certain exceptionalism and a tinge of arrogance. It is a job, being a tenured professor. Just a job. Why not leave?

And so I will. I may still teach at my old college, but I will resign my position as a tenured professor. It would have been an unthinkable move for me when I received tenure; now it seems not only imagin-able, but obvious. My interests have evolved, and I am simply mov-ing along with them. I am not diverting or opting out or making a statement by resigning my tenured post. I am simply taking the next logical step. It's not such a big leap after all.

A POSTSCRIPT

Since this piece was published in *The Chronicle of Higher Education* 16 months ago, I did indeed resign my tenure line. I then accepted a new position at Oberlin College, with a misleading title of Writer-in-Residence (I neither write for them nor am I in residence on campus). What I do in reality, if not in title, is teach two classes per year for Oberlin. I am now in the second year of that position, for which I signed a three-year contract. I enjoy being able to continue to teach, and I do not miss—not for an instant, ever—committee meetings or the bureaucratic drudgery that consumes so much faculty time; my new position's only requirement of me is to show up for class.

That it has only been 16 months since this article appeared (although it will be longer from now when you read this) is unimaginable to me. Although I felt, when writing the piece, I had already largely left academe (I had been on a two-year unpaid leave)—and was showing how "normal" such a move was and could be—when I re-read it, it strikes me as having been written by someone still thinking like an academic, still wrestling with the peculiar socialization and subcultural pressures of academia that force many to think of it in "inside" and "outside" terms, and to consider going "outside" some sign of failure or abdication. Writing in September 2014, this now seems like madness, or cultish behavior.

My work life is now full to brimming: I have started an online magazine and small press (Belt Magazine and Publishing: *Beltmag. com*), and written a book called *The History and Uncertain Future of Handwriting* (Bloomsbury, 2015). I am happier than I have ever been professionally and creatively. I am sustained by what I perceive as meaningful work that makes a difference. It is exciting. People read and interact with my work on a daily basis. It is fun, and it is intellectually demanding and rewarding.

But I cannot end this postscript with "it's all good!" because one basic economic and labor issue is key to my current situation: my healthcare and benefits continue to be provided by the academic institution that employs me half-time. I have not (yet) left those benefits behind (when I was on unpaid leave, I paid my own health insurance, but I was allowed to do so through Oberlin College's group plan. It was expensive, but less expensive than what was available through the Affordable Care Act). For those with the financial benefits that academia provides to many of its employees, consider this asterisk to my story. For those not eligible for those benefits, well, all I can say is this: like all the people I interviewed for the article, I, too, have never looked back.

NOTES

1. Parts of this piece were originally published under the same title in *The Chronicle of Higher Education*, April 8, 2013, accessed September 1, 2014, http://chronicle.com/article/Giving-Up-Tenure-Who-Does/138345/.

2. See Trubek, "When a Spousal Hire Becomes a Single Mom," *The Chronicle of Higher Education*, February 20, 2004, accessed September 14, 2014, http://chronicle.com/article/When-a-Spousal-Hire-Becomes/44769/.

3. Powell, K. "Academia: Off the tenured track," *Nature* 491 (2012): 627–629.

4. Jackson, J. L. Jr. "Opting Out," *The Chronicle of Higher Education*, August 2, 2010, accessed September 14, 2014, http://chronicle.com/blogs/brainstorm/opting-out/25919.

5. "The Professor Who Left After Tenure: Interview with Ann Daly," *techintranslation.com*, February 23, 2011, accessed September 14, 2014, http://techintranslation.com/the-professor-who-left-after-tenure-interview-with-ann-daly/.

6. Kosara, R. "Goodbye, Academia; Hello (Again), Tableau!," *eagereyes.org*, September 16, 2012, accessed September 14, 2014, http://eagereyes.org/blog/2012/goodbye-academia-hello-again-tableau.

7. Lane, T. "On Leaving Academe," *The Chronicle of Higher Education*, August 19, 2012, accessed September 14, 2014, http://chronicle.com/article/on-Leaving-Academe/133717.

8. Lane, T. "I'd Have to be Mad to Leave Here, They Said—and They were Right," *timeshighereducation.co.uk*, August 23, 2012, accessed September 14, 2014, http://www.timeshighereducation.co.uk/420932.article.

9. Wilson, R. "Why are Associate Professors So Unhappy?," *The Chronicle of Higher Education*, June 3, 2012, accessed August 10, 2014, http://chronicle.com/article/Why-Are-Associate-Professors/132071/.

CONTRIBUTORS

Michael Bérubé, Edwin Erle Sparks Professor of Literature and Director of the Institute for the Arts and Humanities at Pennsylvania State University, is the author of several works on cultural studies, disability rights, liberal politics, and debates in higher education. Bérubé's books include *What's Liberal About the Liberal Arts? Classroom Politics and "Bias" in Higher Education* (2006), *The Employment of English: Theory, Jobs, and the Future of Literary Studies* (1998), *Life As We Know It: A Father, A Family, and an Exceptional Child* (1996), and *Public Access: Literary Theory and American Cultural Politics* (1994). In 2012, Bérubé served as president of the Modern Language Association of America.

Margaret Sönser Breen is Professor of English and Women's, Gender, and Sexuality Studies at the University of Connecticut, where she specializes in LGBT literature and queer theory. She is the author of *Narratives of Queer Desire: Deserts of the Heart* (2009) and the editor or co-editor of several volumes exploring issues of gender, sex, and sexuality, as well as questions of good, evil, and wickedness.

Brenda Jo Brueggemann—Professor of English at the University of Louisville—is author of *Lend Me Your Ear: Rhetorical Constructions of Deafness* (1999) and *Deaf Subjects: Between Identities and Places* (2008). She is the co-editor of *Disability Studies: Enabling the Humanities; Women and Deafness: Double Visions; Disability and/in Prose;* and *Disability and the Teaching of Writing: A Critical Sourcebook*. She is former editor of *Disability Studies Quarterly* and the Gallaudet University Press series, *Deaf Lives*.

Claudia Calhoun is Visiting Assistant Professor of Rhetoric at Bates College. Her research focuses on the intersections between popular media and societal change in the United States after World War II. She received her PhD in American Studies and Film and Media Studies at Yale University in 2014. Her current book project looks at the police procedural genre within postwar culture, focusing on the circulation and reception of the radio and television series *Dragnet*.

Christina M. Fitzgerald, Professor of English and Director of the Humanities Institute at the University of Toledo, has published widely on medieval drama and manuscript culture, and recently co-edited *The Broadview Anthology of Medieval Drama* (2012) with John T. Sebastian. But, she is perhaps equally well known among medievalists and other academics as "Dr. Virago," the author of the blog *Quod She* (quodshe.wordpress.com). Frequently linked at *Inside Higher Ed*, *Quod She* is an "academic life" blog, maintained since 2005, which often reports on managing the work–life balance.

Joseph Fruscione taught college English and first-year writing for nearly 15 years in Washington, DC. Currently a freelance editor and writing consultant, he has written a book (*Faulkner and Hemingway: Biography of A Literary Rivalry*), given a lecture at the Library of Congress, and is currently editing the book collection *Teaching Hemingway and Modernism*. He is a regular writer for the *Chronicle of Higher Education*, *Inside Higher Ed*, and *Hybrid Pedagogy*. Joe has twice appeared on PBS NewsHour's "Making Sense" segment (March 2013 and February 2014) to talk about how adjunct issues are affecting higher education, and he has started a monthly column on higher ed for the series. Most recently, he has worked with a group of advocates to petition the US Department of Labor to investigate faculty working conditions and student learning conditions in higher education, which he hopes will lead to better conditions for all faculty and students.

Alex Galarza is a PhD candidate in History at Michigan State University whose research examines soccer clubs and urban life in Buenos Aires during the twentieth century. He is also the Digital Liberals Arts Fellow of the Mellon Scholars at Hope College. He recently returned from conducting dissertation research in Argentina, made possible by a Fulbright IIE Award and a FIFA João Havelange Research Scholarship. Alex co-edits gradhacker.org, a blog and podcast for graduate students, by graduate students and manages footballscholars.org, an online platform for soccer scholarship.

Kristen Ghodsee has her PhD from the University of California-Berkeley and is a Professor of Gender and Women's Studies at Bowdoin College. She has held residential research fellowships at the Woodrow Wilson International Center for Scholars in Washington, DC; the Institute for Advanced Study in Princeton, New Jersey; the Max Planck Institute for Demographic Research in Rostock, Germany; the Radcliffe Institute for Advanced Study at Harvard

University; and the Freiburg Institute for Advanced Studies (FRIAS) in Germany. Ghodsee is the author of five books and numerous articles on communism, postcommunism, and economic transition in Eastern Europe, and was awarded a John Simon Guggenheim fellowship for her work in anthropology and cultural studies in 2012. Her latest book, *The Left Side of History: World War II and the Unfulfilled Promise of Communism in Eastern Europe*, is forthcoming with Duke University Press in 2015. In addition to her work in Eastern Europe, she is the co-author of *Professor Mommy: Finding Work/Family Balance in Academia* (Rowman & Littlefield, 2011).

Tony Grafton, Henry Putnam University Professor at Princeton University, is one of the foremost historians of early modern Europe. His book *Defenders of the Text* (1991) explores the relations between scholarship and science in the early modern period. *From Humanism to the Humanities* (1986), co-written with Lisa Jardine, revised historians' basic understanding of Renaissance education and its legacy. Grafton contributes regularly to such publications as *The American Scholar*, *The New Republic*, and *The New York Review of Books*, including on a range of topics related to the current state of higher education in America. In 2004, the Mellon Foundation awarded Grafton its Distinguished Achievement Award for contributions in the Humanities. He is a past president of the American Historical Society.

Sean Grass, Associate Professor of English at Iowa State University, is the author of *Charles Dickens's* Our Mutual Friend*: A Publishing History* (2014) and *The Self in the Cell: Narrating the Victorian Prisoner* (2003) as well as essays on Victorian writers from Dickens and Wilkie Collins to Christina Rossetti and Charles Reade. He has been a director of graduate studies and an officer for the North American Victorian Studies Association (NAVSA), and he currently serves his department as the Associate Chair for Faculty Development.

Natalie M. Houston, Associate Professor of English at the University of Houston, contributes regular columns on productivity, pedagogy, and technology to the *ProfHacker* blog at *The Chronicle of Higher Education*. Her current research project, *Digital Reading: Poetry and the New Nineteenth-Century Archive*, uses large-scale computational analysis to explore the cultural function of poetry within Victorian print culture. She recently directed an NEH-funded software development project, *The Visual Page*, and is Co-Director for the *Periodical Poetry Index*.

Rob Jenkins is the "Two-Year Track" columnist for *The Chronicle of Higher Education* and the author of *Building a Career in America's Community Colleges*. He has spent 26 years working at two-year colleges as a part-time faculty member, a full-time faculty member, a department chair, an academic dean, and a program director. He currently serves as Associate Professor of English at Georgia Perimeter College near Atlanta.

Brendan Kane, Associate Professor of History and Associate Director of the Humanities Institute at the University of Connecticut, is the author of *The Politics and Culture of Honour in Britain and Ireland, 1541–1641* (Cambridge UP, 2010) and is currently co-editing the collection (with Valerie McGowan-Doyle) *Elizabeth I and Ireland* (forthcoming, Cambridge UP). He co-curated (with Thomas Herron) the exhibition *Nobility and Newcomers in Renaissance Ireland* (Folger Shakespeare Library, January-May 2013).

Stephanie Kerschbaum is Assistant Professor of English at the University of Delaware, where she specializes in composition and rhetoric studies. She is the author of *Toward a New Rhetoric of Difference* (NCTE, 2014) and is currently at work on a collaborative research study of disabled faculty members. She is a 2014–2015 recipient of a postdoctoral research leave fellowship from the American Association of University Women.

Giuseppina Iacono Lobo, Assistant Professor at Loyola University Maryland, has recently published articles in *English Literary Renaissance* and *Exemplaria*, and a chapter in *To Repair the Ruins: Reading Milton* (2012). She is currently working on a manuscript about conscience and national identity during the English Revolution.

Eric Lorentzen is Associate Professor of English at the University of Mary Washington where he teaches a wide variety of courses, but specializes in nineteenth-century British literature, cultural studies and critical pedagogy, and Charles Dickens. He has recently published articles in two collections: one on Charlotte Brontë and alternative literacies, and another on Dickens and cultural studies pedagogy. He is currently working on a book-length project about the nineteenth-century educational praxis known as the "catechistic method."

William Pannapacker is Professor of English and Director of The Andrew W. Mellon Foundation Scholars Program in the Arts and Humanities at Hope College in Holland, Michigan. He is the author of *Revised Lives: Walt Whitman and Nineteenth-Century Authorship* (Routledge, 2004), a monthly columnist for *The Chronicle of Higher*

Education since 1998, and a contributor to *The New York Times* and *Slate Magazine*.

Kristen Poole, Professor of English at the University of Delaware, specializes in early modern religious literary culture. She has written two books on the topic (*Supernatural Environments in Shakespeare's England: Spaces of Demonism, Divinity and Drama* [Cambridge UP, 2011] and *Radical Religion from Shakespeare to Milton: Figures of Nonconformity in Early Modern England* [Cambridge UP, 2000]), as well as numerous scholarly articles. She is the Director of the Luminary iPad edition of *Romeo and Juliet*, and is working on a Master's of Sacred Theology at Lutheran Theological Seminary at Philadelphia, with a major in historical theology.

Claire Bond Potter is Professor of History at the New School for Public Engagement. In addition to her work as a twentieth-century United States political historian, she has blogged at *Tenured Radical* since 2007, where she writes about digital humanities practice, mentoring, the job market, early career decisions, tenure, and balancing scholarship with other forms of academic labor. Her commentary on higher education has been published at *Inside Higher Ed* and *The New York Times*, and she has been a guest on the *PBS News Hour*.

Barry V. Qualls, University Professor of English at Rutgers University, has served as Vice President for Undergraduate Education, Dean of Humanities, and Chair of English. He is the author of *The Secular Pilgrims: The Novel as Book of Life* (Cambridge UP), and of articles and reviews on 19th-Century English literature and on the Bible and its literary impact. In the classroom, he focuses on Victorian literature and on biblical literatures. As an administrator, he has focused on the ways undergraduate and graduate education work together for students in a research university. In 2006, he was named New Jersey Professor of the Year by the Carnegie Foundation for the Advancement of Teaching and the Council for Advancement and Support of Education.

Karen J. Renner has been a lecturer since 2010 at Northern Arizona University where she teaches classes in American literature. She recently edited a collection of essays entitled *The 'Evil Child' in Literature, Film & Popular Culture* (Routledge, 2012) and is currently working on her own book on the same topic. In addition, she is completing a handbook on writing tentatively titled *Reading for the Writer, Writing for the Reader: A Guide to Writing about Literature in the Classroom and Beyond*.

Iris V. Rivero, Associate Professor of Industrial and Manufacturing Systems Engineering at Iowa State University, is Director of Graduate Education and Associate Chair for her department and has delivered talks addressing career development and family balance at international seminars (Women in Industrial Engineering Academia, Istanbul, Turkey), and at universities across the United States (NC State, Georgia Tech, Texas Tech). In addition, she was part of the organizing committee of the ADVANCE Senior Mentoring Summit For Senior Underrepresented Minority Women Engineering Faculty. Her research focuses on biomedical manufacturing.

Cathy J. Schlund-Vials is Associate Professor of English and Asian/Asian American Studies and the Director of the Asian and Asian American Studies Institute at the University of Connecticut. She is the author of two monographs: *Modeling Citizenship: Naturalization in Jewish and Asian American Writing* (Temple University Press, 2011) and *War, Genocide, and Justice: Cambodian American Memory Work* (University of Minnesota Press, 2012). She has three co-edited collections in print and forthcoming; these include *Disability, Human Rights and the Limits of Humanitarianism* (Ashgate, 2014), *Keywords for Asian American Studies* (New York University Press, 2015), and *Asian America: A Primary Source Reader* (Yale University Press, 2015). She presently serves as a series editor for Temple University's *Asian American History and Culture* series.

Greg Colón Semenza, Associate Professor of English at the University of Connecticut, is the author of *Graduate Study for the 21st Century: How to Build an Academic Career in the Humanities* (Palgrave Macmillan, 2005; 2nd ed. 2010). He has also written *The History of British Literature on Film* (Bloomsbury, 2015), as well as numerous books and articles on a variety of subjects ranging from early modern sports to the Sex Pistols. His blog for the *Vitae* section of *The Chronicle of Higher Education*, *This Academic Life*, focuses on work–life issues in academe.

Garrett A. Sullivan, Jr., Professor of English at Pennsylvania State University, is the author most recently of *Sleep, Romance, and Human Embodiment: Vitality from Spenser to Milton* (Cambridge, 2012). He has also edited numerous works, including *The Cambridge Companion to English Renaissance Tragedy* (Cambridge, 2010, with Emma Smith), and along with Julie Sanders is editing for Oxford University Press a new book series entitled *Early Modern Literary Geographies*.

Anne Trubek published *A Skeptic's Guide To Writers' Houses* in 2010 and *Rust Belt Chic: The Cleveland Anthology* in Fall 2012. She is currently working on "The History and Uncertain Future of Handwriting" for Bloomsbury Press USA. Trubek has published articles in *The New York Times, The Atlantic, Wired, Slate, The Washington Post,* and *The Chronicle of Higher Education,* among many others. She is a board member of the National Book Critics Circle and the founder of Belt Publishing.

Valerie Wayne is Professor Emerita of English at the University of Hawai'i at Mānoa. She has co-edited five essay collections, edited Edmund Tilney's *The Flower of Friendship: A Renaissance Dialogue Contesting Marriage* (Cornell UP, 1992), and served as Associate General Editor on the award-winning *Collected Works of Thomas Middleton* (Oxford UP, 2007). A former President of the Society for the Study of Early Modern Women, she has been a Trustee of the Shakespeare Association of America and is completing the Arden 3 edition of Shakespeare's *Cymbeline.*

Linda Woodbridge was Weiss Chair in the Humanities and Professor of English at the Pennsylvania State University. Her many books include *Women and the English Renaissance* (University of Illinois Press, 1984), *The Scythe of Saturn: Shakespeare and Magical Thinking* (University of Illinois Press, 1994), and *Vagrancy, Homelessness, and English Renaissance Literature* (University of Illinois Press, 2001). She is a former president of the Shakespeare Association of America and a Guggenheim Fellow. In 2011, she retired from full-time academic work and, at last, moved back to her home state of Montana.

Simon Yarrow, Senior Lecturer at The University of Birmingham, UK, is author of *Saints and Their Communities: Miracle Narratives in the Twelfth Century* (Oxford, 2006), and of various articles on the material culture of medieval relics, and on gender and world history. *Saints: A Very Short Introduction* (Oxford) is forthcoming in 2015.

CPSIA information can be obtained
at www.ICGtesting.com
Printed in the USA
LVOW04s2015220816

501369LV00047B/1216/P